The Search for
the Beautiful Woman

ASIA/PACIFIC/PERSPECTIVES
Series Editor: Mark Selden

Crime, Punishment, and Policing in China edited by Børge Bakken
Woman, Man, Bangkok: Love, Sex, and Popular Culture in Thailand by Scot Barmé
Making the Foreign Serve China: Managing Foreigners in the People's Republic by Anne-Marie Brady
Marketing Dictatorship: Propaganda and Thought Work in China by Anne-Marie Brady
Collaborative Nationalism: The Politics of Friendship on China's Mongolian Frontier by Uradyn E. Bulag
The Mongols at China's Edge: History and the Politics of National Unity by Uradyn E. Bulag
Transforming Asian Socialism: China and Vietnam Compared edited by Anita Chan, Benedict J. Tria Kerkvliet, and Jonathan Unger
Bound to Emancipate: Working Women and Urban Citizenship in Early Twentieth-Century China by Angelina Chin
The Search for the Beautiful Woman: A Cultural History of Japanese and Chinese Beauty by Cho Kyo
China's Great Proletarian Cultural Revolution: Master Narratives and Post-Mao Counternarratives edited by Woei Lien Chong
North China at War: The Social Ecology of Revolution, 1937–1945 edited by Feng Chongyi and David S. G. Goodman
Little Friends: Children's Film and Media Culture in China by Stephanie Hemelryk Donald
Beachheads: War, Peace, and Tourism in Postwar Okinawa by Gerald Figal
Gender in Motion: Divisions of Labor and Cultural Change in Late Imperial and Modern China edited by Bryna Goodman and Wendy Larson
Social and Political Change in Revolutionary China: The Taihang Base Area in the War of Resistance to Japan, 1937–1945 by David S. G. Goodman
Islands of Discontent: Okinawan Responses to Japanese and American Power edited by Laura Hein and Mark Selden
Women in Early Imperial China, Second Edition by Bret Hinsch
Chinese Civil Justice, Past and Present by Philip C. C. Huang
Local Democracy and Development: The Kerala People's Campaign for Decentralized Planning by T. M. Thomas Isaac with Richard W. Franke
Hidden Treasures: Lives of First-Generation Korean Women in Japan by Jackie J. Kim with Sonia Ryang

North Korea: Beyond Charismatic Politics by Heonik Kwon and Byung-Ho Chung
Postwar Vietnam: Dynamics of a Transforming Society edited by Hy V. Luong
Resistant Islands: Okinawa Confronts Japan and the United States by Gavan McCormack and Satoko Oka Norimatsu
The Indonesian Presidency: The Shift from Personal towards Constitutional Rule by Angus McIntyre
Nationalisms of Japan: Managing and Mystifying Identity by Brian J. McVeigh
To the Diamond Mountains: A Hundred-Year Journey through China and Korea by Tessa Morris-Suzuki
From Underground to Independent: Alternative Film Culture in Contemporary China edited by Paul G. Pickowicz and Yingjin Zhang
Wife or Worker? Asian Women and Migration edited by Nicola Piper and Mina Roces
Social Movements in India: Poverty, Power, and Politics edited by Raka Ray and Mary Fainsod Katzenstein
Pan Asianism: A Documentary History, Volume 1, 1850–1920 edited by Sven Saaler and Christopher W. A. Szpilman
Pan Asianism: A Documentary History, Volume 2, 1920–Present edited by Sven Saaler and Christopher W. A. Szpilman
Biology and Revolution in Twentieth-Century China by Laurence Schneider
Contentious Kwangju: The May 18th Uprising in Korea's Past and Present edited by Gi-Wook Shin and Kyong Moon Hwang
Thought Reform and China's Dangerous Classes: Reeducation, Resistance, and the People by Aminda M. Smith
The Inside Story of China's High-Tech Industry: Making Silicon Valley in Beijing by Yu Zhou

The Search for the Beautiful Woman

A Cultural History of Japanese and Chinese Beauty

Cho Kyo

Translated by Kyoko Selden

ROWMAN & LITTLEFIELD PUBLISHERS, INC.
Lanham • Boulder • New York • Toronto • Plymouth, UK

Published by Rowman & Littlefield Publishers, Inc.
A wholly owned subsidiary of The Rowman & Littlefield Publishing Group, Inc.
4501 Forbes Boulevard, Suite 200, Lanham, Maryland 20706
www.rowman.com

10 Thornbury Road, Plymouth PL6 7PP, United Kingdom

Copyright © 2012 by Rowman & Littlefield Publishers, Inc.

All rights reserved. No part of this book may be reproduced in any form or by any electronic or mechanical means, including information storage and retrieval systems, without written permission from the publisher, except by a reviewer who may quote passages in a review.

British Library Cataloguing in Publication Information Available

Library of Congress Cataloging-in-Publication Data
Cho, Kyo, 1953- author.
    [Bijo to wa nani ka. English]
    The search for the beautiful woman : a cultural history of Japanese and Chinese beauty / Cho Kyo ; translated by Kyoko Selden.
        p. cm. — (Asia/Pacific/perspectives)
    Translation of: Bijo to wa nani ka : nitchu bijin no bunkashi / Cho Kyo. — Tokyo : Shobunsha, 2001. — 464, x, p. : ill. ; 20 cm.
    Includes bibliographical references and index.
    ISBN 978-1-4422-1893-2 (cloth : alk. paper) — ISBN 978-1-4422-1895-6 (electronic) (print)
    1. Feminine beauty (Aesthetics)—Japan—History. 2. Feminine beauty (Aesthetics)—China—History. I. Selden, Kyoko Iriye, 1936- translator. II. Title.
    HQ1220.J3C5313 2012
    305.40952—dc23
                                                                                    2012032384

♾™ The paper used in this publication meets the minimum requirements of American National Standard for Information Sciences—Permanence of Paper for Printed Library Materials, ANSI/NISO Z39.48-1992.

Printed in the United States of America

Contents

Translator's Note	ix
Preface to the English Edition	xi
Prologue: The Search for the Beautiful Woman	1
Chapter 1 Favored Appearances	**15**
1. Lucent Irises, Lustrous Teeth; Moth-Feeler Eyebrows, Willow Waist	15
2. Adoration of White Skin	24
3. Charms of Subcutaneous Fat	28
Chapter 2 Feared Beauties	**41**
1. Beauty Is Ill-Omened	42
2. Beautiful Women Are Cruel	48
3. Beautiful Women Are Hapless	55
4. Enchantresses in the East and the West	61
Chapter 3 The Rhetoric of Representation	**71**
1. Japanese Beauties, Chinese Beauties	71
2. Who Is Beautiful?	76
3. Allegory of Beautiful Women	85
4. Beautiful Women in Art	93
Chapter 4 Beauty as a Construct	**107**
1. Fluctuating Meanings of the Beautiful Face	107
2. Transmission of Safflower	111
3. Whiter Skin, Darker Eyebrows	116
4. Makeup Methods from Ethnic Groups	122

Chapter 5 Beauties in Chinese Verse and Prose, Beauties in Japanese Literature — 131
1. Images of Beautiful Women in Sugawara no Michizane's Chinese Verse — 131
2. Reception and Rejection of Continental Aesthetic Sense — 137
3. Descriptions of Beautiful Women in Japanese Prose — 141
4. Beautiful Women in Japanese Narrative Literature — 149

Chapter 6 Resonance of Aesthetic Views — 159
1. Heian Aristocratic Women — 159
2. Beauty of an Emaciated Look — 165
3. Beautiful Women in Tales of War — 171
4. Yang Guifei and the Image of Beauty — 176

Chapter 7 Edo Culture as a Filter — 185
1. "Adaptations" of the Image of Beauty — 185
2. From Japanese Courtesans to Sino-Japanese Fragile Women — 190
3. Portrayal from *Outlaws of the Marsh* — 195
4. Allegory of Flowers — 202

Chapter 8 Until Naomi Was Born — 215
1. Encounter with Western Beauty — 215
2. Creation of the Image of the Modern Beautiful Woman — 224
3. Physical Appearance as Information on Customs and Manners of the Day — 230
4. Westernization of Heroines — 234

Epilogue: Where Beauty Will Go — 247

Afterword — 255

Glossary of Selected Chinese and Japanese Names, Titles, and Terms — 257

Selected Bibliography — 277

Index — 281

Translator's Note

In the text and glossary, Chinese and Japanese names are given surnames first. In certain cases, well-known Japanese figures are referred to in abbreviated fashion following Japanese practice: Michizane for Sugawara no Michizane (a premodern name), and Sōseki (an independent pen name) for Natsume Sōseki.

This translation benefited from the generous editing assistance of Marc Peter Keane.

Preface to the English Edition

It may be hard for Western readers to believe, but from 2011, double-tooth attachment has become a fad among Japanese girls. Double-tooth attachment involves covering normal canine teeth to make them look more pointed and less straight. Around the time baby teeth are replaced by permanent teeth, children often have an uneven dental alignment. They look sweet when they smile with double teeth. This is why, from long ago in Japan, double teeth were regarded as a symbol of beauty, or sweetness, in young girls. Following the popularity of some recent doubled-toothed young stars, this became a big fad. Teenage girls now rush to cosmetic dentists to have artificial teeth attached to their neatly aligned natural teeth. Naturally, orthodontists have been quick to take advantage of this unexpected windfall. Preparing two types of teeth, removable and semipermanent, and projecting double-toothed stars, orthodontists have waged large-scaled campaigns. A pair of artificial teeth costs $200 at minimum, ranging up to $1,000. Despite the cost, the flow of visitors continues. While schoolchildren often visit orthodontists for teeth straightening in the West, where double or oblique teeth are associated with Dracula, Japanese teenage girls now seek to misalign their teeth so as to appear pretty or cute according to the new fashion.

Another distinctive example of Asian aesthetics is the skin-whitening boom in China. Chinese have long admired white skin. Throughout the modern era, white Westerners were considered to represent ideal beauty, and Chinese women's desire for white skin intensified. The Chinese well know that tanned skin is viewed as beautiful in the West. It is beyond

Chinese people's comprehension that Western women sunbathe or go to tanning salons. By contrast, to minimize exposure to the sun, Chinese women generously apply sunscreen cream and wear broad-rimmed hats low over their face when going out, even in early spring. Even that is not sufficient, and Chinese women now are buying skin-whitening cosmetics as if there was no tomorrow.

Today, with the progress of globalization and the development of telecommunications, cultural information races instantaneously across the world. If one wishes to know what people overseas are wearing and what their tastes are, information is readily at hand. In fact, Western fashion magazines and clothes are widely available throughout East Asia. There nevertheless remains a great gap in aesthetic sense between East and West. What is the reason behind that?

I began writing this book because I wished to know the reason for this. The book does not provide straightforward answers to this question, though it may provide hints. Its explicit purpose is to elucidate the changes in traditional aesthetic sense in Japan and China, particularly to convey how their conceptions of beauty were intertwined, and how they changed over time. For, to compare Asian and Western aesthetics, it was felt necessary to first clarify aesthetic traditions in East Asia.

Stepping into a relatively unexplored area, this book frequently compares Chinese and Japanese poetry, novels, and historical texts to trace the changing depictions of feminine beauty across space, time, and culture. Writing for a Japanese audience, I felt comfortable enough to introduce the topic because of shared Chinese characters as well as the traditional Japanese method that facilitates reading Chinese in Japanese. When a plan to translate this book into English surfaced, I was uncertain about how much could be effectively conveyed without direct quotations from original Chinese and Japanese texts. It was fortunate that Kyoko Selden, with a love for premodern Chinese and Japanese literatures, agreed to translate the book. Her extensive knowledge helped to make the book accessible to English-language readers. In the course of translation, I learned much from her, particularly her refusal to accept the smallest compromise. I was deeply touched by her thoughtfulness and politeness. I am indebted to Marc Peter Keane, who read the entire translation manuscript at an early stage and provided valuable editing assistance.

Starting when translation of this book was projected, I frequently consulted Ako Sahara, then managing director of the Japanese Literature Publishing and Promotion Center, who extended assistance in multiple ways. I wish to thank her.

Publication of this book was supported by the Overseas Outreach Program of Meiji University. I benefited from the instruction and consideration from Professor Takehiko Yoshimura and other members of the committee as well as Chikako Umebayashi of the office. Although the journey was long, the book finally made it to publication. Thank you very much.

Cho Kyo (Zhang Jing)
Meiji University
March 7, 2012

Prologue

The Search for the Beautiful Woman

ARE THERE UNIVERSAL CRITERIA FOR BEAUTY?

What constitutes a beautiful woman? Intrinsically, criteria vary greatly depending upon peoples and cultures. A woman thought of as a beauty in one culture may be considered plain in another. This is not normally in our consciousness. Rather, images of beauty are thought to be universal across all cultures. Marilyn Monroe and Audrey Hepburn gained worldwide fame as beauties, not simply in American eyes but in Asian and African eyes as well. But on what criteria?

Have universal standards for determining beauty emerged with the global reach of consumer culture and of the media? As products of multinational enterprises transcend national boundaries to spread worldwide, people of different races and nations have come to use the same cosmetics, and people of different skin colors and facial and bodily features have come to don similar fashions. As a result, the fact that different cultures have different standards of beauty was forgotten before we realized it.

In earlier epochs, different cultures shared no common conception of beauty. In ancient times, each culture held a different image of beautiful women. This was naturally so when cultures were widely different, say, between Western Europe and East Asia, but images were not identical even between closely connected cultures.

Both Chinese and Japanese are Mongoloid. Moreover, in premodern times China and Japan shared Confucian culture. Despite the fact that cultural ties between the two countries were extremely close, images of beauty in Edo Japan (1600–1868) and Qing China (1644–1911) were strikingly different. For example, while bound feet were a condition for female beauty in China, in Japan blackened teeth were considered beautiful.

At present, with the advance of globalization, the same commodities are not only distributed throughout the world but information easily transcends cultural walls. Boundary crossings represented by satellite television, film, and the Internet have greatly changed values and aesthetics of the non-Western world, but also of the Western world . . . such that the very categories of East and West, and perhaps North and South, are problematized. As American visual culture is being consumed at the global level, the Western sense of beauty inevitably penetrates today's developing countries. But Chinese and Japanese conceptions of beauty have also, at various times, made their way across the globe through art, literature, film, commodities, and communications.

Despite the rapidly advancing standardization of aesthetic sensibility, however, criteria of beauty have not necessarily become uniform. In Sichuan province, a young medical student from the Republic of Mali became acquainted with a Chinese woman. They fell in love and eventually married, the bridegroom staying on in China and becoming a doctor. A *People's Daily* reporter who interviewed him asked, "Would you let us know the secret for winning a beauty like your wife?" "We Mali people have a completely different sense of beauty from yours. A person you regard as a beauty isn't necessarily always beautiful in our eyes," he said by way of preface before answering the reporter's question.

The absence of universal standards for physical beauty was recognized early on along with the discovery of "the intercultural." Ever since Charles Darwin stated that "it is certainly not true that there is in the mind of man any universal standard of beauty with respect to the human body,"[1] many researchers have made the same point. Claude Lévi-Strauss, who observed the body drawings of the Caduveo tribe in Brazil and described them in *Tristes Tropiques*, conjectured as to why many men belonging to other tribes came to settle and marry Caduveo women at Nalike: "Perhaps the facial and body paintings explain the attraction; at all events, they strengthen and symbolize it. The delicate and subtle markings, which are as sensitive as the lines of the face, and sometimes accentuate them, sometimes run counter to them, make the women delightfully alluring."[2] When he wrote this, the aesthetics that greatly differed from the Western sense of beauty did not shock his readers. In their daily lives, however, most people still believe that essential physical beauty exists universally.

HOW FOREIGN RACES WERE REGARDED

It was in the twentieth century that images of beauty became homogenized from the West to Asia and Africa. Before then, not only did aesthetics of facial features differ, but, with some exceptions, different peoples thought one another ugly. The Portuguese Dominican friar Gaspar da Cruz (1520–1570), who visited China in the mid-sixteenth century, portrayed Chinese people, in his *South China in the Sixteenth Century*, as having "small eyes, low noses, large faces."[3] Matteo Ricci (1552–1610), the Italian Jesuit priest who lived in China starting in 1582, wrote, "Men's beards are thin and meager and at times they have none at all. Their hair is rough and straight.... The narrow, elliptical eyes are noticeably black. The nose is small and flat."[4] While neither missionary directly says Chinese are ugly, discomfort lurks between the lines.

Japanese faces looked the same way to Westerners' eyes. The German doctor Philipp Franz Balthasar von Siebold (1796–1866), who resided in Japan in 1823 to 1829 and from 1858 to 1862, states of people of inland Kyūshū, "Their faces are flat and wide, with small and wide noses, large mouths, and thick lips," "wings of the nose pressed deep, eyes wide apart, cheekbones protruding."[5] Swedish botanist Carl Peter Thunberg (1743–1828), who visited Japan in 1775, says, "[Japanese people's eyes] are oblong, small, and are sunk deeper in the head, in the consequence of which these people have almost the appearance of being pink-eyed. In other respects their eyes are dark-brown, or rather black.... The eyebrows are also placed somewhat higher. Their heads are in general large and their necks short; their hair black, thick, and shining from the use they make of oils. Their noses although not flat, are yet rather thick and short."[6] As time passed, exaggerated portrayals of ugliness became fewer, but eyes directed toward Mongoloids did not change much from the cases of Gaspar da Cruz and Matteo Ricci.

Westerners similarly appeared ugly or grotesque in Asian eyes. Yan Shigu (581–645) of the Tang period writes in an annotation in "Traditions of the Western Regions," fascicle 96 of *The Book of the Former Han*,[7] "The Wusun [tribe] have the strangest features among the various peoples of the Western Regions. The reason that today's Hu people [ethnic groups in northern and western regions], with their blue eyes and red beards, resemble monkeys in countenance is that they derive from the same ancestors as the Wusun." When Tang people saw blue (or jasper-green) eyes and red beards, they reflexively thought of animals. Of course, peoples of the Western Regions are not Westerners. But to Tang Chinese, deep-sculpted faces of the Caucasoid type appeared ugly.

Likewise when they directly described Europeans. "Biographies" 213 in fascicle 325 of *The History of the Ming* (1368–1644) characterizes the Dutch as having "deep set eyes and a long nose, with the hair, eyebrows, and beard equally red." Seemingly an objective depiction of physical characteristics, the passage uses the words *deep set eyes and long noses* with a clearly derogatory nuance. The term *red hair* (*hongmao*) as a disparaging alias for Westerners began to be used around then. Likewise, "red hair, jasper eyes" (*hongmao biyan*) was a negative expression. As in Tang China (618–684, 705–907), red hair (or gold hair) and blue eyes were directly connected to the image of wild animals. Such a view finally reversed itself in modern times.

Following the Opium War (1840–1842), China and the West experienced a reversal of power, and Chinese views of Westerners gradually changed. In 1866, the Qing official Bin Chun (1827–1910) was sent as the first formal representative to observe Europe. European women had come to look beautiful in his eyes.[8] Interestingly, his memoir, called *Occasional Jottings aboard a Raft* (*Chengcha biji*), makes no reference at all to the color of hair and eyes.

When looking at people of a different race or ethnicity, whether the observation is of the same gender can affect aesthetic judgments. There are many examples in which, in the eyes of male observers, foreigners of the same gender look ugly, yet women look beautiful. Siebold and Thunberg mentioned above, as well as the German physician and naturalist Engelbert Kaempfer (1651–1716), write in their travelogues that Japanese women are quite lovely. Likewise, even if Western women looked attractive to a Qing government official, he may not necessarily have similarly assessed Western men.

In China, too, once it was recognized that the West had overwhelming power, "red hair" and "jasper eyes" became gradually less ugly. Indeed, in the twentieth century they were transformed into a symbol of beauty. Western fiction in translation exerted great influence on the reversal of the image. Along with that, approaches to the portrayal of Westerners also changed. In Chinese fiction, poetry, and nonfiction, "red hair" changed to "golden hair" (*jinfa*) and "jasper eyes" to "indigo pupils" (*lan yanjing*).

A similar trend was common in Japan as well. There seem to be two stereotypical depictions of Westerners in modern Japanese fiction: extremely ugly or exceedingly beautiful. When portrayed as ugly, physical characteristics suggestive of nonhumans, such as a bearlike huge body, intense body odor, and uncanny blue eyes, are heavily emphasized.[9]

Whether or not people of a different race appear beautiful is less a matter of judgment based on looks and styles than a product of one's evaluation of that race's culture. From the start, it is meaningless to try to determine whether Caucasians or Mongoloids are more beautiful. To compare the appearances of races that differ in eye color, hair, and skull structure is like comparing chow and bulldog, as it were, and judging which animal is more aesthetically appealing. In this sense, the Miss World competition can hardly be expected to have any "fair criteria of judgment." The interracial comparison is predicated on a myth that humans are all the same.

AESTHETICS AND POWER RELATIONS AMONG CULTURES

Judging comparative beauty of two human groups invariably involves a perception of hierarchy, or power relations, between them. Aesthetic judgment about racial and ethnic groups involves power relations between cultures. Stated simply, a people whose civilization is regarded as highly developed is likely to be viewed as physically appealing, whereas an ethnic group deemed "backward" is considered ugly. So long as the "backward" culture remains unaware of its backwardness, members do not think of themselves as ugly. But once hierarchical consciousness is established, the aesthetic of physical features rapidly changes.

This is the reason that, today, Westerners are considered beautiful. It is not just Westerners themselves who think this; people in developing countries also do. Such aesthetic sense perfectly corresponds with ideologies pertaining to "the West" and "the East," and "advanced" and "backward" countries.

The point also can be illustrated by reverse examples. Those who consider Westerners more beautiful than Japanese do not necessarily think that Russians, belonging to the same Caucasoid race, are better looking than Japanese. Some Iranians have looks that can hardly be distinguished from those of Westerners. But when it is known in advance that they are Iranians, few Japanese would feel physically inferior to them.

Take for example the minority Uyghur in Xinjiang, China. Their features divide into two types, one that is close to Mongoloids and another to Caucasoids. The latter, with deep-sculpted faces, resemble Westerners. Uyghur men who used to come to large cities like Shanghai before economic opening were shy about their tall noses. They tried to hide them as much as possible by pulling down their hats.

Other factors can of course shape judgments about beauty. In recent years, young Japanese men and women with darkly tanned faces, pierced ears, and Afro hair can be spotted in Japanese cities. They identify with African American culture, which grew out of slavery and oppression, for a variety of reasons: these include the attraction of rebellion or difference from the

American or Japanese mainstream, or identification with the music and art associated with American blacks. On the other hand, African blacks have not become a target of imitation or emulation by Japanese.

THE FOUNDATION FOR ACCEPTANCE OF A VIEW OF FEMALE BEAUTY

In present-day Japan, an oval face with a tall nose is favored. This is not entirely due to Western influence. The forensic anthropologist Suzuki Hisashi once conducted detailed research on the skeletons of the Tokugawa family and their women. In the early years of the Tokugawa shogunate (1603–1868), political considerations often dominated the choice of formal wives, but from the third generation on, that was no longer necessary, making it possible to factor appearance into selection. In choosing consorts, moreover, there were no political constraints from the beginning. Many of them came from commoner families, and most were chosen for their beauty. The physical characteristics of Tokugawa women should provide insight into Tokugawa conceptions of female beauty.

According to the bone anthropologist Suzuki Hisashi's investigation, many Tokugawa women had narrower faces and relatively tall noses. For example, Tenshin-In (1823–1848), the formal wife of Tokugawa Iesada, the thirteenth shōgun, is described as having "an oval face with large eyes and a straight nose that was not too tall... and is assumed to have been a representative beauty of the Edo period."[10] A long, narrow face and a tall nose were standards for beauty in the Edo period as they are in modern times. Suzuki suggests that the features of shōgun consorts were similar to those of women portrayed in Edo period *ukiyo-e*, a genre of woodblock prints and paintings depicting landscapes, tales, the theater, and the pleasure quarters.

Needless to say, the skull bones alone do not determine facial appearances. Weight, skin color, and so forth greatly influence looks. Nevertheless, judgments about beauty draw heavily on the face. Delicate differences in the size of the mouth and the shape of lips and eyes affect the balance of the face. Whether the eyelids are double or single also greatly affects the appearance, aside from the fundamental question of which was favored in the given age. What can be conjectured from skeletal bones is naturally limited. It is nevertheless possible to estimate Edo taste in facial features.

No similar research on the Chinese imperial household has been conducted, but paintings and photographs portraying court women of the Qing dynasty remain. Those portraits show that women chosen to be empresses and high-ranking consorts are far from unattractive even by today's

Figure 0.1. Portrait of Empress Xiao Xianchun in Formal Court Attire. Qing Dynasty. National Palace Museum (Beijing). *Source:* Qi Gongzhu, ed. *Select Chinese Paintings of Successive Dynasties*, vol. 6 (*Zhongguo lidai huihua jingpin*). Shandong Meishu Publishing House, 2003, figure 248.

standards. Empress Xiao Xianchun (1712–1748), wife of Emperor Qianlong (1711–1799), has such a well-balanced face that she can still be called a beauty today (figure 0.1). Why such aesthetics formed has not yet been clarified. What is certain is that there were at least some points of contact between Western and Chinese or Japanese aesthetics. That laid a foundation in its own way for the Western image of beauty to be accepted and rapidly established in modern times.

BEAUTY AND CHARM

What are the requirements for a beautiful woman? Different people envision different images, such as a slender build, bright eyes, a tall nose, smooth skin. People tend to speak impressionistically about a lovely mouth, clear eyes, and so forth. Cosmetologists and cosmetic surgeons try to understand beauty objectively. Yet, even among professionals, opinion divides over standards of beauty.

What sort of bodily shape appeals as beautiful is a relatively simple question. As a Japanese expression *hattōshin bijin*, a beautiful shape with the head occupying one-eighth of the entire height, suggests, balance can be expressed in terms of height, weight, head-to-body proportion, and so forth.

We should not forget, however, that there is no scientific ground for such criteria and that they are just conventions. The three sizes of bust, waist, and hips, in particular, is a standard of measurement that is formed in relation to *eros*, and its essence is an illusion even as it pretends to be objective.

Compared with bodily types, facial criteria are far more difficult to assess. Specialists have offered various hypotheses, all of which emphasize balance above all. One theory proposes that, dividing the length between the hairline and chin into three equal parts, the distance between the hairline and the eyebrows, that between the eyebrows and the nose, and that between the nose and the tip of the chin should each occupy one-third. Another finds beauty in a profile view in which the height of the nose is one-third of its length and the mouth is contained within the lines connecting the sides of the nose and the jaw.[11]

Reducing a beautiful countenance to numerical values may give an impression that there are absolute, objective criteria to beauty, but it is highly doubtful that this is really the case. In the West, the attempt to try to explain beauty of the highest standard by expressing body proportions numerically goes back to the sixth century BCE.[12] Yet no scientific analysis has demonstrated grounds for defining beauty.

In recent years, a survey using computer technology concluded that female beauty in fact corresponds to an average face.[13] The claim is that a montage photograph based on the mean from a number of computer-processed facial photographs produces a beautiful countenance.[14] But then, the theory that beauty means average was suggested by Darwin early on, and it is hardly new.[15] One may, however, venture to say that there is something new about staging artificial "selection" with the use of the computer.

But a number of counterarguments have already surfaced against the "beauty = average" theory. Faces that deviate from average values seem more attractive.[16] At any rate, there are limits to scientific analyses of beautiful countenances and charms, which are in fact matters related to the heart and spirit. Humans are social animals. Whether or not a person looks beautiful profoundly relates to each observer's human and social orientation.

To begin with, whether someone looks pretty is a matter of consciousness involving individual sentiments. A person who looks exceptionally beautiful to one viewer may not necessarily appear so to others. Evaluation of "charm" is greatly influenced by subjectivity. The expression *kawaii* in Japanese means charming, winning, or cute. It can be considered a typical aesthetic judgment that transcends objective measurement. Someone does not look pretty because of how many centimeters her eyes measure, or how many degrees wide her jaw is. The evaluation is based upon how "her looks speak to me."

"A beautiful woman" is an image as a whole; it is an impression. As long as this is the case, relativity is what matters above all else. There are any number of cases in which a handsome man falls for a plain woman, or a beautiful woman loves an ugly man. "Plain" or "ugly" merely represents the judgment of viewers; the parties involved do not necessarily share the view. The distinction between "beauty" and "nonbeauty" is a product of the relationship between the two individuals. The Japanese saying, "Pockmarks are dimples in the eyes of one in love" (*abata mo ekubo*), demonstrates the mystery of the gaze on a person. Starting with "Love is blind" in English and "In a lover's eyes emerges a Xi Shi" in Chinese, the latter referring to an unsurpassed beauty of the sixth century BCE, we find similar proverbs in almost every language. What is common to those sayings is that judgment of beauty, regardless of culture, is arbitrary and hard to be understood by anyone other than the person concerned.

Particularly with a man and a woman, when something speaks to the heart the moment the one looks at the other, the other person looks most beautiful. Looks are one element, but they are never everything. Rather, the person's air as a whole sometimes gives a stronger impression.

As terms for estimating looks, expressions like *graceful* and *charming* carry an important meaning. They complement evaluation of a person's beauty. When one finds another "charming," behind that feeling is already a judgment that equates likable to beautiful. One's understanding of beauty is also easily affected by psychological elements. Rather than saying that the beautiful woman really exists, we should say that she only exists within the imagination of individuals.

Marilyn Monroe and Princess Diana each became a beauty representing an era, because, through film and media representations of them, an image of beauty as separate from them as individuals was created in people's minds—one that contains fragments of viewers' personal sentiment. The media-formed image evokes personal memories, experiences, and sentiments, and simultaneously functions as the target for emotional self-projection. Precisely for this reason, the status of a universal beauty was attained in these two examples.

BEAUTY AS A METAPHOR

Detailed inspection of changes in aesthetics from age to age clarifies that criteria for "beauty" are affected by elements other than beautiful looks. "Insiders" are beautiful; "outsiders" are ugly. "The noble" are beautiful; "the humble" are ugly. "The upper" are beautiful; "the lower" are ugly. "The affluent" are beautiful; "the poor" are ugly. "The holy" are beautiful; "the secular" are ugly. "The good" are beautiful; "the evil" are ugly. The more we go back to ancient times, the more striking this tendency becomes.

Chinese dynastic histories invariably depict foreign peoples negatively. That is also the case with portrayals of diplomatic emissaries in paintings. This is not limited to foreigners. In writings portraying conflicts, be they historical accounts or fiction, friends tend to have beautiful countenances while foes, both leaders and soldiers, look ferocious. The aesthetics that holds "insiders" as beautiful and "outsiders" as ugly also applies to women. Commoner women rarely appear in literature of ancient times. Nearly without exception, those depicted in poetry and fiction are court women or noblewomen. As in literary works like "The Goddess of the Luo" ("Luoshui-shen fu") by the poet and statesman Cao Zhi (192–232), descriptions of glamorous clothing convey feminine beauty (see figure 3.19 in chapter 3 for a pictorial representation of the poem). Because sartorial splendor was among the requirements for a beauty, women who could not hope for such garb were eliminated as objects of depiction.

That beauty and ugliness are metaphors of vertical relationships is readily apparent in representations of rank among states and races. As mentioned above, in premodern China, foreigners, including those such as Mongols, Tibetans, and Uyghurs living on China's borders, and Europeans, were deemed ugly not only because they were regarded as "outsiders" but because they were "people of lower standing" than the Chinese.

Among the Han themselves, descriptions of beauty and ugliness formed metaphors of vertical relations. The Chinese expression *talented men and fair women* (*cairen jiaren*) by definition implies class origin. The phrase *fair women* does not simply refer to women of lovely appearance but of literary families. In China, where Confucianism was the official learning and the Imperial Examination System processed entrance into the bureaucracy, literary ability was a crucial measure defining social standing. In the fiction of Ming and Qing China (1368–1644, 1644–1911), although women were not eligible to take the imperial examination or become officials, they are never described or depicted as "fair" unless they possess literary talent.

The metaphor most frequently used presumes "holy" to be beautiful and "secular" to be ugly. In every culture, goddesses are without exception depicted as beautiful. Alongside this, the entrance of a beautiful woman into a scene is often portrayed in the same way as the descent of a goddess to the earth. An unparalleled beauty frequently shines dazzlingly as if clad in a halo. Such metaphor, or the interchangeable relationship between a beautiful human and a god or goddess, can be observed in Buddhist images as well.

That "good" is beautiful and "evil" is ugly is a metaphor that has recurred since the oldest days. In literature of all ages and regions, a good woman is almost always beautiful, and a bad woman ugly. We cannot laugh this away as a paradigm in old fiction. In fact, the same pattern is repeated today in Hollywood movies. Yet, the audience does not find it uncomfortable. The metaphor assuming "justice" to be beautiful and "vice" ugly is generally accepted across history.

NARRATING STORIES OF BEAUTIES

"A beauty" is not merely "a beautiful-looking woman" but an indicator of culture that contains multiple meanings. From standards for beauty, we can not only observe the character of each culture but can also study intercultural relationships. Moreover, within the same culture, we note different images of the beautiful woman at different historical moments. From them we can glimpse transitions of customs and aesthetics from age to age. It is also possible to start out with changes in images of feminine beauty to explore intercultural crossings.

Discourse on beautiful women also serves as an indicator, so to speak, of a culture's level of maturity. In general, praise of feminine beauty or descriptions of beautiful women go back to ancient times, but theories of feminine beauty come later. In China, something like a theory of beauty appeared only in late Ming to early Qing. The "Voice and Appearance" chapter of *Occasional Contemplations (Jianqing ouji)* by the seventeenth-century playwright and novelist Li Yu (1610–1680) of the Qing period can be called the first Chinese theory of feminine beauty. As you will see in chapter 1, the author discussed in detail the requirements for a beauty from the aspects of appearance, gesture, makeup, and so forth.

Beautiful women were not always glorified in history. While they were praised as objects of male monopoly in historical and literary works, beautiful looks were also portrayed as masks worn by evil women with destructive power. Beauties were not always associated with status, wealth, and good fortune, but came to be feared as the source of death, downfall, national ruin, loss, and collapse. How such contradictory images were formed, what they meant, and how they functioned are questions to be explored below.

In this book I would like to reflect on issues of beautiful women and beautiful countenances from the angle of comparative cultural history with the above issues in mind. For premodern times, I will focus on cultural intersections within East Asia. I explore the criteria for feminine beauty, and consider when and how changes occurred across history. Changes in aesthetics are often influenced by contact with foreign culture. Examination of the image of a beautiful woman inevitably faces the question of intercultural encounters.

Even within East Asia, things differ greatly between the Han people and diverse ethnic groups, and between the continent and Japan. How do Chinese images of beauty differ from those in Japan, and what are the reasons? These will also be considered.

When exploring ancient images of feminine beauty, written documents are powerful clues, as are works of art. But art and literature do not serve as simple historical evidence. Representations, whether in art or literature, may or may not jibe with images in life. Thus, while examining female images in paintings, we will also observe how beautiful women were portrayed in history books, poetry, fiction, and essays.

In modern times, Western images of beautiful women came to exert overwhelming influence in the East. In particular, I will explore how beautiful women came to be portrayed in China and Japan, and how literary style, vocabulary, and rhetoric changed.

NOTES

1. Charles Darwin, *The Descent of Man*, vol. 2 (John Murray, 1871), 383.
2. John and Doreen Weightman (trs.), *Tristes Tropiques* (first published by Atheneum Publishers, 1974; Penguin Books, 1992), 188.
3. Gaspar da Cruz, *South China in the Sixteenth Century*. Translated into Japanese by Hino Hiroshi as *Jūrokuseiki kanan jibutsushi* (Akashi Shoten, 1987), 293.
4. Louis J. Gallagher, S.J. (tr.), *The Journals of Matthew Ricci: 1583–1671* (Random House, 1953), 77.
5. Philipp Franz von Siebold, *Reise nach dem Hofe des Sjogun im Jahre 1826*. Translated by Saitō Makoto as *Edo sanpu kikō* (Heibonsha, 1967), 77.
6. Timon Screech (editor and annotator), *Japan Extolled and Decried: Carl Peter Thunberg and the Shogun's Realm, 1775–1796* (Routledge, 2005), 88. Cf.: Takahashi Fumi (tr.), *Edo sanpu zuikōki* (Heibonsha, 1994), 218–19.
7. Also called *Book of Former Han*, it was composed by Ban Biao, Ban Gu, and Ban Zhao and completed in 111 CE. It covers the history of China under the Western Han from 206 BCE to 25 CE.
8. Bin Chun, *Occasional Jottings aboard a Raft*. In Zhong Shuhe (editor in chief), *Toward the World Library* (*Zou xiang Shi jie Cong shu*) (Yuelu Publications, 1985), 101.

9. Tsuruta Kin'ya, *Modern Japanese Literature That Boundary-Crossers Read* (*Ekkyōsha ga yonda kindai Nihon bungaku*) (Shin'yōsha, 1999), 10-22.

10. Suzuki Hisashi, *The Bones Tell Their Stories: People of the Tokugawa Shogunate and Daimyō Families* (*Hone wa kataru: Tokugawa Shōgun, daimyōke no hitobito*) (The University of Tokyo Press, 1985), 113.

11. *Da Capo*, vol. 19, issue 12, no. 423 (Magazine House, 1999), 6.

12. Francette Pacteau, *The Symptom of Beauty* (*Essays in Art and Culture*). Translated into Japanese by Hamana Emi as *Bijin* (Kenkyūsha, 1996), 99.

13. Karl Grammer, *Signale der Liebe: Die biologischen Gesetze der Partnerschaft.* Translated into Japanese by Imaizumi Mineko under the supervision of Hidaka Toshitaka as *Ai no Kaibōgaku* (Kinokuniya Shoten, 1997), 168-69.

14. Shioya Nobuyuki, *The Truth of Cosmetic Surgery: Can the Surgical Knife Heal the Heart?* (*Biyō geka no shinjitsu: mesu de kokoro wa naoseru ka*) (Kōdansha, 2000), 50-51.

15. Karl Grammer, *op. cit.*, 159.

16. Ibid., 51.

1

Favored Appearances

1. LUCENT IRISES, LUSTROUS TEETH; MOTH-FEELER EYEBROWS, WILLOW WAIST

Good Impressions Rather than Shapes

What first comes to mind in relation to beautiful appearances is the Chinese phrase *lucent irises, lustrous teeth* (*mingmou haoqi*). To put it in more modern terms, it would be *clear eyes* and *well-aligned, white teeth*. The expressions *moth-feeler eyebrows* (*emei*) and *willow waist* (*liuyao*) also denote a beauty, indicating thin eyebrows with a gentle arc like a moth's feelers and slender waist or lower torso associated with a thin, supple willow branch. As I will discuss later, these clichés were formed partly for rhetorical reasons, and do not mean that feminine beauty is solely judged by the eyes, teeth, eyebrows, and trunk.

On the other hand, regardless of the age or region, in judging beauty, undeniably the greatest emphasis goes to eyes and eyebrows. Eyes are quite a conspicuous presence on the face, and humans habitually turn their gaze to the eyes when coming into contact with one another.[1] When eyes meet, one can instantly read whether the other person takes an interest or has any feelings, favorable or unfavorable. It is hardly surprising that eyes are the first topic in discussing images of beautiful appearance or in describing beautiful women.

Today, partly due to the influence of Western aesthetics, wide-open eyes and double eyelids have come to be seen as symbolic of beauty. Yet in neither ancient China nor Japan were large eyes favored. As is evident not only from literary and historical writings but from visual sources like paintings and sculptures, slim eyes were regarded as beautiful until modern times (see figure 1.1).

Historically, the criteria for "beautiful eyes" have not been immutable. In fact, objective standards for determining eye beauty long remained unclear. In the East in ancient times, the size and shape of the eyes were not particularly important in evaluating female beauty. The expression *lucent irises* plainly indicates that. The term, meaning clear eyes free from clouding, conveys the impression the eyes give to a viewer, but does not describe the external appearance. Naturally, the impression of the eyes is not unrelated to their appearance. But the impression the viewer receives is the more important of the two aspects. The Japanese expression *cool-looking eyes* (*suzushigena me*) must have been created from a similar idea. The English expression *bright eyes* too, while suggestive of wide-open shapes, is more impressionistic than objective. It is no less ambiguous than *lucent irises* and *cool-looking eyes*. In other words, the beauty of eyes is not determined by whether they are large or double lidded but rather by the impression they convey.

Eyes Are Judged by Their Expressiveness

Such aesthetics go back to ancient times. The rhyme-prose "The Divine Woman" ("Shennü fu") by Song Yu, a poet of the Warring States period (403–221 BCE), describes the eyes of a beautiful goddess: "Her irises are radiant and luminous, glistening with much beauty to behold." To put it simply, her eyes are bright and shiny. The passage is loaded with poetic diction, but every epithet emphasizes the shiny appearance, not the shape, of the eyes. Such a view of the eyes is common in later literature as well, although varying in vocabulary, rhetoric, and mode of expression.

This is not limited to literary depiction; the same applies to writings discussing women's appearances and cosmetic methods. *Occasional Contemplations* (*Jianqing ouji*) by the Qing period dramatist Li Yu (1610–1680) contains a section touching on the criteria of female beauty. "Favored Appearances," the first chapter of volume 6 titled "Voice and Appearance," contains a section called "Eyebrows and Eyes," where the author exclusively discusses how to evaluate eyes and eyebrows. According to this source, the beauty of eyes is determined by three elements: the size, movements, and relative proportion of the black and white parts. Regarding size, it says that women with slim eyes are of tender nature, whereas those with large eyes are hussies. It further states that women with agile eyes, in which the white and black parts are distinct, are clever. Women whose eyes are dull, without movement, and predominantly white or predominantly black lack

Figure 1.1. Zhao Bingzhen, *Overnight on a Lotus Boat* (*Lianzhou wanbo*). Qing Dynasty (1644–1911). National Palace Museum (Taipei, Taiwan). *Source:* National Palace Museum Editorial Committee, ed. *Shinühua zhi mei* (*Glimpses into the Hidden Quarters: Paintings of Women from the Middle Kingdom*). Palace Museum, 1988, hereafter *Glimpses*, 44.

intelligence. It is insightful of Li Yu to include among the criteria for female beauty the ability to respond quickly in communication.

Similar aesthetics exist in Japan. *Customs, Manners, and Fashions of the Capital* (*Miyako fūzoku kewai den*) by the cosmetics researcher Sayama Hanshichimaru, published in 1813, states the criteria for beautiful eyes: "Because the eyes are at the center of the face and the first in bringing out the facial features, they should have dignified strength. Yet, eyes that are too large are unsightly. Some people narrow their eyes, forcefully attempting to make them smaller, but the eyelids and outer corners of the eyes become wrinkled producing a squint. This worsens the looks of the eyes." The expression *dignified strength* refers to the gaze, and does not mean large eyes. As is clear from the statement that *eyes that are too large are unsightly*, in the Edo period (1600–1867) large eyes were deemed rather unattractive.

These accounts suggest that the messages that eyes convey were noted long ago. In other words, eyes that convey a good impression to the viewer are beautiful, while those unaccompanied by feelings are not felt attractive. A gaze, because it creates an emotional connection between the viewer and the viewed, is far more important than external looks in judging whether or not eyes are beautiful. This is also why the same face can look totally different depending upon the viewer.

Narrow Eyes Are Beautiful

Later in China, however, detailed references began to be made regarding eye shapes. Particularly interesting is *The Grotto of Immortals* (*Youxian ku*), a tale of the strange by Zhang Wencheng (also Zhang Zhuo, 660?–741?) of the Tang period (618–907) about an encounter with two immortal women dwelling in a cavern. It offers a criterion different from today's emphasis on big, bright eyes as charming and pretty:

Her heart is vacant, hard to fathom,
Her eyes are narrow, they strongly engage my heart.
Turning herself around she's already in my arms,
Yet to be seen whether she has an amorous voice.[2]

The second line here, "Her eyes are narrow, they strongly engage my heart," merits particular attention. Opinion may be divided as to whether "eyes are narrow" means that the woman has narrow eyes, or refers to narrowed eyes in a moment when passion is difficult to resist. Either way, the interesting fact remains that narrow-looking eyes were favored. From the viewpoint of eroticism, half-closed eyes may in fact be more attractive in a bedroom than glaring eyes.

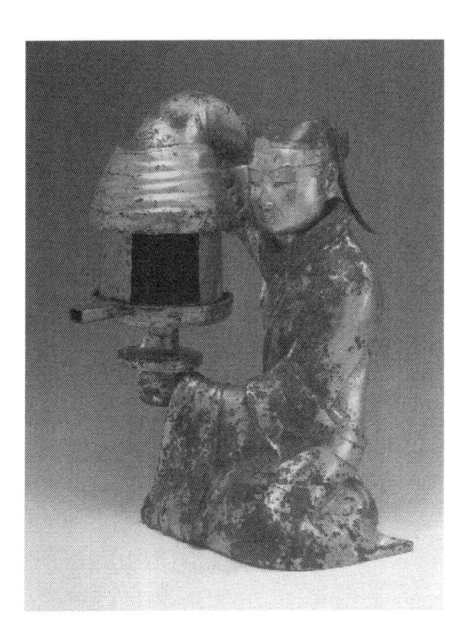

Figure 1.2. Zhangxin Palace Lantern (Zhangxingong deng). Former Han Dynasty (206 BCE–9 CE). Hebei Provincial Museum (Hebei). *Source:* Wang Chaowen, ed. *Zhongguo meishu shi* (*History of Chinese Art*). Qilu Shushe and Mingtian Publishing House, 2000, the Qin-Han volume, figure 254.

However, "eyes are narrow" in *The Grotto of Immortals* probably indicates narrow eyes as a physical feature rather than a facial expression of the moment. This is because, in China, narrow eyes were long considered beautiful. We can glimpse this, for example, when looking at a figurine from the Han period (figure 1.2). The same aesthetics appears also in a Daoist source discussing bed-chamber skills. *Jeweled Chamber Secrets* (*Yufang mijue*), ascribed to the Six Dynasties period (222–589), characterizes the ideal woman:

> Ideally, a woman should be young, firm-breasted, well filled out, fine-haired, small-eyed with clear distinction between the white and black parts of the eyes; her facial and bodily skin finely textured and smooth, her voice and way of speaking pleasant to the ear; not large-boned, but rather well rounded from the neck down so that no angularity shows.

Here the author clearly defines "small eyes" as ideal. This statement is also quoted in *The Essence of Medical Prescriptions* (*Ishinbō*, compiled by Tanba no Yasuyori, 984), the earliest extant Japanese medical text and a compendium covering all areas of health, including the art of love. A similar view is found here and there in other writings on the art of the chamber as well.

Of course, Daoist philosophy is richly present in *Jeweled Chamber Secrets*, and sex is discussed as one approach to health. However, because it states that health improves through intercourse with a beautiful woman, it is evident that a small-eyed woman was considered beautiful.

Slim, Long Eyebrows, White Teeth, and Red Lips

Second in importance after the eyes are eyebrows. In comparison to the eyes, nose, and mouth, mere makeup can transform the external appearance of eyebrows and the impression they convey. In fact, every culture has a long history of eyebrow makeup. In ancient Egypt, there was a custom of dyeing eyebrows black, letting them grow long, and also dyeing eyelashes black.[3] In ancient Greece, women dyed eyelashes and eyebrows black with antimony as a form of makeup.[4]

In Japan there was a method of makeup that involved painting eyebrows, and such references already appear in the *Record of Ancient Matters* (*Kojiki*, 712), *Chronicles of Japan* (*Nihon shoki*, 720), and *Anthology of Myriad Leaves* (*Man'yō-shū*, mid-eighth century).[5]

China has a culture that is more obsessed than any other with the beauty of eyebrows. I will discuss this in greater detail in chapter 4, but in a word it is safe to say that China is unparalleled in terms of the length of history of eyebrow makeup and diversity of method. Whether natural or painted, in China long and thin eyebrows were long considered a requirement for beauty.

As seen in the phrase *lucent irises, lustrous teeth*, teeth were also a criterion of female beauty in ancient China, along with eyes and eyebrows. We find the expression, *her teeth are like gourd seeds* as early as "The Grand Beauty" in the "Odes of Wei" section of *The Book of Songs* (*Shi jing*) compiled in the Zhou period (1027–256 BCE). "Gourd seeds" is a metaphor for well-aligned, white teeth. The rhyme-prose "On Deng Tuzi as a Sensualist" ("Deng Tuzi haose fu") by the above-mentioned Song Yu of the Warring States period has a phrase *her teeth are like shells held in the mouth*, and "The Goddess of the Luo" by Cao Zhi of the Later Han (25–220 CE) includes the expression *white teeth gleaming within*.[6] All these viewed teeth as a condition for a beautiful countenance. However, as time passed, the degree of attention to teeth seems to have waned. The *Occasional Contemplations*, cited above, makes no mention of teeth.

Aesthetics of teeth differed greatly between Japan and China. In Japan, a makeup method of teeth blackening emerged in the Heian period (794–1185/1192).[7] The "Safflower" chapter of *The Tale of Genji* contains a passage that goes in Royall Tyler's translation, "Her teeth had not yet received any blacking, but he had had her made up, and the sharp line of eyebrows was very attractive."[8] As is clear from this, blackened teeth were considered beautiful. Aside from this example, teeth blackening is mentioned in over forty books from the Heian to the Edo period.[9]

In China, greater attention went to lips than to teeth. Song Yu's "The Divine Woman" ("Shennü fu") contains a description, "her vermilion lips are bright like cinnabar," while Cao Zhi's "The Goddess of the Luo" also mentions "red lips that shed their light abroad."[10] Red lips symbolize feminine beauty in both. As for the mouth, it was thought that the smaller, the prettier. In contrast to the decreasing attention to the teeth with the passage of time, a small mouth was long regarded as a basic condition for female beauty. Not just literary works but paintings also testify to this.

Entrance of Tall Noses

Chinese literature presents an interesting phenomenon. Verse and prose depicting a beautiful woman indicate standards of beauty concerning eyes, eyebrows, mouth, and lips, but they hardly ever refer to the nose. This is especially notable in literary Chinese. Only after fiction in the vernacular emerged in the Song period (960–1279) did descriptions of beautiful noses appear. In portraying the beauty of the female main character Pan Jinlian (or Golden Lotus), the second installment of *The Plum in the Golden Vase* (*Jinping mei*, early eighteenth century), long fiction composed in the vernacular, takes up her nose after her black hair, narrow eyebrows, clear eyes, and small mouth, introducing a straight nose as an element of beauty. But such a description is rare even in vernacular fiction.

In comparison, there was an awareness of a straight nose as something beautiful in Japan already in the Heian period. *The Tale of Middle Counselor Hamamatsu* (*Hamamatsu Chūnagon monogatari*, eleventh century) contains a reference to a "countenance neither narrow nor round but just right, with the center of the face rising a little." The last part means that her nose was somewhat tall. Based on this account, the cosmetic culture researcher Murasawa Hirohito argues that a straight-nosed face came to be regarded as beautiful by the late Heian period.[11]

As we can see from the description in *The Plum in the Golden Vase*, in China a face with a nose with a straight ridge had been favored before the arrival of modern Western culture. In paintings throughout the generations, no examples are found in which flat noses were portrayed as good-looking. In this sense, aesthetics favoring a shapely nose can be said to have a certain degree of universality. In China, however, northern riders from the steppe reigned several times, and this should be factored in when considering the concept of beautiful women.

The Ideal Body Shape

In the same way as "lucent irises" and "moth-feeler eyebrows" are metaphors for a beautiful countenance, "willow waist" is a metaphor for the ideal, slender body shape, *waist* (*yao* in Chinese, *koshi* in Japanese) meaning the middle section of the body including the lower torso and hips. *Willow waist* is also called *the State of Chu waist*, Chu referring to a kingdom in the Spring and Autumn and Warring States periods (722–481 BCE, 403–221 BCE). Originally referring to the slender body, later it became synonymous with a beautiful woman. The history of favoring a thin torso goes back to the Warring States period. Because King Ling of the State of Chu loved a slender beauty with a narrow waist, court women ate less in order to become slim. Some are said to have died from excessive dieting ("Strategies of Chu" in *Strategies of the Warring States, Zhanguo ce*, compiled between the third and first centuries BCE and finalized by Liu Xiang, 77 BCE–6 CE). The preference for slenderness continued after that as well (figure 1.3).

Later, some changes occurred in these aesthetics. Rhyme-prose pieces like "The Divine Woman" and "The Goddess of the Luo" indicate that medium height and build came to be regarded as beautiful, and that a narrow lower torso was not necessarily emphasized. In the Tang period (618–907) in particular, though only temporarily, plumpness was preferred.

Such aesthetic preference in ancient East Asia, including China and Japan, not only shared few similarities with dominant conceptions in the West, but often seems exactly the opposite.

Views of the body, among others, differ greatly. In particular, no literary writings or pictorial representations addressing the beauty of the breasts are found in ancient East Asia. The Roman poet Ovid (around 34 BCE–17 CE) depicts an ideal woman in *Amores*, book 1, number 5:

I got her garment off and she stood enjoying my gaze:
not a blemish on any part of her:

What shoulders she had! Arms ripe for caresses!
Nipples the perfect shape for a little tweak.

And God—that flat stomach beneath the compact breasts!
That taut, muscled flank! Those girlish thighs![12]

Praise of the naked body and description of the breasts are totally absent in ancient East Asia. One reason may be that, in periods when Confucian ethics prevailed, open praise of the naked body was not permissible. That is not the only reason, however. In China's amorous literature and erotic paintings, domains where Confucian precepts did not reach, interest in breasts was low. Until the late Qing period, or late nineteenth to early twentieth century, Chinese people did not demonstrate much interest in them. Women appearing in old paintings were flat-breasted without exception (figure 1.4). A Qing literary work on courtesans titled *An Account of Seaside Excursions* (*Haizou yeyou lu*) introduces discourses at length on bound feet, but it includes no mention whatsoever of the breasts. This is not unrelated to the cultural tradition in which they were regarded mostly as nursing organs.

Figure 1.3. *A Human, a Dragon and a Phoenix, a Silk Painting* (*Ren'wu longfeng pohua*). Warring States Period. *Source: Zhongguo meisu shi*, the Xia-Shang-Zhou Volume, figure 208.

Figure 1.4. Ascribed to Gu Kaizhi, *A Woman Writes a Letter of Advice* (*Nüshi zhen tu*). Eastern Jin. British Museum. *Source:* Liu Changluo et al., ed. *Zhonghua guwenmin daituji* (*Collection of Ancient Chinese Culture*). People's Daily et al., 1992, part 7 ("Customs and Manners"), 7.

2. ADORATION OF WHITE SKIN

Raw Materials for Cosmetic Powder

Concrete descriptions of faces are limited in Chinese literary works, but white skin was emphasized from early on as a condition for a beautiful woman. In Japan, too, such works as *The Tale of Genji* and the *Diary of Murasaki Shikibu* from the early eleventh century already contain references to powder, indicating that white skin was regarded as beautiful. Because such aesthetics and makeup methods are related to Chinese influence, however, I would like to further detail them in chapter 6.

Now, was the preference for white skin in China due to the original sense of beauty or to intercultural influence? What processes did the use of powder go through until today? These questions require examination.

According to *The Origins of Things* (*Shiwu jiyuan*) written by Gao Cheng of the Song period (960–1279), women started using powder during the reign of King Wen (around 1100 BCE), and at the court of the first emperor of Qin (third century BCE); all of the imperial consorts and ladies-in-waiting used rouge and drew eyebrows, thus marking the beginning of facial makeup. Gao Cheng gives no proof whatsoever, and it is difficult to judge whether this was true.

Still, there is no doubt that powder was used from the old days. The "Strategies of Chu" chapter in *Strategies of the Warring States*, compiled by Liu Xiang (77–6 BCE), recounts that women of the State of Zheng stood by the roadside with faces powdered, eyebrows inked. This was during the reign of King Hui of Chu, in other words between 329 and 299 BCE. This indicates that a fairly advanced makeup method had already developed before the Qin period.

In China, cosmetic powder is traditionally called *fen* (etymologically meaning "split rice") or *qianfen* (lead powder). Each is made from a different material. According to the *Etymological Dictionary of Names* (*Shiming*) by Liu Xi of the Later Han (25–220), *fen* was so named because it was made by pounding and crushing rice grains, and when it was dyed red, it was called *chengfen* (double-dyed red powder) and was applied to cheeks. If we follow this account, cosmetic powder was made of rice in the ancient times.

The other kind, lead powder, is also called *hufen*, or "Hu powder," *Hu* meaning northern and western ethnic groups in Chinese history. Lead powder is literally made of lead. In the "Things" category of *A Treatise on Curiosities* (*Bowu-zhi*), the compiler Zhang Hua (232–300) wrote, "Zhou burnt lead and tin to make powder." In other words, in the time of King Zhou (?–c. 1122 BCE), the art of producing powder from lead had already developed. However, this account also provides no proof, and thus cannot serve as the basis for determining the date of the development of lead powder. On the other hand, judging from the fact that an expression *decorate the face with Hu powder* appears in the *Book of the Later Han*, volume 63, "The Biographies of Li and Du," lead powder had been in use at the latest by the time of Emperor Shun (ruled 125–144) of the Later Han.

With Men, Too, Being White-Skinned Meant Being Handsome

Cosmetic powder made of rice seems to predate that made of lead, but whether the former continued to be used after the appearance of the latter is unclear. However, by the Six Dynasties period (222–589), lead powder had already become the mainstream among aristocrats. In "The Goddess of the Luo," Cao Zhi praised the beauty of the river goddess's pale flesh: "No scented ointments overlaying it, / No coat of leaden powder applied."[13] In the Tang period, the makeup practice with the use of lead powder became more or less established, and we find many examples in Tang poems, including the phrase *lead flower smiles at my scowling blue eyebrows* in the "Song of a Sleepless Night" ("Yezuo yin") by Li He (791–817).

When white skin is favored, it does not, naturally, mean that it suffices that the face is white. Application of powder to the face aims, from the beginning, at suggesting that the skin of the entire body is white. Thus, it is necessary to apply powder not only to the face but to other exposed areas like the hands, arms, and neck. Interestingly, there was a custom in ancient China of applying powder to areas covered by garments like the chest, shoulders, and back. The oldest related record goes back to the Han period.

"The Biographies of the Thirteen Sons of Emperor Jing," volume 53 of the *Book of Han*, introduces the following episode: Liu Qu, or Prince Hui of Guangchuan, favored a beautiful woman by the name of Tao Wangqing. Out of jealousy and with intention to harm her, his queen, Yangcheng Zhaoxin, one day told the prince, "Tao Wangqing exposed her skin before the court painter, with powder applied to her chest and arms." The queen's stratagem succeeded, and Tao Wangqing was cruelly punished.

The problem with Tao Wangqing's conduct was not the makeup method but the exposure of the skin before a man. Still, the episode suggests that application of powder to the chest and arms was normal in those days. "An Account of the Wo People," a section on Japan contained in the "Book of Wei" portion of the *Records of the Three Kingdoms* (*Sanguo zhi*, compiled around 280–290), says, "They apply red paint on their body, which resembles the use of powder in China." This indicates that powdering continued during the Six Dynasties (222–589).

Tang poetry includes frequent references to the same. "Viewing a Beauty" by Shi Jianwu (780–861) contains a line, "Long keeps the white snow present before the breast." In "Dedicated to a Beauty" Fang Gan (dates unknown) also says, "Powdered breast, half veiled, suggests the clear snow." This of course refers to the exposed areas of the breast, but all the same, application of powder to the breast was a common makeup method.

It is interesting that men also wore powder in the Han period. The expression, *embellish the visage with Hu powder* in the "Biographies of Li and Du" in the aforementioned *Book of the Later Han*, occurred when military commander Li Gu was slandered. This custom did not decline even during the Six Dynasties period (222–589). According to "Attitude" in *A New Account of Tales of the World* (*Shishuo xinyu*, fifth century), a man called He Pingshu was handsome and extremely white-skinned. Cao Cao, the warlord and penultimate chancellor of the Eastern Han dynasty (also the father of Cao Zhi, mentioned above), suspected that He Pingshu wore powder, and had him eat a hot wheat flour dish on a midsummer day. Perspiring profusely, He Pingshu wiped his face with his red robe after the meal, but his facial complexion grew even whiter.

Whiteness as a Symbol

In these literary pieces, whiteness of the skin represented "beauty," and powder was frequently used in order to emphasize white skin.

However, in the Tang period, while white skin was still admired, the practice of making up the face with rouge also began to be seen. "Early Spring's Faint Rain" by Li Shanfu (mid to late Tang) contains a couplet that goes, "Dancing sleeves of blue silk mingle as they flare / The crimson face's beads of tears are suppressed as they swirl." The expression *crimson face* here is likely to mean not just a beautifully radiant face but a face actually rouged. Even if we put aside the rhetorical reason for using "paired phrases" in a couplet, such a face cannot be thought of as sheer fiction. In fact, the following lines from "Viewing a Courtesan" by Sikong Shu (eighth century) introduces the same expression without a particular rhetorical demand: "the pale green eyebrows and crimson face are unable to stand the emotion / With the broken flute and remaining strings she raises one voice." The "crimson face" here must be "realistic." In "The Woman in Mount Hua" ("Huashan-nyu shi"), the reknowned poet and essayist Han Yu (768–824) also sings, "White throat, red cheeks, blue eyebrows long / she comes forward, ascends to the seat, performs the Daoist ritual." In depicting a beautiful woman, all that these poets list are a white neck, red cheeks, and long, blue eyebrows.

Tang period paintings unearthed in recent years also attest to that point. One example is *Ladies-in-Waiting at the Go Board* (*Yiqi Shinyü tu*, figure 1.5), from a tomb in Turpan in Xinjiang. As this painting shows, Tang period women made up their faces singularly red. According to *Memorabilia of the Kaiyuan and Tianbao Eras* (*Kaiyuan Tianbao yishi*) attributed to Wang Renyu (880–956), Yang Guifei, the favored consort of Emperor Xuanzong of the Tang, perspired so much in the summer that her towel turned pink when she wiped herself. This description, if we take the above-mentioned painting into consideration, probably realistically reflects the makeup method of those days.

Figure 1.5. From *Ladies-in-Waiting at the Go Board* (*Yiqi Shinyü tu*). Tang. Museum of Xinjiang Uyghur Autonomous Region (Urumqi). *Source: Museum of Xingjiang Uyghur Autonomous Region*, Kōdansha, 1987, figure 147.

However, whether rouge makeup began in the Tang period is unclear. For example, "crimson face" is mentioned in "A Court Lady's Frailty of Fortune" (*Qie boming ci*) by Emperor Jianwen (503–551) of Liang, from the Six Dynasties period. This would mean that application of rouge to the cheeks was used from early days. The only difference is that, in the Tang period, the makeup rather went to extremes, and as we can tell from extant pre-Tang mural paintings, it is certain that the application style of rouge as in *Ladies-in-Waiting at the Go Board* had not existed earlier.

When we view paintings from the Five Dynasties (Five Dynasties and Ten Kingdoms, 907–960) that followed the Tang, we no longer find the makeup method of applying rouge to the entire cheeks. On the other hand, the taste for white skin was still strong, and powder has been applied by women ever since.

These sources clarify that, in China, aesthetics holding white skin beautiful existed from olden days. There may have been cultural influences among different ethnic groups behind the emergence of this sense of beauty. However, even if that were the case, it would have been limited to the East Asian cultural sphere. At least, it was irrelevant to the admiration of fair skin that existed in Western culture.

The question is why white skin was considered beautiful in the East as well. Intrinsically, we find no physiological or psychological reason for thinking white skin, excessively white at that, beautiful. White skin may of course evoke a sense of beauty by conveying an impression of cleanliness, but that alone does not sufficiently explain the taste. Indeed, the passion for white skin was singularly intense.

What comes to mind is the symbolic meaning of white skin. White skin normally conveys an impression that its owner does not engage in physical labor or does not leave the house at all, hence an association with affluence. White skin then can convey two symbolic meanings: protective shelter and high social standing.

This is not limited to China. In the Classical period (5–4 centuries BCE) in ancient Greece, women began to be confined to their chambers, and as a result their skin turned extremely pale.[14]

Thus seen, aesthetics that respects white skin is not unrelated to the formation of male-dominant society. In fact, research in cultural anthropology hardly ever reports on a preference for white skin in matriarchal society.

3. CHARMS OF SUBCUTANEOUS FAT

Chinese Culture That Respects Slimness

Is a well-rounded form appealing, or a slim body shape? That differs depending upon the culture and the age. As the Japanese expression *slim beauty* (*yasebijin*) indicates, at present, slender women are certainly considered beautiful. Many young women sacrifice health and shy away from favorite foods to concentrate on losing weight. This applies to contemporary China as well.

And yet, the concept of a slim body as beautiful has an unexpectedly short history. Despite the fact that both the idea and the method of dieting come from the West, until a little over one hundred years ago, an ample body still represented female beauty in Europe as well. As exemplified by Pierre-Auguste Renoir's paintings, women in paintings all possessed full bodies.

It was in the late nineteenth century that slim women came to be considered beautiful in Europe. Edward Shorter points out in his *Women's Bodies: Social History of Women's Encounter with Health, Ill-Health, and Medicine,* that this is related to the changes of the female body in modern times. In the nineteenth century, European women's body shape went through major changes. Food became richer, bringing good nutrition. Women became taller, their body frame stronger. As they came to be able to eat equally well with men, they removed their body-compressing corsets. Due to such changes in objective circumstances, female bodies became larger and plumper. There was scarcity value in a voluptuous body when small, slender women were the majority, but when full-bodied women increased, slimness came to be valued—so the critic Unno Hiroshi convincingly argues in his *History of Dieting* (*Daietto no rekishi*).[15]

While this theory closely matches Western culture, it may not fully explain the phenomena in East Asia. In China, slim women were considered beautiful from ancient times. The term *Chu waist* (or the slim torso that women of the State of Chu emulated) goes back two thousand years, and the surpassing beauty Lin Daiyu in *A Dream of Red Mansions* (*Honglou meng,* mid-eighteenth century) is also slender. Although we lack statistical data, viewing descriptions in literary works and the height and external appearances of unearthed remains (for example, the mummified corpse from Mawan-dui, an archaeological site located in Changsha, Hunan), the average physique of women long ago was never large. Not a few examples praise petite bodies in literary works. In his rhyme-prose on "Jiangfei" ("Jiangfei fu"), Xie Lingyun (385–433) described the legendary goddess with the phrase "small hips and delicate bones, vermilion lips and lustrous teeth." The reference to "delicate bones" clearly illustrates the aesthetics that regards the petite as beautiful.

With the fashion of foot binding that seems to have started in the mid-tenth century, it became difficult for women to become plump due to physiological restrictions. But, prior to that, many women were thin to begin with in ancient China. If I were to follow Unno Hiroshi's logic, plump body shape should have been considered superior. The reality is the opposite, however.

Despite the fact that the majority of women were petite, slim bodies continued to be favored.

In East Asia, it is only since modern times that a tall, slender shape has been admired as proof of health and well-developed physique.

Plumpness Was Admired in the Tang Period

Erik Heuer perceived China as "a culture that totally rejected the opulence of the female body,"[16] but that is a complete misunderstanding. It is true that from the Spring and Autumn (722–481 BCE), and the Warring States periods (403–221 BCE) down to the Qing dynasty (1644–1911), the times when slender bodies were considered beautiful overwhelmingly predominated. However, there was an era, if short, when plumpness, or sometimes even a physique that could only be called obese, was thought to be beautiful.

Reproductions of Tang paintings and mural paintings of unearthed tombs contain many images of women. They reveal that most women of a certain era of the Tang were quite round. We may comfortably assume that those painted in pictures were considered to be beautiful women.

In examining these beauties, the short and plump shape is notable. "Willow waists" that had been admired from the Spring and Autumn period completely disappeared, and robes without sashes seem to have liberated the wearers from the constriction given to the waist. The full-moon facial shape exceeds plumpness, nearly reaching the point where it may even suggest obesity. The full-cheeked face, which later came to be regarded in Japan as beautiful, called *shimobukure* (rounder toward the bottom of the face), recurs in Tang paintings (figure 1.6). This indicates that an aesthetic sense that finds beauty in voluptuousness had already been established.

A similar tendency is also found to some extent in literary representations. Descriptions in poetry do not necessarily match reality, which I would like to discuss in greater detail later. Skipping poetry for now, I will here concentrate on prose, which is free from poetic conventions, ruling forms, and metric patterns.

The *Old Book of Tang* (*Jiu Tangshu*), volume 51, "Biographies 1, Empresses and Imperial Consorts 1," describes the imperial consort Yang Guifei as "full and enchanting in appearance, skilled in singing and dancing." Opulence must have been emphasized as descriptive of Yang Guifei's physical beauty, precisely because a round body shape was thought beautiful. Unfortunately, the standard of fullness is unknown. Taking into account such elements as the age when there was no custom of measuring body weight and the fashion of robes without sashes around the body, it is more or less

Figure 1.6. *Music and Fun at Court* (*Gong'yue tu*), Detail. Tang. National Palace Museum (Taipei, Taiwan). *Source: Glimpses*, 9.

certain that it was not the level just above what is now called standard body weight. Probably Yang Guifei was so plump that a glance was sufficient to notice how round she was.

However, already by the Song (960–1279), such plump women rarely appear in paintings. Exactly when they disappeared is as hard to specify as when they appeared. Such sort are not picked up in official histories, which only record great men and major events. The insufficiency of materials that would provide proof makes chronological investigation difficult. However, as seen in mural paintings in the Li Shou Tomb (631), the burial site of the cousin of the Tang founder Li Yuan, and the tomb of Li Feng (675), Li Yuan's fifteenth son, women of early Tang were still slender (figure 1.7). Yet, in the high Tang (712–765), images of plump women appeared in mural paintings of tombs belonging to important personages. A lady-in-waiting with such a physique is painted in the tomb of the military leader Su Sixu, constructed in 745 (figure 1.8).

The same tendency is observed in silk paintings as well. The high Tang painter Zhang Xuan portrays plump women in *Spring Outing of the Lady of the State of Guo* (*Guoguo Furen youchun tu*, figure 1.9) and *Preparing Newly-Woven Silk* (*Daolian tu*). His somewhat later contemporary Zhou Fang (c. 730–800) also painted women of similar physique in *Courtiers Playing Backgammon* (*Neiren shuanglu*, figure 1.10).

Figure 1.7. Mural Painting from the Li Feng Tomb. Tang. Shaanxi Provincial Museum (Xi'an). *Source:* Shaanxi Provincial Museum, ed. *Shaanxi Provincial Museum*. Kōdansha, 1981, figure 162.

Figure 1.8. Mural Painting from the Su Sixu Tomb. Tang. Shaanxi Provincial Museum (Xi'an). *Source:* Xu Guangji, ed. *Zhongguo chutu bihua quanji*, vol. 7 (*Complete Collection of Unearthed Chinese Mural Paintings*). Kexue Chubanshe, 2012, figure 345.

Images of beautiful women depicted in literature may deviate from facts for rhetorical effect, but some pieces offer portrayals close to reality. In the "Farewell Poem for Li Yuan Returning to Bangu, with a Preface," the Tang essayist and poet Han Yu has a phrase, "carved eyebrows and full cheeks, clear-voiced and lithe-bodied." This indicates that the plump shape of the face, full in the lower half, remained a sign of a beauty. Han Yu was born in

Figure 1.9. From Zhang Xuan, *Spring Outing of the Lady of the State of Guo* (Also Known in English as *Spring Outing of the Tang Court*). Tang (Copy from the Song period). Liaoning Provincial Museum (Shenyang City). *Source:* Liaoning Provincial Museum, ed. *Liaoning Provincial Museum.* Kōdansha, 1982, figure 93.

768 and died in 824. From the late eighth century to early ninth century, an opulent body shape may still have been considered beautiful.

At the latest in the tenth century, however, the trend toward ampleness must have waned. For instance, in *Han Xizai's Night Revels* (*Han Xizai yeyuan tu*, figure 1.11), painted in mid-tenth century, ample women no longer appear. Depending upon the region, the tendency to favor voluptuous body shape may have still remained. Although from the same Five Dynasties period (907–960), women who appear in *Folk Performance, a Relief* (*San'yue tu fudiao*) unearthed in Quyang County, Hebei province, from the tomb of the regional military governor Wang Chuzhi (863–923), for example, are still full-bodied. In the Song, the majority of beautiful women appearing in paintings became slender. On the other hand, as in *Cooling Off by the Palace Pond* (*Gongzhao naliang*) by an anonymous painter (figure 1.12), images of a beauty of the opulent type are found here and there. However, given the Chinese proclivity to imitate painting styles of an earlier period, it is unclear whether Song period painters who depicted obese women in fact consciously intended to represent reality. For example, *Beautiful Women's Outing* (*Hua liren xing*, figure 1.13) by Li Gonglin of the Song period reproduces the earlier composition and drawing technique of *Spring Outing of the Lady of the State of Guo* and may not represent contemporary taste.

Figure 1.10. Zhou Fang, *Courtiers Playing Backgammon*. Tang. National Palace Museum (Taipei, Taiwan). *Source: Glimpses*, 10.

Figure 1.11. From Gu Hongzhong, *Han Xizai's Night Revels*. Five Dynasties Period (907–960). Palace Museum (Beijing). *Source:* Yang Baida, editor-in-chief. *Gugong wen'wu dadian* (*Antiques Canon, The Palace Museum*, hereafter *Antiques Canon*), I (Paintings). Fujian Renmin Publishing House, Jiangxi Educational Publishing House, Zhejiang Educational Publishing House, Forbidden Palace Publishing House, 1994, figures 48–49.

Figure 1.12. *Cooling Off by the Palace Pond*. Song. National Palace Museum (Taibei, Taiwan). *Source: Glimpses*, 29.

Figure 1.13. From Li Gonglin, *Beautiful Women's Outing*. Song. National Palace Museum (Taibei, Taiwan). *Source: Glimpses*, 14.

Why Opulence Was Liked

But why did well-rounded women gain favor? Paintings of plump women suddenly appeared in the Tang. However, no cause is found from within the culture for such an abrupt change. Based on the mild speed of social development and pattern of cultural transition of those days among other things, it is hard to imagine that it derived from internal cultural changes.

The most probable reason is intercultural influence. Many northern people were involved in the founding of the Sui and Tang dynasties (581–618, 618–907). Both Sui and Tang emperors descended from the Xianbei, a nomadic people residing in northeast China and Mongolia, and, in the Tang period in particular, there were many military leaders called "barbarian officers" (*fanjiang*). Following military victories, equestrian peoples of remote regions moved southward in large groups and settled in the regions populated by the Han people.

Those groups made hunting and cattle raising their major means of production. Their staple food was probably meat rather than grains. Judging from the production standards of those days, they would not necessarily have been able to consume sufficient meat while leading a nomadic life. However, having made their mark as warriors and come to settle in cities as military officers or high-ranking officials, the situation should have greatly changed. While meat remained the staple food, the amount eaten at each meal must have increased greatly. Needless to say, such a sudden change in eating habits would result in corpulence. And women who hardly exercised must have been more prone to adding surplus fat.

However, that alone cannot cause the 180-degree reversal of aesthetic appreciation. As stated earlier, by the time of the founding of the Tang, many military leaders of ethnic groups became aristocrats and held high positions and power as military officers or government officials. Customs of food, clothing, accessories, and makeup may spread from the upper to lower classes in any culture, but the reverse is impossible. In the first place, there is no absolute criterion for "beauty." In any era, as stated earlier, "aristocratic" is beautiful, and "humble" ugly. "Upper" is beautiful, and "lower" ugly. "Affluent" is beautiful, and "poor" ugly.

This paradigm can also explain the changes in aesthetics during the Tang. It is not hard to conjecture that Tang commoners were influenced by criteria of beauty in upper-class women wearing lovely clothing and seated on gorgeous palanquins. The aesthetic view favoring plump body shapes probably developed in this manner. In other words, what began to show through the thick, subcutaneous fat was the reversal of power relations. External conditions that made it difficult for Han women, whose staple food was grains, to become plump even if they wished to, must have also accelerated the reversal of aesthetics.

The return to the taste for slimness, starting in the Song period (960–1279) and particularly during the Southern Song (1127–1279), is also inexplicable if we ignore the changes in racial relationships. In reaction against the invasion of different ethnic groups from remote regions during the Five Dynasties and Ten Kingdoms period, the Southern Song ruled by the Han took a rather negative attitude toward minority cultures. Defeated in the war against Tungusic people from the north and driven southward where they reestablished their dynasty, in the Southern Song period Han xenophobia became particularly intense. This, too, must have contributed to the return to ancient aesthetics.

Return to Slimness

Aside from the exceptions in the Tang period, it is rather rare in Chinese history to find ampleness viewed as beautiful. However, praise of a rich female body is not totally absent. In Song Yu's "The Divine Woman," we encounter the description, "her form richly full and solemnly beautiful, holding a warm, jewel-like face." The expression *richly full* is synonymous with *voluptuous*. However, the definition of *voluptuousness* may vary depending upon the era. However, in verifying the common image of feminine beauty, if we reference visual arts such as painting and sculpture we can roughly surmise the implication of such an expression.

Mural and cloth paintings unearthed from tombs of the Warring States and Han periods include no images of plump women, at least as far as is presently known. Thus, with respect to the expression *opulent*, we can assume that the gap in sensibility was fairly large between the Tang and earlier ages.

That also applies to the Song. Eliminating some exceptions, until the Qing period (1644–1911) we hardly find examples depicting opulent women as beauties. The thirtieth installment of *A Dream of Red Mansions* contains an interesting reference to physical shape. While the protagonist Jia Baoyu is conversing with a female cousin Xue Baochai, whose name means Jeweled Hairpin, she mentions her low tolerance to heat. Jia Baoyu carelessly responds as follows:

> "No wonder they compare you to Lady Yang, you're both 'plump and sensitive to the heat.'"
> Baochai was so enraged by this remark that she could have flown into a temper, but she restrained herself. This quip rankled so much, however, that she reddened and laughed sarcastically.
> "If I'm so like Lady Yang," she retorted, "it's too bad I've no brother or cousin able to be another Yang Guozhong."[17]

Judging from the portrayal of a young woman angered and embarrassed at mention of her plumpness, we can presume that being plump was regarded as a shortcoming in those days. In other words, in the eighteenth century, at least among the rich aristocracy, there was no awareness of voluptuousness as beauty.

NOTES

1. Kōhara Yukinari, *A Book of Faces* (*Kao no hon*) (Chūō Kōronsha, 1989), 140.
2. Zhang Wencheng, *The Grotto of Immortals* (*Youxian ku*). Translated by Imamura Yoshio as *Yūsenkutsu* (Iwanami Shoten, 1990), 36.
3. Dominique Paquet, *Miroir, mon beau miroir: une histoire de la beauté* (Gallimard, 1997). Translated by Kimura Keiichi under the editorial supervision of Ishii Mikiko as *Bijo no rekishi* (Sōgensha, 1999), 21.
4. Ibid., 25.

5. Murasawa Hirohito, *Cultural Accounts of Faces* (*Kao no bunkashi*) (Tokyo Shoseki, 1992), 11.
6. Burton Watson (tr.), "The Goddess of the Luo." In *An Anthology of Translations: Classical Chinese Literature*, vol. 1, edited by John Minford and Joseph S. M. Lau (Columbia University Press, The Chinese University Press, 2000), 315.
7. Murasawa Hirohito, *op. cit.*, 35.
8. Royall Tyler (tr.), *The Tale of Genji*, vol. 1 (Viking, 2001), 130.
9. Hara Mitsumasa, *Inquiry into Ohaguro* (*Ohaguro no kenkyū*) (Ningen no Kagakusha, 1984), 57-64. His examples include *Categorized Compendium of Ancient Matters* (*Koji ruien*, compiled in the Meiji era), *The Pillow Book* (*Makura no sōshi*, ca. 996), *The Murasaki Shikibu Diary* (*Murasaki Shikibu nikki*, assumed to have been completed by 1010), *The Tales of Riverside Middle Counselor* (*Tsutsumi Chūnagon monogatari*, ca. 1055), *The Tale of Flowering Splendor* (*Eiga monogatari*, late Heian) from the early centuries, and *Miscellaneous Notes on a Journey to the East* (*Tōyū zakki*, 1788).
10. Burton Watson, *loc. cit.*
11. Murasawa Hirohito, *op. cit.*, 45.
12. Ovid, *Amores*. Translated with an introduction by Tom Bishop (Routledge, 2003), 9.
13. Burton Watson (tr.), *An Anthology of Translations: Classical Chinese Literature*, vol. 1, 315.
14. Dominique Paquet, *op. cit.*, 23.
15. Unno Hiroshi, *A History of Dieting* (*Daietto no rekishi*) (Shinshokan, 1998), 40-45.
16. *Sittengeschichte*, translated into Japanese as *Bi to miryoku no rekishi*, vol. 1, by Takayama Yōkichi (Tōkō Shoin, 1973), 15.
17. Cao Xueqin and Gao E, *A Dream of Red Mansions* (*Honglou meng*). Yang Xianyi and Gladys Yang (trs.), *A Dream of Red Mansions*, vol. 2 (Foreign Languages Press, 2003), 843. Lady Yang refers to Yang Guifei mentioned earlier in this chapter. Her cousin Yang Guozhong became prime minister through nepotism.

2

Feared Beauties

People admire beautiful women and praise beautiful countenances. When using the expression *a beautiful woman*, we sometimes assume her personality will be nice as well. Unlike "beauty" as abstraction, however, beautiful looks are physical characteristics. One does not necessarily possess superior virtue because one looks beautiful. Naturally, some beautiful persons are good, and others wicked. They are not to be admired simply for the reason that they possess attractive features. Notwithstanding, a beautiful woman is frequently regarded as a symbol of goodness. Goddesses that embody goodness, in fact, are always beautiful. This is a universal cultural phenomenon, and it was an ancient Greek notion that "what is beautiful is good."[1]

In China, for a long time a beautiful countenance was a metaphor for virtue. Vassals not appointed to positions of trust by the emperor likened themselves to forsaken beauties, and loyalty to him was compared to profound female affection for a man she cares about. Because of this rhetorical practice, beautiful women were, until a certain time, depicted in literature in combination with goodness.

On the other hand, we also see totally contradictory phenomena. Both in ancient Greek myths and Chinese tales of the strange of the Six Dynasties (222–589), the majority of goblins are female beauties. Foxes, snakes, and ghosts always disguise themselves as attractive women. Male demons and ghosts also appear at times, but they are ugly and frightful-looking from beginning to end. We hardly ever encounter a setting in which an apparition in the guise of a handsome man deceives a woman.

Today, too, side by side with fondness for beautiful women, we hear such labeling as "beautiful women are wicked" or "beautiful women are cruel." It is difficult to confirm whether this has become a commonly accepted idea, but it is a fact that such comments frequently occur in conversations among males. While beauties are liked, dread of them as fearful beings always lurks deep down in men's hearts.

When and how did the view that beautiful women are wicked originate? According to the historian and cultural specialist Inoue Shōichi, arguments for "rejecting beautiful women" and "encouraging ugly women" began to appear in Japan in moral education textbooks in the Meiji era (1868–1912). Books on the philosophy of life have also thoroughly looked down upon beautiful women. Inoue points out that the association of beautiful women with evil goes back to the Edo period, using as examples *Lessons with Illustrations for Admonishing Women* (*Jokai e-iri onna jitsugo-kyō*), published in 1695, and *Treasury of Great Learning for Women* (*Onna-Daigaku takarabako*) of 1716. Moreover, he argues that Meiji ethics further reinforced the Edo idea that beautiful appearances lead to vice.[2] The core of his theory is that changes in social relationships created an ethical view that is harsh on beautiful women. Namely, in modern times, as the fixed-class system disintegrated, equality of opportunity was realized to some degree. Thanks to this newfound freedom, beautiful women could use their appearances as weapons to help them rise from a lower to a higher class. Jealousy related to class ascendance took the form of ascribing evil to beautiful women.

In interpreting the Meiji view of beauties, this has certain persuasiveness. However, the equation of beautiful women with vice is not peculiar to modern Japan. Similar beauty bashing existed earlier. Again, it was not limited to Japan. In the first place, where did the Edo association between beautiful women and evil come from? It is sometimes said to originate in Chinese classics, but whether that is indeed the case is a question. What is more important is how the concept of beauties as evil is expressed in literary works, and how it affected the formation and establishment of the "beauty = sin" image. I would like to discuss these issues in this chapter.

1. BEAUTY IS ILL-OMENED

Beautiful Women Cause Calamity

In a nonfiction work I read in China as a junior high student, the father of a lovely girl laments: "The presence of such a beautiful child in our poor house may cause disaster." I did not then think this line particularly strange. I had frequently heard similar words. The idea that beautiful appearances brought forth misfortune was partly a matter of common sense.

In those days in China, when a girl in a commoner's household was reputed to be "a beauty," the parents, especially the mother, tended to feel anxious. Parents always love good-looking children, and people around them may also praise a child for her winning appearance. On the other hand, neighbors often bad-mouth, saying that beauty "incurs trouble" (*re shifei*) or "brings disaster" (*re huo*). Now that society has changed, this is not necessarily always the case, especially in urban areas. Until just decades ago, however, such views were common. Those of us belonging to the generation over age forty have carried from childhood an idea of "beautiful appearances = disasters."

Even today, incidents that demonstrate the "accuracy" of that "law" sometimes occur. In 1971, in an attempt to flee the country, Mao Zedong's heir apparent Lin Biao crashed to his death in the Mongolian territory. Following this "9.13 incident," rumors of "princess selection" for his son Lin Liguo raced through the streets. After the Cultural Revolution ended, a book provided details of the event.

One or two years before the "9.13 incident," Lin Biao's wife, Ye Qun, issued an order to military circles to find a bride for her son. After several months of "screening," they found an outstanding beauty. Lin Liguo's "princess" was a woman by the name of Zhang Ning. She was born into the family of an active military officer, who died of illness when she was small. Because she was pretty, she joined a military opera troupe while in elementary school and received special training to become an actress. She was chosen to be Lin Liguo's "princess bride" at around twenty years of age. The path of life she trod was indeed the very picture of "beautiful appearances = disasters." Right after the wedding, her husband Lin Liguo died in a jet crash along with his father. Not only was she detained, but her family was implicated in the Lin family's alleged coup attempt. She remarried after the Cultural Revolution but parted from her husband after having one child. When the child, her only son, became an elementary school pupil, he was killed by her former lover. The man had resented her for having spurned him. Because of beautiful looks, as it seems, not only she herself but her family members repeatedly suffered great damage.

History of Femme Fatale Legends

When did the concept that beautiful women are inauspicious and beautiful looks bring forth disasters take root in China? While difficult to date, evil women recorded in historical documents can be considered one origin of the association. The legend of Bao Si (eighth century BCE) is typical. This beautiful woman who wed King You of Zhou refused to smile after becoming his queen. Wishing to see her lovely smile at any cost, the king devised an ultimate strategy. For a supposed emergency, he lighted a signal fire on the beacon tower to summon his lords and their troops. Looking at the great confusion of the lords who gathered, Bao Si burst out laughing for the first time. Because King You tricked the lords again and again thereafter, nobody came to the rescue when the Quanrong nomads invaded.[3]

This legend is not found in historical writings. *The Annals of the Zhou Dynasty*, volume 4, of the *Records of the Grand Historian*, does refer to Bao Si, but she is described from a different angle, and the content is not exactly the same. The *Records* traces the ruin of the Eastern Zhou Dynasty (1027–771 BCE) to Bao Si's family background. In other words, King You's favor is seen as inescapable fate. The legend probably amplified this view.

There are other legends of beauty as a source of disaster. Take for example Li Ji (seventh century BCE), a concubine and later wife of Duke Xian of Jin, who caused the death of Shensheng, his heir, and also Daji (twelfth century BCE), a concubine of King Zhou of Yin (Shang), who caused the downfall of the Yin dynasty. Viewed chronologically, Daji and Bao Si are earlier than Li Ji, but if we view the order of recordings in historical documents, the story of Li Ji in *The Commentary of Zuo* (twenty-eighth year of the reign of Duke Zhuang of Lu and the fourth year of the reign of Duke Xi of Lu) antedates the account of Bao Si in the *Records*. Li Ji, a consort of Duke Xian of Jin, gave birth to two children, Xiqi and Zhuozi. She plotted to have Xiqi succeed to Duke Xian's seat, and conspired with the duke's favored vassals Liang Wu and Dong'guan Wu to have the heir Shensheng and two other princes, Chong'er and Yiwu, dispatched to the borderlands on the pretext of needed defense against foreign tribes. Further, she used slander to kill Prince Shensheng and banish the other two princes.

While Bao Si and Li Ji are historical characters, their accounts have been handed down as didactic stories about beauties bringing forth disasters. As I discuss below, *Biographies of Exemplary Women* (*Lienü zhuan*, ca. 18 BCE) by Liu Xiang of the Han period is an extremely important book.

Beautiful Countenances Beckon Death

The common idea that beauties bring about disasters was not established by these legends alone. *Biographies of Exemplary Women* chapters included in historical records reinforced this concept from a totally different direction.

We find a number of patterns among characters included in *Biographies of Exemplary Women*. One is the constant woman who guards her chastity at the cost of her life. Plundered by thieves or rebels and on the verge of being raped, she takes her own life in order to remain pure. This conduct is extolled as virtue. Such cases abound in biographies of exemplary women of different generations and are particularly numerous during the disturbances of war. In such records, beauty and violence form causal relationships. As a result, they convey to the reader an impression that beauty invites disgrace and ultimately causes death.

Folk tradition, which provides source materials for vernacular fiction from the Song dynasty (960–1279) on, also played an important role in establishing the idea that beautiful women brought about misfortune. One example is "The Pledge of Mandarin Ducks unto Death" in *Qingpingshan Studio Promptbooks* (*Qingpingshantang huaben*) of the Ming period (1368–1644). While portraying the unrestrained life of a woman by the name of Jiang Shuzhen, this story conveys a lesson that a beautiful woman is inauspicious and that a man enticed by one is always ruined in the end. The piece exerted great influence in the formation of common sense.

The protagonist of this fiction is exceedingly fond of men. She marries twice, and along the way has relations with a number of men. Strangely, not only her husbands but also all others who have had carnal relations with her either die unnaturally or commit murder. A poem by Zheng Ao of Later Jin (936–946), quoted in the story, best represents this theory of beauty as inauspicious:

Moth-feeler eyebrows are in truth belles' blades
They kill all the dandies of the world.

In other words, good looks are beautiful blades and end in ruining every playboy in society. The idea of beauty as vice, initially born of the Confucian view of history, permeated popular culture through storytelling and so forth.

Deceiving Men

Legends of evil women are also connected with the idea that beautiful women are frightening. This is another side of the Chinese image of beauty.

The *Analects of Confucius* (*Lun yu*) contains a phrase, "Women and underlings are difficult to handle."[4] As these words indicate, from the beginning Confucian ethics carried deep-rooted contempt of women.

The association between beauty and lasciviousness already existed in a poem called "The Lament" ("Lisao," also translated as "Encountering Trouble") by the poet and statesman Qu Yuan (340–278 BCE) of the State of Chu, a representative piece in the *Songs of the South* (*Chu ci*): "All your ladies were jealous of my delicate beauty / In their spiteful chattering they said I was a wanton."[5] This association developed hand in hand with Daoist asceticism in the Han and Six Dynasties periods through such expressions as *the hatchet that cuts nature* (carnal pleasure that takes men's lives), into the image of beauty beckoning death.

Bewitch the lord and lead the state to downfall. For self-interest's sake, harm a rival cruelly. Although the means they use differ from case to case, these two approaches are patterns common to evil women. Not just those concerned, even we of later times cower at their cruelty. The gap between beauty and cruelty is endlessly interesting. It is quite natural to receive from these records the impression that beautiful women are dangerous. Thus, the legend that "beauties are frightful" was born.

Among popular tradition, what spread this concept was probably tales of the strange, of which many appeared in the Six Dynasties period. There is a variety of types like ghost stories and tales of animal metamorphoses, but when those beings disguise themselves as humans, they invariably present themselves as beautiful women. Now, why did ghosts and foxes in tales of the strange assume the shape of a beautiful woman instead of a beautiful man? Basically, two reasons can be given. The structure of patriarchal society, especially, can be considered the greatest source of such fantasy.

With the establishment of patriarchal society, which occurred fairly early in China, women were excluded from major social activities, and their status naturally was reduced as well. In particular, from the Han period when Confucianism became the official learning, women began to be confined to homes. Their roles being limited to child raising and housework, they were virtually deprived of a social life.

Tales of the strange were mainly written with an assumed male audience. This determined, a priori, the gender definition of goblins in this genre. In real life, men could use their ability, be it power or money, to get beautiful women as they wished. They had no need to take the trouble to assume the shape of beautiful men to flatter or deceive women. Conversely, women could not gain power or money unless they used such guile. Imagination about bewitching women offers unexpectedness and fascination precisely within the reality of male predominance over females. To put it differently, the structure of a beauty bewitching a man itself demonstrates the power relationship between men and women.

The Metaphor of Power Relationship

Men seem to intrinsically harbor a kind of masochistic desire such that they greatly enjoy stories in which a male character suffers torture by a ghost in the shape of a beautiful woman. However, we cannot overlook a desire to confirm the power relationship that lurks behind this surface narrative. The fantasy about a superior person suffering a reversal of positions and battling to overwhelm the inferior one, in other words, contributes to reaffirming the hierarchy.

This does not occur only between men and women. A similar desire exists in every hierarchical relationship. Kings and rebels, Central States and "barbarians," heirs to the crown and usurpers—there are many variations. Today, the same is reproduced in Hollywood movies in the form of the police versus criminals, white settlers versus "barbarous Indians," good American citizens versus Arab terrorists.

The other reason is the remarkable one-sidedness in the gender of the readership. Tales of the strange, written in literary Chinese, were intended for men.

In premodern China, education was basically a system that presupposed screening of candidates for government officials. Forbidden to become government officials, women in general were not even given opportunities to receive education. Excluding such occupations as courtesans, women had no need to acquire basic cultivation in literary arts. It sufficed that they could read and write at a level necessary for daily lives. Literary Chinese differed from the vernacular, and its acquisition required professional training. Basically, only men could receive such training. In fact, private academies prohibited the entrance of girls. Even in affluent homes, the best the parents did was merely to keep a home tutor until a daughter reached adulthood.

The pattern seen in supernatural tales of goblins disguised as beautiful females is a result of assuming male readers in male-centered society. There might have been some variations in style, had female readers existed.

In fact, starting in the Ming period (1368–1644), with the development of the art of printing, women began to read books in their chambers. Amidst the massive production of "talented men and fair women fiction," beautiful females who deceived men disappeared. There, the conflict between good and evil evolved between the inelegant rich and the talented poor, and corrupt bureaucrats and pure-minded public servants. It is no mere coincidence that in *Strange Tales from the Make-Do Studio* (*Liaozhai zhiyi*, late seventeenth century by Pu Songling), which was intended for male intellectuals and written in difficult literary style, foxes still appear disguised as attractive women. The author's subconscious might have been at work.

That all transformations take the form of a beautiful woman is related to the transmission of Buddhism as well. From the start, in Buddhism, carnal desire was something to refrain from, and it was also the greatest "enemy" of ascetic practices. Among Buddhist tales, such as those collected in the *Forest of Gems in the Garden of the Dharma* (*Fayuan zhulin*, completed in 668), there are numerous episodes such as that of a man who, seduced by a demon in the guise of a beautiful woman and about to be devoured, has a narrow escape thanks to invoking the name of Amitabha Buddha. The embodiment of carnal desire that appears in these tales is invariably a beautiful woman. The more attractive her appearance, the stronger her seductive power. Ghosts and goblins that appear in Buddhist tales, too, have to be enchantresses in view of the structure of the narrative.

2. BEAUTIFUL WOMEN ARE CRUEL

A Cold-Blooded Beauty with a Smiling Face

Goblins disguised as beautiful women are frightful. But beautiful women in reality are even more terrifying. This is because they ruin men and cause them to die.

The Qing period fiction *A Dream of Red Mansions*, installment 12, introduces an episode in which Wang Xifeng, or Sister Phoenix, the wife to the main character's paternal first cousin, lays a trap and in the end causes a young man, Jia Rui, to die. Falling in love with her at first sight despite the fact that she is a married woman, Jia Rui confesses his love and proposes a tryst. Sister Phoenix takes no liking at all to him, but offhandedly accepts the offer just to teach him a lesson.

When Jia Rui appears in the backyard at the appointed time, Sister Phoenix has the doors on both sides of the pathway locked, leaving him to stand all night in the cold midwinter wind. Enraged by Jia Rui's conduct of "staying out overnight" for the first time, his serious, honest grandfather and guardian beat him. Even then the young man cannot see through Sister Phoenix's real intention. He reproaches her for having failed to keep her promise. Unable to give up, he entreats her to meet him yet again. Sister Phoenix again agrees, but has two ruffians, Jia Rong and Jia Qiang, ambush him. His shameful behavior thoroughly exposed, Jia Rui is finally released after drafting a bond of debt for fifty silver *liang*. On his way home, human waste falls suddenly on the exhausted young man's head from the second story. Having been deceived by Sister Phoenix and now doubly shocked, he becomes seriously ill and eventually dies.

If we assume that Jia Rui is a playboy and that his difficulties flow from that, then that is that. On the other hand, Sister Phoenix's cruelty is cast into relief through this event. While Jia Rui entertains wicked intentions, if she had remonstrated with him, or guided him to give her up, he would not have lost his life. She, however, does not do so. As if catching a prey, she sets double and triple traps to slowly drive him to his death.

Sister Phoenix's cold-bloodedness is not only directed to Jia Rui. She is even more merciless toward Second Sister You. Sister Phoenix's husband, Jia Lian, secretly makes Second Sister You his concubine. After learning of this, Sister Phoenix sets out to retaliate, while pretending to be warmhearted in Second Sister You's presence. Sister Phoenix is finally satisfied when she has Second Sister You killed cruelly.

Wicked Women in the Street

One who is even crueler is Pan Jinlian, or Golden Lotus, in *The Plum in the Golden Vase* (*Jinping mei*), a late Ming period novel partially based on *Outlaws of the Marsh* mentioned below. A concubine of an old merchant, after his death she is made to marry the dwarf Wu the Elder. On becoming acquainted with the rich, lustful merchant Ximen Qing, she falls in love. In order to continue the illicit relationship, together with him she poisons her husband to death.

At any rate, many of the women who have appeared in Chinese fiction are weak-willed. They can do nothing about the arrogance of government officials, their own poverty-stricken life, and their husbands' worldly pleasures. Among numerous such women, Sister Phoenix of *A Dream of Red Mansions* and Golden Lotus of *The Plum in the Golden Vase*, each capable of frightening men, cut striking figures.

Both Sister Phoenix and Golden Lotus are beautiful. This is no mere coincidence. For an ugly woman is never characterized as brutal in Chinese fiction, whether written in literary language or in the vernacular. "The Jealous-Woman River" ("Dufu Jinxiang") in the "Records of the Moon" ("Nuogao ji") section of *Miscellaneous Morsels from Youyang* (*Youyang zazu*, the Tang period) is a story in which an ugly woman takes revenge in the form of a ghost on a man who favors beautiful looks. The ugly woman's retaliation springs from intense jealousy, but her conduct is more likable than brutal. A situation in which an ugly woman is cruel is devoid of interest and is hard to develop into a successful story.

When did the image of a cruel beauty appear? Historical documents now and then present wicked women, but is that indeed where the pattern originated?

The aforementioned historical consorts Daji, Bao Si, Li Ji, and others are typical wicked women. They enchanted their monarchs and lords, and spurred them toward tyranny. However, they did not directly treat others cruelly. The *Commentary of Zuo* contains a description of Lady Xia (seventh century BCE), a princess of the State of Cheng. She was a lascivious woman, but did not do anything particularly cruel. *Records of the Grand Historian* details the dreadful way in which Empress Dowager Lü (second century BCE) treated Consort Qi. Lü's conduct is so cruel that it makes the reader shudder, but she is neither beautiful nor ugly.

In historical writings, cruelty and beauty do not seem to have been necessarily connected. Another important point is that wicked women who appear in histories are without exception ladies of the rear palace. Their cruelty was necessitated in order to protect themselves amidst intense survival battles. We find no records of ordinary women, like the above-quoted Sister Phoenix and Golden Lotus, who end in committing atrocities that they should have been able to avoid had they so wished.

Behind Fragility

What about old fiction? Putting aside tales of goblins and limiting to pieces portraying human lives, women who appear in Tang romances are far from cruel; they do not even dominate men. The heroine Yingying, or Oriole, of "The Story of Yingying" ("Yingying zhuan") only endlessly sheds tears when discarded by a man. When Xiaoyu, or Small Gem, of "The Story of Huo Xiaoyu" ("Huo Xiaoyu zhuan") reproached her sworn lover Li Yi for his mercilessness, she only "stretched her left hand to grasp Li Yi's elbow, hurled a wine cup to the ground with her right, wailed aloud a few times, then expired." These women are mercilessly forsaken after being toyed with to men's satisfaction. Before the selfish men, the beautiful women simply dissolve into tears. We only see there the image of womanhood as wronged and oppressed.

When did cruel beauty emerge? Aside from goblins disguised as enchantresses, the oldest examples from fiction, including stage plays, go back to promptbooks (*huaben*, anthologies of materials for narrative performances). A typical example is Qingnu, the central character of "The Golden Eel Brings Calamity to Officer Ji" in *Stories to Caution the World* (*Jinshi tongyan*) from Southern Song (1127–1279). Using her beauty as a weapon, she randomly forms relationships with men. When having a tryst with a man by the name of Zhang Bin, she happens to be caught by a boy called Fulang. She mercilessly kills the seven-year-old boy, fearing the exposure of her affair. Although written as a story of retribution, such characterization never appears in fiction in literary Chinese. Again, in "Cao Baiming Is Mistaken for a Robber" in *Qingpingshan Studio Promptbooks* of the Ming period, a tale based on what is said to be a real story from the Yuan period (1260–1368), the protagonist Xie Xiaotao, or Little Peach, hatches a plan with her lover in order to trap her husband. The image of such a woman recurs fairly frequently in Ming period fiction.

Why was the image of a cruel beauty created? Some vernacular novels in the Ming period made use of Song narrative scripts; authors of others collected and rewrote tales from popular tradition. The greatest characteristic of vernacular novels is the didactic theme recommending the good and punishing the evil. But this didacticism originally derived from popular morality often portrayed in folk performing arts. Fiction of the evil beauty type was perhaps naturally born of such street morals.

Upon reading such stories, we find a common narrative setting. Namely, the central male character always marries, or takes sexual interest in, a woman beyond his circumstances. Wu the Elder in *Outlaws of the Marsh* (*Shuihu zhuan*, Ming period; also translated as *All Men Are Brothers* and *Water Margin*) is short and extremely ugly. Yet he married a rare beauty, Golden Lotus, a setting repeated in *The Plum in the Golden Vase*. The young man Jia Rui in *A Dream of Red Mansions* is not particularly ugly, but between him and Sister Phoenix, the woman he adores, is an insurmountable difference in social standing, of which he is totally oblivious.

What type of woman a man marries indicates a symbolic relationship. Intrinsically, status and money alone guarantee monopoly of feminine beauty. Therefore, government officials and the rich naturally have good-looking wives and concubines, but men of no political or financial power must content themselves with the position of "the weak" in terms of sexuality. While women are allowed to climb higher and higher, overriding class stratification in exchange for beauty, men basically lack such opportunities. I say "basically," because, in legend, Empress Consort Wu (Zetian Wu Hou, or Wu Zetian, 624–705) is said to have kept male concubines, or more literally, men of lovely "face and head" (*mianshou*). But this is an exception.

In that sense, stories of cruel beauties were originally intended to inculcate in men "the horror of marriage beyond one's means," rather than providing a moral that beauty is cruel. In fact, in such stories men who act beyond their social standing are fiercely ridiculed. The message is that weak men cannot expect salvation, that the weak should rest satisfied with marriages that befit the weak.

Interestingly, however, the moral conveyed by those stories resulted in reinforcing the concept that beautiful women are cruel.

As Long As the Heart Is Beautiful

The common idea that beautiful women are cruel goes hand in hand with the Confucian view of women, especially the formation and spread of the legend of ugly women. In other words, the moral view that a woman, even if ugly, is an ideal woman so long as she has virtue, is related to the formation of the image of a beauty as cruel. Behind it is the idea that a woman's beauty is the source of vice.

In Japanese we find such expressions as *pernicious woman* (*dokufu*) and *evil woman* (*akujo*), but there is none at all in modern Chinese. The phrase *cruel woman* (*hendu-de nüren*), literally "cruelly pernicious female," is in use in Chinese, but the expression *cruel* (*hendu*) can be used as an adjective not only for women but men as well, along with another phrase meaning *cruel* (*edu*), literally "evilly pernicious." The term *pernicious old lady* (*du poniang*) that appears in Ming vernacular fiction is now obsolete. Instead, *outpouring woman* (*pofu*) and *wild woman* (*hanfu*) are still in frequent use today. Neither is equivalent to Japanese *pernicious woman*. Rather, they mean intractable "hussy." Again, in modern Chinese we have *destructive woman* (*huai nüren*), but it carries a different nuance from *pernicious woman*, and the history of its usage is short.

The same applies also to "cruel beauty." Even as it established itself as an important human image, the Chinese language lacks terms that express it. Whether Golden Lotus or Sister Phoenix, their "pernicious" manners were portrayed through concrete events and scenes; it was not that the expression *pernicious woman* was used to describe them in the text.

The widely accepted concept that beautiful women are cruel is reinforced by legends of ugly women, and understood in the context of praise of ugly women. The idea that a woman is good as long as her heart is beautiful even if she looks ugly goes back to Liu Xiang's *Biographies of Exemplary Women*, compiled toward the end of the Former Han dynasty. The legend of Zhongli Chun in the category of "Accomplished Speakers" is particularly well known. Her head resembled a millstone, and her eyes were sunk. Her hands were knotty, her fingers fat. Because she was ugly, at age forty she could not find anyone to marry her.

One day, humbly clad, she visited King Xuan, the monarch of the State of Qi. She said to the official in charge, "I am an unwed woman of Qi. I have heard of the king's saintly virtue, and would like to sweep the rear palace for him." Court attendants burst out laughing, covering their mouths, but the king was curious enough to grant her an audience. Zhongli Chun remonstrated the king: even as the kingdom faced the threat of two powerful neighboring states, his palace was luxuriously decorated, nefarious vassals surrounded him, and, unaware of the crisis, he daily indulged in eating and drinking. At this rate, she said, the state would be imperiled. Impressed by her eloquent admonition, King Xuan took her as his queen. He followed her advice by ousting treacherous retainers and ending his extravagant lifestyle. Because he enriched the state treasury and strengthened the military, government stabilized and the economy prospered.

Aside from Zhongli Chun, the same chapter of the *Biographies of Exemplary Women* also records the deeds of "Permanent Lump Woman" ("Suliunü") and "Outcast Orphan Woman" ("Guzhu-nü"). The woman nicknamed "Permanent Lump Woman" had a large protrusion on the nape of her neck, the story goes, but became queen because she counseled King Min of the State of Qi, and later helped the king to build prosperity. "Outcast Orphan Woman," also ugly, was highly virtuous, so she became the wife of the chief minister of Qi. Strangely all three are women of Qi, but in any case Liu Xiang's *Biographies of Exemplary Women* offers a sense of value by which virtue is far more important for women than appearances.

Why Is Ugliness Noble?

Although Liu Xiang's *Biographies of Exemplary Women* is the origin of the praise of ugly women, it did not immediately permeate throughout the culture. Naturally, for the concept of beauties as cruel to be formed, many other causes must have also existed. In fact, after *Biographies of Exemplary Women* circulated, feminine beauty continued to be admired, and a beautiful woman as a metaphor for a loyal vassal remained in use.

The fact that the idea of fidelity as more highly valued than appearance became universally accepted in Chinese culture is not unrelated to the fact that "biographies of exemplary women" became a category in history books. *Book of Later Han (Hou-Han shu)*, volume 84, was the first to set up "biographies of exemplary women" as a classifier. Drawing on this source, the same category was set up in the *Book of Jin* (volume 96), *Book of Wei* (volume 92), *Book of Sui* (volume 80), *History of Northern Dynasties* (volume 91), *Old Book of Tang* (193), *New Book of Tang* (volume 205), *History of Song* (volume 460), *History of Liao* (volume 107), *History of Jin* (volume 130), *History of Yuan* (volumes 200, 201), *History of Ming* (301, 302, 303), *Draft History of Qing* (volumes 508, 509, 510, 511), and so forth. Among the Twenty-Five Histories, every history of a unified dynasty includes "biographies of exemplary women," and starting with the *History of Song*, the category is found in other historical works. Moreover, as time passes, the number of women handled increases, expanding to a massive amount, especially from the Ming period on.

An "exemplary woman" means a woman of integrity and chastity. Thus, individuals taken up under this category are originally irrelevant to what their appearances are. However, in biographies of "exemplary women" in history books, physical beauty continues to be portrayed in negative terms.

A Virtue of Refraining from Beauty

In "Lessons for Women" ("Nüjie") the woman author Ban Zhao of the Later Han describes concrete criteria of women's "virtue." According to this work, women have four kinds of virtue: "womanly virtue," "womanly words," "womanly bearing," and "womanly work" (*fude, fuyan, furung, fugong*). "Womanly bearing" does not, it says, signify "beautiful countenance" (*yanse meili*); rather, "To wash and scrub filth away with a basin of water, to keep clothes and ornaments fresh and clean, to wash the head and bathe the body regularly, and to keep the person free from disgraceful filth may be called the characteristics of womanly bearing."[6] In short, it suffices to take timely baths to stay physically clean, and wash clothes well to look neat and tidy. Here the idea of denying attractive looks is clearly emphasized. In addition, the piece considers that "enchanting manners" (*yaotiao zuodai*) displayed before people, or dressing up prettily and acting coquettishly, goes against virtue.

Starting in Wei and Jin (220–265, 265–420), "biographies of exemplary women" gradually began to handle and extol daughters pious to their parents and women who commit suicide in order to protect their chastity or faithfulness. Writings touching directly upon the relationship between physical appearance and feminine virtue became fewer, and from the Song period on, integrity rather than beauty became a crucial standard for evaluating women.

Confucianism had, from the outset, the tendency to find aesthetic value in negative sentiments such as associations with severe poverty, misfortune, grief, and solitude. There is a saying, "accepting poverty and enjoying humbleness" (*anpin luojian*), meaning that one should endure poverty and be satisfied with low rank. As this phrase indicates, it was regarded as lofty not to seek success and fulfillment of desires, and virtuous to retain human dignity in the face of ill luck and hardship. Although it was not that abstinence was advocated unconditionally, desire was basically considered something to be controlled. In this context, it came to be thought that beauty of the heart was to be prized above beauty of appearance, and that beautiful looks, to the contrary, presaged disasters.

3. BEAUTIFUL WOMEN ARE HAPLESS

Crimson Face Means a Hapless Fate

Not only do beautiful women invite misfortune to their families and others, but their own lives are also unlucky. In China there is an expression, "crimson face, hapless fate," meaning that a beauty is fated to lead an unfortunate life. Deeply rooted in popular culture, the phrase is frequently used in daily lives, even today.

A Ming period play called *The Peony Pavilion* (*Mudan ting*) by Tang Xianzu introduces a song:

Wherefore in this world
Does a crimson face simply mean hapless fate
With such forlorn pain and utter solitude?[7]

Because drama is close to street life, the expression "crimson face, hapless fate" came to be widely used from early on.

The origin of this set phrase is not known, nor is it clear when it first appeared. Li Yu of the Qing period once referred to its etymology in his *Occasional Contemplations*: "The loveliest [of flowers] is peach [blossoms], and the shortest-lived is also peach [blossoms]. The theory of crimson face and hapless fate stems from this." However, the expression *crimson face* goes back to "Dancing, a Rhyme-Prose" ("Wu fu") by Fu Yi of the Han period, and "Lady Li, a Rhyme-Prose" ("Li-furen fu") by Emperor Wu of Han also uses it in the sense of feminine beauty. The theory that it developed as a metaphor from association with peach blossoms must be groundless conjecture.

The old four-character set phrase *crimson face, hapless fate* goes back to Yuan period drama. In act 10 of *Romance of the Western Bower* (*Xixiang ji*, early fourteenth century) is a dialogue line, "The beauty always has a hapless fate, / And never bold is a scholar great."[8] In act 3 of the poetic drama *Mandarin-Duck Coverlet* (*Yuanyang bei*), also of the Yuan, we come across a line: "Be it this life or a former life, after all I am of crimson face, hapless fate." Examples of the phrase increase as time passes, particularly frequently appearing in vernacular fiction.

Those examples suggest that the concept of "crimson face, hapless fate" was formed in the Yuan period. However, the Northern Song poet Su Shi (1036–1101) had written a piece titled "Poem on a Hapless Beauty" ("Boming jiaren shi"). It contains the lines: "From the olden days, beauties are fated to be hapless / The gate closes, spring ends, willow flowers scatter." Although the exact phrase *crimson face, hapless fate* is not used, the meaning hardly differs. If so, the concept that "beautiful persons are unlucky" already existed in the Song. This leads us to think that the idea that "beautiful women live short lives" was first formed as common sense, and then later the phrase *crimson face, hapless fate* was created.

Evil Women Are Also Hapless

But what does "crimson face, hapless fate" really refer to? Xie Zhaozhe of the Ming period offers a detailed explanation in his *Five Miscellanies* (*Wu zazu*), referring to historically famous women:

> There are many beautiful women. But some wander around various places, stumble and fall, and others are married to unsuitable spouses. Is this what the hapless fate of crimson-faced beauties is all about? Or is the Creator jealous of them? No need to discuss the type like Moxi and Xiaji, but there are countless examples of things not turning out to be as wished: for example, Xi Shi ruined herself at the King of Wu's palace, Wang Zhaojun spent her miserable life in a foreign land, the sisters Zhao Feiyan and Zhao Hede at the Zhaoyang Palace ended in bringing disasters to the court, and Yang Guifei took her own life with a short braided cord. Zhuo Wenjun's relationship with Sima Xiangru and Lü Zhu's service for Shi Zhong were exceptions, probably because they were as talented as they were beautiful, and they were thus heaven-made spouses. The one type, with the heart of a zither, sets a jade in place at the beginning; the other, with the transience of dew by the roadside, ends in crushing a jewel so that they make others shed tears with deep chagrin even after one thousand years. It is useless to question the heavens.[9]

Becoming a vagrant or beckoning death precisely because of beautiful looks—this is the substance of "crimson face, hapless fate." Although marriage to an unsuitable spouse is also mentioned, under the marital system based on parental decisions, undesirable marriage was not, from the start, exclusively a misfortune of beautiful women. Xie Zhaozhe may have written the above with cases in mind in which women were seized because of their beauty by men of power.

The view of beautiful women as wicked reflects the perspective of the sovereign or national interest. When we view such a person as an individual woman, we see a different side.

After the death of her husband Duke Xian of Jin, Li Ji was killed in 651 BCE by Li Ke, a minister. Consort Yang Guifei was ordered to kill herself for the alleged responsibility for An Lushan's rebellion (755). Both cases are unnatural deaths. Golden Lotus in *The Plum in the Golden Vase* might not have had illicit relationships with Ximen Qing had she not married Wu the

Elder. Much less would she have poisoned her husband. Ultimately, beauty is the cause of everything. Unless a woman is beautiful, she does not meet such destiny. In other words, rather than that a beautiful evil woman is also hapless, it could be said that evil women and frailty of fortune are two sides of the same coin.

Beauties, Courtesans, and Hapless Fate

The commonly accepted concept of beautiful persons as hapless is, in any particular case, the same as that "beautiful persons are inauspicious." While the former speaks about the fate of a beautiful person herself, the latter points to those around her. The formation of such an idea is related to the image of courtesans.

The theory of beauties being unlucky did not exist from ancient times. It can be traced to a poem by Bo Juyi of a court lady who laments her white hair, but there is scant proof that it had by the Tang period become a generally accepted idea. At least we cannot say that literary works depicting beauties as unfortunate had by then formed a story line. Whether in free-style prose unrestricted by rhetorical conventions, fiction in literary Chinese in the tradition of the supernatural, or fiction in the vernacular, the discourse of beauty causing misfortune drew attention from the Song on, and began to be seen in striking numbers in the Ming.

Changes in the culture of the pleasure quarters can be given as a reason. To begin with, the word *beauty* is often used as a synonym for *courtesan*. This is particularly so in early modern times when licensed quarters developed.

Visitors to licensed quarters in the Tang period were basically government officials or candidates for government office. The status of courtesans was relatively high. However, with the passage of time, as commercial culture developed, working as a courtesan came to be an established occupation. Agriculture, commerce, and manufacture achieved stable development in the 276 years of the Ming. The scale of cities grew, wealth accumulated, and as a result commoners also came to be able to visit pleasure quarters. As is clear from a tale called "The Oil Peddler Wins the Queen of Flowers" in *Stories to Awaken the World* (*Xingshi hengyan*, late Ming), a man of the meager occupation of an oil vendor was able to buy a famous courtesan if only he saved money. This is not a piece of fiction that ignored reality. Such a work appeared precisely because men of lower social strata were now able to buy women.

Changes in society and customs thus transformed the culture of the pleasure quarters. As before, high-class courtesans entertained high-ranking men, but on the other hand, pleasure quarters targeted at commoners grew in the form of houses of prostitution.

The environment for low-class courtesans was far inferior to that for high-class entertainers. It is easy to imagine human trafficking and abuse. In Edo period Japan, courtesans had a path for marriage after working a fixed number of years. In comparison, reality was far harsher in China. Once a woman became a courtesan, there was absolutely no possibility for respite. When they aged, they were often chased out of the quarters and set adrift on the streets. Thus, the association of "beauty = courtesan" may have created the associative circuit of "beauty = courtesan = ill luck."

In the Ming period, syphilis introduced by Western sailors further worsened the image of courtesans. Once contracting syphilis, a courtesan was thrown out of the pleasure quarters with no choice and had to drag her decaying body to beg on the streets. As a matter of fact, documents recording such scenes remain. This is the very image of the idea that beautiful appearance invites disaster. Even if born into a similarly poor house, a girl with plain looks did not suffer the woe of becoming a courtesan. Harsh reality made persuasive the common idea that beauty brought ill luck.

Aesthetics of Fragility

"Crimson face, hapless fate" is associated with another concept: beautiful women are physically fragile. When this aesthetics was formed is also difficult to determine. If we go back, related imagery is seen early on in the depiction of feminine beauty.

Admiration for a slender physique must be the original cause for connecting beauty with fragility. "Seven Explications" ("Qishi") by Wang Can (177–217) of the Later Han dynasty contains an expression, "rich skin and supple flesh, weak bones and slender shape." The phrase assumes that a thin, frail shape is more attractive than a robust form. The aesthetic sense favoring fragility must have formed from within the culture that preferred slender physique and slim lower torso. Expressions like "weak arms," "weak shoulders," and "weak steps," all denoting delicate tenderness, are also based upon the same concept.

The late Tang author Zhang Mi writes of Empress Zhao Feiyan (Flying Swallow) of the first century BCE in "Not Up to a Spoon and Chopsticks" in *Accounts of Women's Chambers* (*Zhuanglou ji*): "Feiyan was arrogant and willful. Whenever she felt even a little out of sorts, she stopped eating and drinking. The Emperor himself had to hold a porcelain spoon and a pair of chopsticks for her." The original uses the word for *faintly ill* (*weibing*).

The emperor took pains to care for her perhaps because she looked all the lovelier in her illness.

But Zhao Feiyan is a woman of the Han period, while the author Zhang Mi belongs to the Later Tang (923–936) of the Five Dynasties period. It is not clear whether or not a generally accepted concept that delicate constitution was beautiful had existed in the Han. Even so, the context unmistakably goes back at the latest to the Five Dynasties Ten States period, in which Zhang Mi lived.

The Relationship between Illness and Love

A typical example of "fragility is beautiful" is Lin Daiyu, or Blue-Black Jade, the younger first cousin of the protagonist Jia Baoyu in *A Dream of Red Mansions*. Blue-Black Jade is not only lean but "too weak to resist the wind" and too ill to stand on her feet as she likes. Yet she is extolled as supreme feminine beauty. Going beyond the idea of slender physique as beautiful, this is open admiration of ill health.

Contrarily, opulence is ridiculed. Xue Baochai, or Jewelled Hairpin, Jia Baoyu's other first cousin, is not obese but merely full-bodied as well as well educated. Despite that, Jia Baoyu thoroughly mocks her.

The idea of fragility as a metaphor for love's longing does not begin with *A Dream of Red Mansions*. In *Beginner's Guide* (*Meng Qiu*), an eighth-century reader in verse for young children, we find an expression referring to a sixth-century BCE beauty sent for strategic reasons from the king of Yue to the king of Wu: "Xi Shi holds her heart, her beauty increases all the more." Ill and unable to withstand the pain, she put her hands against her chest, eyebrows knit; and in this posture, she looked absolutely beautiful. Although *Beginner's Guide* is a Tang era book, this legend may go somewhat further back.

The image of delicate health is also related to love. An example of using frail constitution as a symbol of love's longing is found in *Romance of the Western Bower* (early fourteenth century), a dramatic adaptation of a Tang story called "The Story of Yingying." In this play, longing is expressed as "love sickness," in other words, as illness. In a scene in act 12, the heroine's maid Hongniang sings the following:

She won't attend to needle and thread
Nor renew the rouge and powder on her face.
Spring sorrow knits the brows on her forehead,
Which only mutual love can erase.[10]

In this song, "sickness" and "love" are mutually metaphorical. An expression *mutual-love sickness* (*xiangsi bing*) also appears in the same play. This indicates that an admiring view of "sickness" associated with love as feminine beauty already existed in the Yuan period.

Obeisance and Dependence

The work that represented illness as physical beauty with greatest exaggeration is *The Peony Pavilion* (late sixteenth century). In this drama, love sickness forms a key point in the story's development. At the beginning of the play, the heroine Du Liniang becomes unable to walk by herself, and barely manages to appear onstage, supported by her maid Chunxiang. Her fragility is expressed in her physical motions.

Praise of illness appears in many places in songs in the same play as well. "Sick and lost / wherefore wasting away?" (Chunxiang's song); "My frail mind / my slender waist / would I be able to withstand my prolonged illness?" (Du Liniang's song); "For whom do you knit your eyebrows / for whom do you waste away / for whom does your heart ache? (Chunxiang's song); and so forth—there are endless lines that can be quoted. Based on such context, the author of *A Dream of Red Mansions* portrayed the first female protagonist Blue-Black Jade's ill health as beauty. At the same time, being ill and unable to live long became a characteristic of "crimson face, hapless fate."

The formation of the common concept that physical fragility is beautiful is naturally based upon the basic emotional relationship between men and women characterized by "dependency" and "encouraging dependency." In order to clarify the relationship between "being romantically impressed" and "romantically impressing," it is not rare that one resorts to unconventional conduct or expression, or seeks such. For example, a man and a woman in love often use baby talk or act like babies in their private space. This is because childlikeness symbolizes unconditional obeisance and dependence.

In like manner, the unconventional relationship in which the one is physically frail and the other is devoted to caring for the sick also symbolizes unconditional love. Whether Zhao Feiyan of the Han history or Yingying of *Romance of the Western Bower*, in each case fragile health was attractively portrayed in presenting a loved beauty. Eventually, such fragility was detached from "love" and came to simply characterize a beautiful woman.

4. ENCHANTRESSES IN THE EAST AND THE WEST

Beautiful women are cruel and frightful—such a notion is not limited to China, but is fairly universal whether in the East or in the West. Agrippina, the fourth and last wife of Claudius, the fourth emperor of the Roman Empire, is known as a wicked woman in the West. Great-granddaughter of the first emperor, Augustus, she was at once beautiful and blessed with keen intelligence. She used artifice to marry her uncle Claudius, and exercised influence as empress to her heart's content. In order to put her son Nero on the throne, she poisoned Claudius. Nero, who later won a worldwide reputation as a tyrant, became the fifth Roman emperor just as she wished.

The topic of wicked women of the Roman period also brings up the name of Messalina. This third wife of Emperor Claudius was extraordinarily lascivious. She pursued one handsome man after another, without satiation. In the end, she even stole out of the palace to act as a prostitute in town. If anyone dared criticize her, she killed the critic on a false charge. She was, so to speak, a typical wicked woman.

From the Middle Ages on, the number of historical personages passed down as cruel beauties further increases. Countess Elizabeth Báthory Erzsébet of Hungary, who, in order to retain her youthfulness and beauty, killed young women and applied their blood to her skin in place of cosmetic lotion; Françoise Athénaïs de Montemart, marquise de Montespan, who vied for the king's favor and, out of jealousy, attempted to poison Louis XIV; Madame de Pompadour, the official *maîtresse-en-titre* of Louis XV, who squandered money to satisfy her vanity until state finances were impoverished—there are numerous examples.

Western literature has an image of the femme fatale. The term refers to the type of woman who entices men with bewitching appearances, deceives them with sexual charm, and ultimately ruins them. Physical beauty is not necessarily presented as the direct cause of cruelty. But it is made easy to imagine that beautiful women are dangerous sources of tragedy for men. Whether in historical legends or literary works, the associative circuit "beauties are cruel" clearly exists in the West.

The Countenances of Enchantresses

Among evil women appearing in Japanese history and literature are the eighth-century female monarch Shōtoku Tennō, who loved the charlatan Priest Dōkyō, and the ninth-century empress at the Somedono, who was possessed by an evil spirit.[11]

However, in Japan the idea that "beauties are cruel" was not commonly accepted early on. As I will discuss later, I think it was first established in the Edo period through reception of Chinese vernacular fiction. At least, it seems that in medieval times (the Kamakura and Muromachi periods, late twelfth to late sixteenth century) the concept was not yet widespread.

For example, while Shōtoku Tennō is labeled as an evil woman, she was not reputed as a beauty. Above all, she did nothing cruel. Favoring Priest Dōkyō is her only scandal. In the first place, a person like Shōtoku Tennō is prone to large transformations as a literary character, regardless of historical facts. It would not be at all strange if, for example, she is depicted as a terribly cruel beauty in medieval tales. Yet, not a single such literary piece appeared. At most, she was talked about as a lustful woman. That alone hardly leads to saying that "beautiful women are cruel." The same applies to the empress at the Somedono.

Narrating about beautiful looks as a metaphor for destruction is, rather, related to the transmission of Buddhism. "Priest Kyata Goes to the Land of Rākṣasa" in *Stories Gleaned at Uji* (*Uji shūi monogatari*, early thirteenth century), volume 6, is a story of a beautiful monster. While Priest Kyata of Tenjiku (India) was voyaging with five hundred merchants, they drifted to an unknown land and were welcomed by good-looking women.[12] Each of the merchants married and settled, but finding one day that the women were monsters, they all managed to flee just in time. When the monsters noticed their escape and chased after them, "the women instantly turned into demons some ten meters tall and jumped over forty meters into the air, shouting aloud." Later, the demon that had been the priest's wife found her way to his house and demanded to be reunited, but was angrily spurned. The king fell for her at first sight, however, and invited her to his chamber. The beautiful woman, whose "atmosphere, form, and carriage were endlessly fragrant and charming," was quite otherwise on the third morning: "The look in her eyes having changed, she appeared extremely frightening. There was blood around her mouth. She looked around for a moment, then, seeming to leap from the eaves, disappeared into the clouds." The beautiful woman was in truth a dreadful vampire.

In this manner, along with the reception of Buddhism that entered Japan via China, religious ethics admonishing against infatuation with women also came to be accepted.

Fearsome beauties appear not only in Buddhist tales but also in shorter stories known as *kanazōshi* ("tales" in *kana*, Japanese phonetic script). *Tales for Comfort* (*Otogi monogatari*, late seventeenth century), volume 5, number

4, introduces an episode in which a ghost appears in the form of a beautiful woman and tries to deceive a man. Tales of ghosts and goblins disguised as a beauty formed a type also in folklore.

Edo Period Views of Beautiful Women as Vice

A large transition occurred in the Edo period. First there was the reception of the so-called "Three Words and Two Slaps" (*sanyan erpai*). This refers to the Chinese anthologies of stories in the vernacular published in the Ming: *Constant Words to Awaken the World, Comprehensive Words to Caution the World, Illustrious Words to Instruct the World*, and *Desk-Slapping Wonders, First Collection* and *Desk-Slapping Wonders, Second Collection*. These Chinese vernacular stories were widely read in those days in Japan, and were adapted by the mid-Edo author, Confucian scholar, and doctor Tsuga Teishō (1718–1794?). The "Three Words and Two Slaps" played the greatest role in the spread of the female image of "dreadful beauties."

"With a White Falcon, Young Master Cui Brings an Evil Spirit upon Himself," story 19 of *Stories to Caution the World*, contains the following verse:

Lust! Lust!
Hard to be rid of, easy to be lured.
It lurks in the boudoir and on willow-lined paths,
Aiding petty rogues, ruining gentlemen's morals.
The King of Chen's talent did him no service.
King Zhou's mighty strength was rendered useless.
The killer with the painless knife
Is the very one in front of your face.
Her lovely eyes are in fact sparkling waves
That drown the good as well as the foolish.[13]

"Sparkling waves," or more literally "sidelong waves," refers to a beautiful woman's flirtatious glance cast at men. The original Chinese word for *beauty* here is *se* (色 countenance, expression, beautiful looks, color, sensual desire), meaning attractive women. The verse directly expresses the idea that beautiful women destroy men's lives.

A poem at the beginning of "Qiao Yanjie's Concubine Ruins the Family," chapter 33 of *Stories to Caution the World*, contains the lines: "Those who run the state and the family / Are men with a weakness for the other sex." The poem at the end of the story includes the line, "Lust brings ruin to family and home."[14] Both phrases warn that sensual pleasures lead men to catastrophe.

Such a concept was accepted into Edo literature through adaptations from Chinese stories. "Kurokawa Genda-nushi Enters the Mountains and Gains a Path to Longevity" in *A Garland of Heroes* (*Hanabusa sōshi*) argues: "There are women who are licentious by birth. Even if they are married, they conduct themselves in questionable ways like having illicit lovers. Their husbands, indulging in carnal love and misled by the words spoken in bed, become, through those words, unfilial to their parents or disloyal to their lord. This happens to many, including men of power or learning. But how can this be the case with truly accomplished men?"[15]

Such a statement itself expresses the view of morality in the line of the "Three Words and Two Slaps." Again, the preface to *Tales of Overgrown Fields* (*Shigeshige yawa*), by the same author, introduces a Tang period romance called "Legend of Dame Ren" ("Ren-shi zhuan") as a story "admonishing against wicked sensual pleasures that soften a person's heart." This, too, is based upon the same idea.

Concepts in the Manner of *Outlaws of the Marsh*

What further strengthened that sort of consciousness is such fiction in the vernacular as *Outlaws of the Marsh* (*Shuihu zhuan*, fifteenth century).

The femme fatale Golden Lotus, mentioned earlier, first appears in the twenty-fourth installment of this novel. In the Rong'yu Studio edition (which is fuller than other editions), the installment starts with a poem that foreshadows the development of the Golden Lotus episodes of plots, adultery, and deaths. The poem, which is too long to quote here, cites ancient and contemporary examples to illustrate how beautiful women entrap loyal vassals and ruin good men.

Installment 44 of the same novel inserts the following poem after portraying the countenance of the wife of Yang Xiong, an executioner and prison warden:

At age twice eight the beautiful body resembles dairy cream
A blade worn on the waist, she kills her foolish husband
Although she does not see a human head fall
Unbeknownst to him she makes his bone marrow dry out.[16]

This poem, with little connection to the development of the story (he kills her after she admits to her relationship with a monk), delivers instruction that beautiful women can destroy men's lives. Particularly worthy of attention is lines 3 and 4. These two lines are based on the Daoist theory of the body. According to Daoist theory of health maintenance, semen is the essence of life and source of energy. If one indulges in sensual pleasures and excessively wastes it, the theory holds, it harms health and can in the end even cause death.

To begin with, eschewing sensual pleasures was regarded from long ago as a condition for longevity. The philosophical treatises *Laozi* and *Zhuangzi*, attributed to Laozi of around fifth century BCE and Zhuangzi of the third century BCE respectively, contained words warning against *se*, or amorousness, but from the Han dynasty on, direct attacks against beautiful women emerged. In the chapter on *xuan* (玄 the mystery, which is the source of all things) in *Baopuzi* (*The Master Who Embraces Simplicity*, the author's alias), the author Ge Hong (283?–343?) states that "charming visages and enchanting forms with faces made up with powder chop off life spans."[17] This is originally a sentence found in the "Noble Life" ("Guisheng") section of *Mr. Lü's Spring and Autumn Annals* (*Lüshi Chunqiu*), but it was passed down to the age when Ge Hong lived. Later, with the spread of Daoism, aversion toward beautiful women further permeated. In Japan, the idea was partially accepted by Kaibara Ekiken in *Life-Nourishing Principles* (*Yōjō-kun*, 1713), and in literature, it became known with the reception of Chinese fiction in the vernacular.

Loyal Retainers: Outlaws of the Marsh (*Chūshin Suikoden*, 1799), a Japanese adaptation by Santō Kyōden (1761–1816), contains a sentence about the fourteenth-century Japanese warrior Kō no Moronao, famous for an episode of failed love for another warrior's wife and subsequent tragic events: "From indulgence in lust and love of sensual pleasures, he stirred an incident, in the end destroyed his household, ruined himself, and suffered the hatred of commoners of a thousand years" (part 1, volume 2). This adheres to the traditional lesson in Chinese fiction in the vernacular. An inserted verse, after the manner of poetic insertions in *Outlaws of the Marsh*, follows to repeat the same admonition:

Indulgence in flowers consumes the heart that desires them,
The body loses the spirit and hidden virtue.
I encourage you to stop plucking any flower you happen on,
Buddhism, in the first place, warns against sexual misconduct.

This warning is based on Buddhist ethics, but the expression *the body loses the spirit* is also suggestive of Daoism. It reflects the pattern common in the "encourage the good and punish the evil" genre in the style of *Outlaws of the Marsh*. Not just in content, this poem stylistically imitates Chinese vernacular fiction in adopting, among other things, the form of verse interspersed in prose.

"A Serpent's Lust" in the *Tales of Moon and Rain* (*Ugetsu monogatari*) by Ueda Akinari (1734–1809) provides a Japanese version of the "beautiful woman is frightening" idea. Manago, a surpassing beauty, later brings about an ill-fated result. An old man who sees through her identity says to the young man Toyoo: "That demon is a giant snake and very old. Having a lascivious nature, it is said to bear unicorns when it couples with a bull, and dragon steeds when it couples with a stallion. It appears that out of lust, inspired by your beauty, it has attached itself to you and led you astray. If you do not take special care with one so tenacious, you will surely lose your life."[18] The first part of this statement is a quotation from *Five Miscellanies*, but the admonition, "If you do not take special care with one so tenacious, you will surely lose your life," precisely expresses the concept that "beautiful women ruin men." Here, the images of fair ladies, monsters, lascivious women, and so forth converge, crystallizing as a character called Manago. Although the material is derived from Chinese vernacular fiction, it is re-created in a Japanese way. Given its great influence on later literature, we may assume that the association of "a serpent and a beautiful woman" was already established.[19]

The "serpentine woman" who bewitches men not only exists in the East but is found in Western culture as well.[20] It appeared in Greek tales long ago, and some argue that this was transmitted to China through Asia Minor.[21]

The late Edo author Takizawa Bakin's long fiction also introduces "pernicious women" and "enchantresses" who bewitch men. Funamushi (Sea Slater), who appears in *Eight Dog Chronicles* (*Nansō Satomi hakkenden*, 1814–1842) does such things as killing a traveler for valuables, or pretending to be a prostitute to lure a man and biting off his tongue while making love, then carrying off his money and belongings.

It is clear that the concept that "beautiful women are frightening" was accepted with the reception of Chinese vernacular fiction. Conversely, there is no trace of the idea having been transmitted through such Confucian texts as the Four Books and Five Classics. In passing, Noh drama has a category known as the female demon type (*kijomono*). Plays in this category contain scenes that remind us of the formula, "beautiful women are frightening."

The idea that beautiful women are unfortunate also was transmitted to Japan during the Edo period through "crimson face, hapless fate." In chapter 15 of *The Full Account of Sakurahime: Dawn Light Storybook* (*Sakurahime zenden akebono sōshi*) by Santō Kyōden, Bakin's close contemporary, we find phrases such as "Grieving over her hapless fate, Sakurahime takes to bed again." But in most cases, those expressions remain imitations of Chinese diction. Again, the image of a hapless beauty does not seem to have been handed down to, and reproduced by, later generations.

In Meiji (1868–1912), some authors accepted the femme fatale image of the West. For example, it has been pointed out that Natsume Sōseki portrayed similar images under the influence of fin de siècle literature in pieces like *Ten Nights of Dream* (*Yume jūya*).[22]

However, the "enchantress" imagery appearing in Sōseki's fiction did not derive from Western literature alone. *Red Poppy* (*Gubijinsō*, 1907) has a passage that runs: "One who pours one's soul into lovely-eyed beautiful looks is bound to be devoured.... One who commits one's life to charming, sweet smiles is bound to kill another." Such a way of thinking clearly goes back to Chinese literature through Edo authors like Kyōden and Bakin. Regarding the female central charater Fujio in *Red Poppy*, the novelist Mizumura Sanae points out that the "ornate style" here helped create the association with "enchantress."[23] However, the diction of the "ornate style" itself carries no such connotation. Rather, the image of "enchantress" depends upon how a beautiful countenance is grasped and what results it brings forth. In fact, Chinese expressions like "lovely-eyed beautiful looks" and "charming sweet smiles" themselves have no nuance that hints at "enchantress." In Kyōden's or Bakin's fiction, there is no correspondence between those expressions and "pernicious woman" either.

As seen above, the view of beauties as sinful is neither peculiar to modern times nor limited to Japan. It can be considered a universal concept seen in every patriarchal society.

In matriarchal society, which is based upon natural relationships, kinship structure is firm. In comparison, patriarchal society is constructed as culture. In order to reinforce the brittleness of what is man-made, it inevitably produced the view of beauties as sinful. In fact, in the Heian period when marriage by commuting (*kayoi-kon*) still remained, the view of beauties as sinful did not emerge from within. Not only that, there is also no trace of that view having been introduced from China as Confucian ethics. Descriptions from "biographies of exemplary women" that had tremendous influence in China drew no attention whatsoever in Japan, either. It is not by coincidence that views of female morals based upon Confucian ethics, represented by Great Learning for Women, finally appeared in the Edo period. The reason is that, following the spread of patrilocal marriage, in which the bride moves in with the groom's family, patriarchal society suddenly needed moral views to consolidate its foothold.

It was probably for the same reason that, despite the fact that the Chinese view of beautiful women as sinful can be traced back to pre-Han days, in

Japan it was accepted only in the Edo period. Moreover, at first it was accepted through vernacular fiction. Introduction of the same view written in literary Chinese lagged one step behind. In addition, the majority of it was first accepted only after being diluted via popular reading materials. The influence in premodern Japan of the "beauty = sin" view found in Chinese classics including history books is extremely thin.

NOTES

1. Nancy Etcoff, *Survival of the Prettiest: The Science of Beauty* (Anchor Books, 2000). Translated into Japanese by Kimura Hiroe as *Why Do Beautiful Women Alone Benefit? (Naze bijin dake ga toku wo suru no ka)* (Sōshisha, 2000), 54.
2. Inoue Shōichi, *On Beautiful Women (Bijinron)* (Asahi Shinbunsha, 1995), 10–19, 59–63.
3. The Quanrong were an ethnic group active in the northwestern part of China during the Zhou (1046–221 BCE) and later dynasties.
4. Simon Leys (tr.), *The Analects of Confucius* (W. W. Norton & Company, 1997), 89.
5. David Hawkes (tr.), *An Anthology of Translations: Classical Chinese Literature*, vol. 1 (Penguin Books, 1985), 243.
6. Nancy Lee Swann (tr.), *The Columbia Anthology of Traditional Chinese Literature* (Columbia University Press, 1994), 537–38.
7. Tang Xianzu, *The Peony Pavilion: Returning to Life (Mudanting: huanhun ji)*. Translated by Iwaki Hideo as *Returning to Life (Kankonki)* in *Collection of the Drama*, vol. 2 (Chūgoku Koten Bungaku Taikei, hereafter CKBT, 1970, 53), 63. The song is introduced in scene 16.
8. Xu Yuanchong (tr.), *Romance of the Western Bower* (Library of Chinese Classics, Hunan People's Publishing House and Foreign Languages Press, 2000), 151.
9. Translated from the Japanese translation by Iwaki Hideo (CKBT 52, 1970), 64.
10. Xu Yuanchong, *op. cit.*, 181–83.
11. Tanaka Takako, *On Evil Women ("Akujo" ron)* (Kinokuniya Shoten, 1992), 25–40, 87–94.
12. Watanabe Tsunaya and Nishio Kōichi (annotators, CKBT 27), 210–16.
13. Translation by Shuhui Yang and Yinqin Yang (University of Washington Press, 2005), vol. 2, 302.
14. Ibid., 566 and 580.
15. Tale 4 in volume 2. Nakamura Yukihiko (annotator and translator, Nihon Koten Bungaku Zenshū, 48, Shōgakukan, 1973), 129.
16. Komada Shinji (tr.), *Suikoden*, vol. 2 (CKBT 29, 1968), 89–90.
17. He Shuzhen (annotator, Zhonghua Library, 2002), 26.
18. Anthony Chambers (tr.), *Tales of Moonlight and Rain* (Columbia University Press, 2007), 173.

19. The point is discussed in Takada Mamoru, *Women and Snakes (On'na to hebi)* (Chikuma Shobō, 1999).

20. Nanjō Takenori, *The Legend of the Serpentine Woman—To the East and West Tracing the "White Snake Legend" (Hebi-on'na no densetsu—"Baishe-zhuan" wo otte higashi e nishi e)* (Heibonsha, 2000), 104–11.

21. Ibid., 202–10.

22. Yoon Sang In, *The End of the Century and Sōseki (Seikimatsu to Sōseki)* (Iwanami Shoten, 1994). An English translation of *Ten Nights of Dream* is available in *Ten Nights of Dream, Hearing Things, The Heredity of Taste*, translated by Aiko Itō and Graeme Wilson (Tuttle Publications, 2004), 318.

23. Mizumura Sanae, "'Man and Man' and 'Man and Woman'—Fujio's Death" ("'Otoko to otoko' and 'otoko to onna'—Fujio no shi") in *Hihyō kūkan*, no. 6, 1992, 165.

3

The Rhetoric of Representation

1. JAPANESE BEAUTIES, CHINESE BEAUTIES

Differences between Japanese and Chinese Paintings of Beautiful Women

Both Japanese and Chinese are said to be of the Mongoloid race, with close cultural ties from ancient times to the mid-nineteenth century. Nevertheless, observing the genre of art called "pictures of beautiful persons" (*bijinga* in Japanese), we note that their views of beauty greatly differ.

I would like to first consider two pictures for comparison's sake: *A Beauty under Cherry Blossoms* (*Kaka bijin zu*, figure 3.1) by the Edo Japanese artist Chōbunsai Eishi, and *A Beauty with Infants at Play* (*Meiren yingxi tu*, figure 3.2), a New Year picture (*nianhua*) from the Qing period in China. The former dates from the Kansei era (1789–1801), while the exact production date of the latter is unknown. Judging from the composition, painting style, and coloring, it can be roughly estimated to belong to the time between the Qianlong (1735–1795) and Guangxu (1875–1908) eras. New Year pictures are woodblock prints used for decorating the inside and outside of a house with good-luck wishes for a thriving business, household stability, flourishing posterity, and so forth in the New Year. Normally, these prints do not indicate the artist's name. That is also the case with this piece.

The production dates of *A Beauty under Cherry Blossoms* and *A Beauty with Infants at Play* do not differ greatly. However, on comparing these two pieces, we realize afresh how different Japanese and Chinese images of beauties in art were in the eighteenth and nineteenth centuries.

Figure 3.1. *A Beauty under Cherry Blossoms.* Chōbunsai Eishi, Private Possession. *Source: Ukiyo-e, Nihon bijutsu zenshū*, vol. 2. Kōdansha, 1991, 42.

Figure 3.2. *A Beauty with Infants at Play.* Qing Dynasty. Tianjin Art Museum (Tianjin). *Source:* Tianjin Art Museum, ed., *Tianjin Art Museum.* Kōdansha, 1982, figure 262.

Chōbunsai Eishi's *A Beauty under Cherry Blossoms*, a typical Edo-period portrayal of a beautiful woman (*bijin-e* or *bijinga*) in the *ukiyo-e* tradition, depicts an elite courtesan standing under cherry blossoms, looking back. Her face is slightly long, and her daintily painted, small mouth conveys sensual charm. Her eyes are narrow and turn slightly upward toward the edges. A minimal amount of ink is used to depict her nose, line-drawn to show just the contour. Such a representation of the five sensory organs is common for pictures of this genre. Particularly worthy of note is the body shape. A glance suffices to see that she has a narrow waist and slender body. In the Edo period, a slim, elongated body where the proportion of the head to the body is one to eight seems to have been favored.

A Beauty with Infants at Play from the Qing period conveys totally different aesthetics. The oval face is emphasized to excess with the result that the chin is so pointed that the shape of the head nearly goes out of balance. While the mouth is small as in the Japanese painting, the eyebrows, much more distanced from the eyes, exemplify the conventional representation common to New Year prints of those days. The well-shaped eyes are somewhat narrow as in the Edo period painting, but they differ from their Japanese counterparts in that they are clearly double-lidded.

Agreement between New Year Prints and Literati Paintings

A Beauty with Infants at Play was produced at Yangliuqing to the west of Tianjin City, a town that was a center for New Year prints. New Year print studios started to appear in late Ming, and by mid-Qing, there were specialty stores all over town. During the Guangxu era (1875–1908), the number of artisans working on carving and printing alone is said to have exceeded three thousand. While some New Year prints were produced on the basis of preliminary paintings by literati, not a few were by professional painters specializing in this genre. The latter frequently portrayed scenes of ordinary people's lives, introducing customs and fashions. The portrayal of clothes and accessories in *A Beauty with Infants at Play* suggests that the practice of those days was fairly accurately reflected. The representation of the countenance is also in accord with the Qing view of beautiful women and their methods of makeup. New Year prints are closer to commoners' lives than are literati paintings.

When comprehensively taking into account the development, targeted market, and producers of New Year woodblock prints, we realize that, even after the Opium Wars (1839–1842, 1856–1860), they were, for some time, hardly influenced by Western paintings. As in Japan, beautiful women appearing in early pictures and sculptures in China had single eyelids without

Figure 3.3. Chen Hongshou, *Female Immortals, a Scroll*. Ming. Palace Museum (Beijing). *Source: Antiques Canon, The Palace Museum*, 411, figure 194.

exception. But women with double eyelids began to be portrayed starting in the Ming period, as can be observed in *Female Immortals, a Scroll* (figure 3.3). It is not clear whether Qing period New Year prints simply held on to the preceding dynasty's aesthetic sense, or more realistically expressed commoners' sense of beauty of their time. Those prints, however, clearly share the taste of literati paintings. In fact, not only in *A Beauty with Infants at Play* but in other New Year prints as well, double eyelids are depicted as a symbol of beauty. Naturally, it is impossible to assert that the aesthetic preference for double eyelids had already been established. But there is no doubt that double eyelids were at least also thought beautiful. Moreover, this bore no relation to the influence of modern Western culture.

Grounds for Comparison of Pictures of Beautiful Women

When comparing Japanese and Chinese pictorial representations of beautiful women, we encounter a number of difficulties. First, there is the question of what to compare with what. Pictures vary in genres; histories and backgrounds of production differ; techniques also differ.

In addition, there is the question of which historical periods to turn to for comparison. For example, the results will differ depending upon whether the Genroku era (1688–1704) of Japan is mechanically contrasted with China's Kangxi era (1661–1722), or eras with similar economic and societal conditions are compared. According to the Japanese scholar of Chinese literature Yoshikawa Kōjirō, Chinese culture traveled to Japan in the Heian period (794–1185/1192) with a lag of about fifty or one hundred years. Was there a similar cultural lag in early modern times as well? If so, how should we handle that?

Third, there is the issue of assessing Chinese influence on Japan. Chinese paintings were transmitted to Japan before modern times. Naturally, we ought to take into consideration Japanese acceptance and rejection of Chinese art, or production with awareness of Chinese art.

The three issues are equally important, and each merits research. Here, however, I have in mind roughly the following grounds for comparison. First, both New Year pictures and *ukiyo-e* representations of feminine figures are prints, and both combine practical and ornamental characters. If we consider this a premise, limited comparison is possible. Second, in terms of the relationship with Western culture, early modern China and Japan can be considered to share similar backgrounds in the sense that modernization was yet to occur. Third, Edo-period *ukiyo-e* exhibit skills of expression that surpass those of Chinese prints, and there was little influence

Figure 3.4. Leng Mei, *Out in the Garden on a Moonlit Night."* Qing. National Palace Museum (Taipei). *Source: Glimpses,* 45.

on them from Chinese New Year prints. In this chapter I do not intend to discuss art. Rather, I would like to limit my focus to how feminine beauty was represented. On the above premises, and if one also keeps the limits of comparison in sight, it should be possible to meaningfully compare Chinese and Japanese artworks focusing on feminine beauty.

Naturally, there is the question of how representative New Year prints are of Qing art. Depiction of beautiful persons in them reflects the aesthetics of the age quite well, as we can tell when comparing Qing period literati paintings as illustrated by the Qing court painter Leng Mei's *Out in the Garden on a Moonlit Night* (*Yueye youyuan*, figure 3.4). New Year prints do not greatly differ from literati paintings in either composition or human representation.

Loved by people as auspicious items, New Year prints had from the start certain compositional patterns. Many designs also imply wishes for affluence, fecundity, family harmony, and so forth. Despite such an allegorical nature, however, they do not deviate much in representation from common norms of artistic expression. On the contrary, in order to respond to the demand for standard representation, New Year print makers seem to have been fairly conscious of the drawing technique of literati paintings.

2. WHO IS BEAUTIFUL?

Eroticism of the Lips

Since the Tang period, there were close links between Japanese and Chinese paintings, and in particular Japanese painters invariably kept in view the paintings from the continent. In pictorial representations of feminine beauty, Japan surpasses China by far in both the number of pieces and the height of the level of achievement, but depiction of the face emphasizing line drawing is common to both. Because artists do not give a three-dimensional expression to the face with the use of shading in color, emphasis of depiction goes to the brilliance of clothing rather than to facial expression. For this reason gorgeous robes, dazzling hair ornaments, and specific gestures were stressed almost to excess.

Stylization created a variety of conventions. Both in Japan and China, the willowy torso and sloping shoulders are emblematic of feminine beauty, so that as long as these are depicted, the object is recognized as a beautiful person regardless of how other parts of the body appear. As *willow eyebrows* (*liumei*) was a fixed phrase referring to a beautiful woman in literature, so were, in art too, long eyebrows with a gentle curve a metaphor for a favored countenance. Likewise, small lips also suggested a beautiful countenance. There is a fair amount of commonality between China and Japan in this kind of rhetoric for shaping images.

On the other hand, we also note great differences. In representations of beautiful figures in the Edo period, the posture is rich in variation, and gestures are also diverse. In comparison with Japanese full-color woodblock

Figure 3.5. *A Beautiful Woman Wiping Rouge.* Detroit Museum. Source: Ukiyo-e, Nihon bijutsu zenshū, vol. 20. Kōdansha, 1991, 443.

prints (*nishiki-e*), there is greater stylization in Chinese pictures of fair objects. In postures and gestures in particular, a limited number of patterns are constantly reproduced in China.

To those familiar with Chinese representations of feminine beauty, *A Beautiful Woman Wiping Rouge* (*Kuchibeni wo fuku bijin*, figure 3.5), produced by the *ukiyo-e* master Utagawa Toyokuni around 1800, is extremely refreshing. The woman's gesture of pressing tissue to her lips after applying rouge conveys indescribable charm. Not only that, this momentary gesture contains a story. The minutely depicted hair on the sides of her face, sensual in itself, looks even more so, helped by the contrast against the rest of the hair that is put up pristinely. The woman has painted her eyebrows neatly, applied powder down to her neck and chest, and added rouge to her lips. She is finishing the last step of her makeup in order to show herself at her best when the man she expects arrives.

The Tricks Used in *Ukiyo-e*

What is interesting here is that the time of the woman's gaze and the time of the piece as a whole are not the same. Despite the fact that this is a makeup scene, the sidelong glance of the character in the picture is clearly the kind that is meant for a person of the opposite sex. In other words, the artist, anticipating her gaze in the next scene, synthesized it into this makeup scene.

So intricate an artifice is nowhere to be found in Chinese art. The beautiful woman in a picture either stands or sits—there are only these two patterns. In particular, Ming and Qing portrayal of postures is monotonous, with scant attempt at stylistic variation. *Four Beautiful Women* (*Si meiren tu*, figure 3.6) by Tang Yin of the Ming period presents the front, side, and rear views, but offers little differentiation of posture. The Qing New Year picture titled *Su Little Sister Thrice Fools Her Bridegroom* (*Su Xiaomei sannan xinlang*, figure 3.7) portrays standing and seated women, but the poses taken by the four resemble those in other New Year prints.

Though all involve seated postures, designs differ between, for example, *Young Woman and a Cat at a Kotatsu* (*Kotatsu no musume to neko*, figure 3.8) by Utagawa Kunimasa, Toyokuni's student, and *Three Fashionable Beauties Cooling Off in the Evening* (*Fūryū yūsuzumi san-bijin*, figure 3.9) by Kikukawa Eizan, who produced numerous woodblock prints of female portraits in the 1830s before moving on to painting. In China, as seen in *Gold and Jewels Fill the House* (*Jin'yu mantang tu*, figure 3.10) from the Qing period, seated postures are practically the same even in portrayals of daily lives.

Figure 3.6. Tang Yin, *Four Beautiful Women*. Ming. Palace Museum (Beijing). *Source: Zhongguo meishu shi* (*Chinese History of Art*), the Ming volume, figure 47.

Figure 3.7. *Su Little Sister Thrice Fools Her Bridegroom*. *Source:* Tianjin Art Museum, figure 260.

Figure 3.8. Utagawa Kunimasa, *Young Woman and a Cat at a Kotatsu*. Tokyo National Museum. *Source: Ukiyo-e, Nihon bijutsu zenshū*, vol. 20 (*Comprehensive Collection of Japanese Art*), Kōdansha, 1991, 34.

Figure 3.9. From *Three Fashionable Beauties Cooling Off in the Evening*. *Source:* Kikukawa Eizan, Hiraki Ukiyoe Foundation. *Nihon bijutsu zenshū*, vol. 20 (*Comprehensive Collection of Japanese Art*), Kōdansha, 1991, 35.

Figure 3.10. *Gold and Jewels Fill the House.* Qing. Tianjin Art Museum. *Source: Tianjin Art Museum,* figure 258.

Figure 3.11. Kitagawa Utamaro, *Young Women's Sundial: The Hour of the Horse.* Boston Museum. *Source: Ukiyo-e, Nihon bijutsu zenshū,* vol. 20, 20.

In order to complement the monotony of facial expression, Edo period representations often use the technique of emphasizing the movement of the mouth. *Young Women's Sundial: The Hour of the Horse* (*Musume hidokei uma no koku*, figure 3.11) by Kitagawa Utamaro, a celebrated printmaker and painter particularly known for his artful studies of female figures, depicts a woman after a bath holding a rubbing bran bag in her mouth. *Ten Types of Women's Physiognomies* (*Fujin sōgaku jittai*), also by Utamaro, includes a portrait of a woman blowing into a glass toy pipe. Through these devices, artists made efforts to add variation to representations that contain few motions. Such designs and devices are scarcely found in Chinese literati paintings or New Year prints.

Courtesans' Sexual Attractiveness

While beautiful women portrayed in the Edo period are long-bodied, those who appear in Qing period representations are mostly petite. They are slender, but, as exemplified in *A Beautiful Woman with Infants at Play*, they are clearly short judging by the proportion of the head to the body. In fact, we find few Qing examples in which a tall and slender body shape is depicted as beautiful.

Such aesthetics is not necessarily traditional. Literati paintings portrayed both women of average height and tall persons. *A Lady-in-Waiting by Plum Blossoms* (*Meihua shinü*) from the Yuan period (1260–1368; figure 3.12) is one example of a tall woman. However, such is hardly seen in Qing New Year prints.

Edo period representations of women greatly surpass contemporary Chinese counterparts in terms of stylistic elaboration. Particularly striking is the representation of sexual charm through composition. Utamaro's *Array of Supreme Beauties of the Present Day: Takigawa* (*Tōji zensei bijin zoroe, Takigawa*, figure 3.13), which portrays a popular courtesan at the Yoshiwara licensed quarters, focuses on the head and the upper torso, intentionally omitting portions of the body. The curved lines of the gorgeous robes flow vertically and diagonally, while the head of this top-ranking courtesan is held nearly horizontally as she absorbedly reads a letter she has kept under her kimono lapel. Such bold composition is unimaginable in Chinese art. Seated postures do appear in the late Qing, but not a portrayal with the delicate relationship between composition and framing.

Shyness symbolic of sexual charm is common to Japan and China, but in expression of sexuality, they greatly differ. In Edo color prints, the nape of the neck is the most important part that expresses eroticism, and every

Figure 3.12. *A Lady-in-Waiting by Plum Blossoms.* Yuan. National Palace Museum (Taipei). *Source: Glimpses,* 34.

Figure 3.13. Kitagawa Utamaro, *Array of Supreme Beauties of the Present Day: Takikawa.* Tokyo National Museum. Source: *Ukiyo-e, Nihon bijutsu zenshū,* vol. 20, 23.

Figure 3.14. *Twelve Hours of the Green Houses: The Hour of the Bull.* Source: Musées Royaux d'Art et d'Histoire (Belgium), 21.

bijinga without exception strongly emphasizes its curve. No such convention is found in Chinese pictorial representation. Nor is there any example in China of exposure of a leg from the knee down as in Utamaro's *Twelve Hours at the Green Houses: The Hour of the Bull* (*Seirō jūni-toki tsuzuki, ushi no koku*, figure 3.14). Instead, a glimpse of the tip of a bound foot at the hem of the robe was often depicted as sexually appealing.

3. ALLEGORY OF BEAUTIFUL WOMEN

Symbolism of Motherhood

In Chinese portrayals of beautiful women, the body vaguely seen through thin, translucent, silken clothing conventionally represents sexual appeal. *After Bathing in the Huaqing Pool* (*Huaqing chuyu tu*, figure 3.15), a painting of Yang Guifei, the beloved consort of the Tang emperor Xuanzong, by Kang Tao of the Qing, is representative, but many others can be quoted from illustrations in woodblock printed books. The technique of line drawing of the body, faintly visible through a thin garment, is used with particular frequency in erotica. Such portrayals can be divided roughly into two types. One is the so-called literati paintings. The other belongs to woodblock illustrations in amorous popular literature like *The Plum in the Golden Vase*.

Women in literati paintings are often placed in specific cultural contexts. For example, they embody a generally accepted concept of the enchantress "who has beautiful looks, entices men with her body, and at times brings about a disaster grave enough to ruin the nation." Take the woman in *After Bathing in the Huaqing Pool* (figure 3.15). Although a typical beauty, Yang Guifei is also portrayed as an "evil" temptress in power who caused the An Lushan Rebellion (755–763), bringing serious damage to the Tang court.[1] The translucent, silken robe is a symbol of lasciviousness and a metaphor for seduction. In this case, along with sexual charm, the beautiful countenance is represented as immoral. Thus, beautiful women in paintings were intended to convey a historical lesson, or point to something to guard against. Tang Yin's *Four Beautiful Women* is an exception, but that is because he was not depicting historically known beauties but, instead, a wife and concubines. I will discuss this later.

Because beautiful figures appearing in printed illustrations in erotic literature were portrayed as "lascivious women," needless to say, viewers judged them accordingly.

Women in New Year prints are cast in a totally different context. Erotic beauties are not represented at all, and those portrayed are always "likable" women.

Figure 3.15. Kang Tao, *After Bathing in the Huaqing Pool.* Qing. Tianjin Art Museum.
Source: *Tianjin Art Museum,* figure 25.

Strictly speaking, *A Beautiful Woman with Infants at Play* (figure 3.2) is not a "picture of a beautiful woman." As mentioned before, New Year prints originated as good-luck ornaments. Judging from the clothes and accessories in this piece, the woman is clearly not a woman servant but a married, upper-class woman. In Qing China, clothing indicated social status, and thus a look at the outfit in a portrait suffices to determine whether the character is a noble lady or a maid. In this piece, too, there is no room at all for misunderstanding.

The belongings are meaningful as well. Held in the two infants' hands are stems of lotus blossoms, a wind instrument called *sheng*, and some fragrant olive blossoms. The names of the three good-luck items and the word for children are pronounced in Chinese *lian, sheng, gui,* and *zi* respectively. Put together, they are identical to the four-character set phrase *liansheng guizi* (successive births of children who will join the nobility), thus forming a double meaning with "prosperity of posterity." Even an illiterate viewer can grasp the allegory of this picture at a glance. Further, the beautiful mother and healthy infants are an allegory of family harmony. In New Year prints, women were portrayed as bearers of children rather than as objects of sexual interest. Their feminine beauty is expressed only secondarily in ways that deprive the representation of sexuality.

Why the great difference between Japanese and Chinese representations of feminine beauty? The limitations of China-Japan exchanges in art in the Edo period and the differences in production techniques may be relevant. But there are other causes.

The monotony of postures in Chinese representations of beautiful figures is related more than anything else to restrictions based on Confucian ethics such as separation between the genders and prohibition for women to leave home. The majority of artists were men, who had few opportunities in their daily lives to associate with women except those of their families and of the pleasure quarters. They had to use their wives and concubines as models, or only reproduce beauties from paintings of the past or portray women in imagination.

Another reason is bound feet. When I was a junior high school student in China in the 1970s, there were still old women with bound feet in the neighborhood. Even to be courteous, I cannot say the way they walked was beautiful. A seated posture aside, when it comes to a forward-bending posture as in the *ukiyo-e* artist Isoda Koryūsai's *Beautiful Woman in the Snow* (*Setchū bijin zu*, figure 3.16), it is hard for one with bound feet even to maintain such a posture. New Year prints, which focus on the customs of the age, were not expected or required to represent an unusual posture like that.

Figure 3.16. *Beautiful Woman in the Snow. Source:* Isoda Koryūsai.

Moreover, *bijinga* (female portraits) of the *ukiyo-e* type and Qing period Chinese counterparts handle different objects. In Japan, *ukiyo-e* portray merchant lives, and at least in principle merchants were the assumed viewers. There was no room, and perhaps no need, for warrior-class morals and aesthetics to interfere. The majority of Edo period female portraits represented courtesans, or used courtesans as models. In *ukiyo-e*, in many cases, "a beautiful person" is an alias for *oiran*, a top-ranking courtesan. The reason is that artists "did not try much to portray family lives."[2]

Fictitious Mother-Child Images

Naturally, it was not that *ukiyo-e* never portrayed family women, or the so-called *ji-on'na* (women not of the entertainment profession). From the start, *ukiyo-e* had a wide scope of expression. Its range included lives of ordinary citizens in daily life. In fact, *ukiyo-e* artists Suzuki Harunobu (1725?–1770) and Torii Kiyonaga (1752–1815), among others, created mother-child images. Harunobu's *Mother and Child by the Mosquito Net* (*Kaya no oyako*, figure 3.17), *An Insect Cage and a Little Child* (*Mushikago to shōni*, figure 3.18), Utagawa Toyohiro's *The Twelve Seasons of the Year by Toyokuni and Toyohiro, the Third Month* (*Toyokuni Toyohiro ryōga jūni-kō, sangatsu*), each represent a likable scene from daily life.

Figure 3.17. Suzuki Harunobu, *Mother and Child by the Mosquito Net*. Source: *Harunobu—botsugo 200-nen kinen* (*Harunobu: Two Hundredth Anniversary of Death*). Tokyo National Museum, 1970, catalogue, figure 225.

Figure 3.18. Suzuki Harunobu, *An Insect Cage and a Little Child*. Source: *Harunobu—botsugo 200-nen kinen*, figure 218.

At a glance, these paintings seem to portray amateur women. But the image of the two mothers hardly differs from that of courtesans in other portraits. In other words, courtesans and family women shared the same hairstyle, clothing, and makeup. In the Edo period, married women were expected to shave their eyebrows. Both in Suzuki Harunobu's and Torii Kiyonaga's mother-child paintings, however, eyebrows are present on the mother's face. How would that be possible?

According to *Morisada's Rambling Writings* (*Morisada mankō*), a comprehensive recording of Edo customs and manners by Kitagawa Morisada (1810–?), in the Edo period women originally blackened their teeth when they married, but in reality unmarried women too did so at age twenty in the Kyōto-Ōsaka area, and before twenty in Edo (present-day Tokyo). They powdered the nape of the neck more generously than the face. Around 1813, Edo women thickly rouged their lips to a deep brass color, but later they came to paint them more lightly. Most important were the eyebrows.

> Married Kyōto-Ōsaka area women who have not yet blackened their teeth nor changed their hairdo switch to the style with two chignons (*ryōwa*) and so forth and shave their eyebrows around the fifth month of pregnancy. In Edo, unmarried and married women with blackened teeth always change into a hairstyle with a flat chignon in back (*marumage*) and shave their eyebrows. Brides of the warrior class in Edo blacken their teeth and wear a chignon but do not shave their eyebrows until they reach twenty-three or twenty-four years of age.
>
> When Kyōto-Ōsaka area brides do not become pregnant at twenty-one or twenty-two years of age, they change their hairstyle and shave their eyebrows.[3]

As this description suggests, even women who did not shave their eyebrows following marriage always did so when they became pregnant. Warrior-class women reaching "twenty-three or twenty-four" but not shaving their eyebrows would mean they are not yet pregnant at that age. According to Kitagawa Morisada, maids of warrior households "always dyed their teeth, shaved their eyebrows, and changed their hairstyle"[4] at age sixteen or seventeen, even if they were not married. In other words, there is no possibility that the women in the mother-child paintings can be woman servants.

Could they be courtesans? Kitagawa Morisada explains:

> Kyōto and Ōsaka courtesans and young geisha dye their teeth alike. It seems they wear the Shimada-style hairdo [the kind mostly worn by unmarried women], and do not shave their eyebrows. Even at a mature age, those women keep their eyebrows and hairdo.[5]

"Mothers" in mother-child portraits have good-looking eyebrows. They are dressed like courtesans rather than ordinary women. Of course, paintings do not necessarily copy reality. Kitagawa Morisada states:

> *Ukiyo-e* artists, who focus on worldly themes, portray beautiful women in certain ways. Today, women under thirty years of age and above twenty always shave their eyebrows, but in *ukiyo-e* art, eyebrows are intentionally drawn. Without eyebrows, the woman in a picture would seem over forty years old. Thus, this deliberate practice. The future generations will certainly err when they use this as proof of a fact.[6]

In short, *ukiyo-e* artists drew eyebrows even on ordinary women's faces when emphasizing youth. If so, it can be considered artistic license that mothers in mother-child paintings did not shave their eyebrows.

But how were those paintings actually received? Mothers appearing in mother-child paintings are portrayed as beautiful women. An important hint is concealed therein. To begin with, *ukiyo-e* representations of attractive figures were often of courtesans. In that sense, it would be fair to say that *bijinga* were produced with an awareness of sexually oriented consumption. Thus, there is no need to portray family women, who are deprived of sexuality and eliminated from the world of romantic love, as beautiful persons. The emphasis on youth and beauty itself indicates that they are likened to courtesans rather than represented purely as mothers. In fact, Harunobu's mother-child paintings accentuate the woman's sexual appeal. Such paintings should be considered not as representing family images but as belonging to one of the many *bijinga* variants. Children portrayed in the paintings are no more than stage props like combs, mirrors, and folding screens.

People in those days must have known this well. Or rather, they must have been enjoying the images of beauties—courtesans—in the guise of mothers. Precisely because those paintings depicted courtesans, they were able to boldly emphasize feminine sexuality. In fact, the gesture of the mother in *An Insect Cage and a Little Child* hardly differs from that of a courtesan. A mother playing with a toddler looks like a courtesan—this indicates that "mother-child pictures" were produced on the assumption of noneveryday fantasies and wishes of townspeople, for whose appreciation the artworks were intended.

Sequestered Beauties

Pictorial representations of beautiful figures in China portray courtiers as well as wives and consorts of famous people, but we find no examples depicting courtesans. From the start, few titles of Chinese paintings and drawings include the characters for "a beautiful person" (in Chinese *meiren*, Japanese *bijin*). To my knowledge, the earliest use of the term can be traced no further back than to the Ming period. Tang Yin's painting discussed above is indeed titled *Four Beautiful Women* (*Si meiren tu*, figure 3.6), but there are few other examples among paintings of the same period. This painting portrays a wife and concubines living in a large residence, not courtesans.

Although New Year prints were produced for commoners, in Ming and Qing China, where Confucian ethics filtered deep into the customs of daily life, in contrast to Japan's townsfolk, merchants remained unable to create their own culture and place their stamp on morality. In Ming and Qing China, affluent merchants patronized artists, purchased literati paintings, or economically supported artists' livelihood and artistic production.[7] As this indicates, merchants were also fond of literati paintings, and their standards of appreciation did not at all differ from those of court officials and intellectuals. Or rather, merchants sought to emulate the literati's elegant accomplishments, separating themselves from the vulgar as much as possible.

As long as Confucian ethics influenced the content of law, even commoners were unable to free themselves from its strictures. Thus, there was no room to begin with in New Year prints for beauties to appear. What surfaced, then, was the acceptable image of a good wife and wise mother. As seen in *A Beautiful Woman with Infants at Play*, women in Qing period New Year prints, in many cases, are mothers handling children or good wives supportive of husbands. Without resorting to such "cover-up operations," it might have been impossible to portray beautiful women at all. The reason is that, as suggested by the expression "crimson face, hapless fate" (meaning that beautiful women are often unfortunate), a woman's beauty often signified inauspiciousness for the family. But when she hides behind a mask of either a mother or a wife, the obstacle to artistic expression is cleared, and the work can be enjoyed as a good-luck omen.

If the beautiful person represented is a wife or a mother, loose or suggestive postures cannot be portrayed. Worse, an exposed lower leg would be outrageous. As mentioned earlier, *After Bathing in the Huaqing Pool* was painted on the historical assumption that the imperial consort Yang Guifei was an evil woman who brought disaster to the nation, and the curved lines of the legs seen through her thin robe could be drawn precisely because they suggested lasciviousness. A beautiful figure as an ideal image of a woman, inevitably, had to be a good wife and wise mother. This made it impossible to portray courtesans in paintings. In other words, while "shared" beauties were depicted in Japan, in China only "monopolized" beauties were allowed to appear in art. Deep-rooted Confucian concepts, or its ethical views that permeated into commoners' customs and manners, greatly restricted even the production techniques for the representation of beautiful women.

4. BEAUTIFUL WOMEN IN ART

Differences between Literature and Art

There was a stereotype of some sort among images of beautiful figures in Chinese literature, which did not change much until modern times. Intrinsically, Chinese poetry was strongly lyrical, its epic functions never being overly emphasized. On the other hand, "literary Chinese" (*wenyan*) used in prose literature became divorced from the spoken language and was fossilized like Latin. For this reason, it was unable to develop within the everyday language environment. As pursuit of excessive conciseness in literary Chinese created a unique aesthetics of expression, it deprived itself of the potential for detailed description. This undermined the motivation to realistically present the objects of narration. Conventions of literary allusion and competition in rhetorical skills also reinforced the tendency to make light of reproducing reality.

Naturally, the images of women in Chinese literature are not unrelated to reality. In some pieces, we can read about makeup methods and hairstyles of the old days. As a whole, however, we find descriptions of the viewer's emotion at seeing a beautiful appearance far more often than those of a person's body shape or countenance. Not limited to attractive women, it is a universal trend with descriptions of characters, including men. For this reason, throughout different ages, images of beautiful persons portrayed in verse and prose changed little.

But even if images of beauties in literature froze into certain standardized types, did similar stereotyping occur in the visual world far from conventional literary representation? In order to examine this, we need to consider images of women in art forms that are close to real life. The question is whether beautiful figures in pictorial art are the same as in literature. If different, I would like to pinpoint the differences and understand how they arose.

Chinese portraits go back to the Warring States period from the fifth century BCE. Extant paintings from those days mostly remain in the form of tomb murals and burial accompaniments. They were created as practical items rather than works of art in today's sense. We can assume that they are closer to real life. However, it is difficult to easily confirm whether or not all women appearing in them were intended to be beautiful.

Pictures Inspired by Literature

The oldest pictorial representation of feminine beauty we can view now is *The Goddess of the Luo Illustrated* (*Luo-shen fu tu*) by Gu Kaizhi (344–408?) of the Eastern Jin (317–420).

Five copies are extant. Figure 3.19 (portion) is from the one in the possession of the Palace Museum, deemed as authentic in part I of the three-part *Court Library's Treasury Cases* (*Shiqu baoji*, compiled 1743–1861). As apparent from the title, this portrait was inspired by a rhyme-prose by Cao Zhi (192–232) titled "The Goddess of the Luo." For Gu Kaizhi, born in 344 BCE, Cao Zhi was a person one-and-a-half centuries earlier. Thus, the artist did not experience the age in which the poet lived. Still, the second century did not belong to a remote past totally unfamiliar to the artist. In ancient agricultural society, changes are thought to have occurred relatively slowly. It would be fine to assume that the conception of beauty in this artwork did not differ greatly from that in Cao Zhi's age.

Figure 3.19. From Gu Kaizhi, *The Goddess of the Luo Illustrated*. Jin. Palace Museum (Beijing). *Source: Antiques Canon*, figure 1.

On a long, silk-screen scroll measuring 27.1 centimeters in height and 572.8 centimeters in width, the artist illustrates the content of the rhyme-prose, "The Goddess of the Luo," dividing it into a number of separate scenes. Besides human forms, we see natural landscapes with mountains and waters and trees as well as carriages, horses, and boats. Given that Fufei, the goddess of the Luo River, is said to have been exceedingly beautiful, Gu Kaizhi must have portrayed her as a beauty. As long as the portrait is made on the basis of a literary piece, naturally it should be restricted to a certain degree by the original work. However, it is reasonable to consider that it reflects the aesthetic sense of the artist's age fairly accurately, and presents the image of feminine beauty that the people of those days had in mind.

As in his other paintings, Gu handles the goddess's clothes with fine details. This suggests that glamorous clothing was an important aspect in lending pictorial expression to a beautiful figure. The somewhat exaggerated sloping shoulders are in accord with the description in the poem, "With shoulders shaped as if by carving," an indication that, in the Six Dynasties period (222–589, a collective noun for six dynasties during the periods of the Three Kingdoms, Jin dynasty, and Southern and Northern dynasties), such shoulders were an essential condition for a beauty. The hair, carefully depicted with tall loops at the top, suggests something about hairstyles of those days. It lets us imagine the kind of hairdo to which the expression in the poem, "Cloud-bank coiffure rising steeply" (*yunji e-e*), referred.[8]

The goddess's face in the painting is rather plump and rounder toward the bottom. Her eyes are slim and long, slanting upward toward the outer corners, while her eyebrows are horizontal. She has a straight nose and a mouth that is quite small. Although these features convey a sense of beauty in the Six Dynasties period, portraiture focusing on line drawing does not tell us anything beyond that. It was from the Tang period on that painters gradually learned the technique of surmounting, through color shading, the deficiency of line drawing.

Realistic Paintings of Court Ladies

The Goddess of the Luo Illustrated has the character of a picture with a story to be explicated by a narrator. Moreover, it is not a painting purely of human figures. Later, during the Tang, portraits, especially of beautiful women, began to appear. Particularly noteworthy is "picture of court ladies" (or more literally, "pictures of ladies-in-waiting," *shinü-hua*).

"Pictures of court ladies" are also called "pictures of upper-class women," pronounced identically but written with a different character for *shi*, and originally referred to portraits of noblewomen. The appellation "court lady" (or "upper-class lady") itself first appeared in the Tang period, but it was only in the Song that it began to signify a beautiful woman. Still, even before the Song, depending upon the attribute of the object of representation, in many cases this type of picture actually portrayed beautiful figures, or presented women as such. Because "pictures of court ladies" developed in order to respond to the demands of court life, naturally they had existed before the term was born. But they were first established as a genre in the Tang, and moreover began to be abundantly produced then.

Zhou Fang can be cited as a representative artist of Tang portraits of court ladies. His portraits realistically capture not only the external appearances of characters but also their expressions and postures. Only a few pieces are extant, including *Court Ladies with Floral Hair Ornaments* (*Zanhua shinü tu juan*) and *Court Lady Holding a Fan* (*Huishan shinü tu juan*, figure 3.20). Though limited in number, every piece typically expresses the distinctive character of Tang portraits of court ladies.

Each of the women appearing in *Court Lady Holding a Fan* is plump. As discussed in chapter 1, the high Tang period valued plumpness in women.

Figure 3.20. Zhou Fang, *Court Lady Holding a Fan*. Tang. Palace Museum (Beijing). Source: *Antiques Canon*, figure 1.

Burial stone images unearthed from tombs constructed between the seventh and eighth centuries as well as mural paintings of women in those tombs are full-bodied almost without exception. In contrast, women just one age earlier still had slender figures (figure 3.21).

The same trend is observed in high Tang pictures. In chapter 1, I referred to Zhang Xuan's *Spring Outing of the Lady of the State of Guo*, but Zhou Fang is a slightly later artist. Normally, in poetic theory the high Tang roughly refers to the years from the Kaiyuan era (713–741) to the Dali era (766–779). From the angle of cultural history, it might be best to interpret it somewhat more loosely. The dates of birth and death of Zhou Fang are unclear, but he was appointed to a government office around the thirteenth year of the Kaiyuan era (725). There is no doubt that he was a high Tang artist.

Women appearing in *Court Lady Holding a Fan* reveal the proportion of the body to the head as nearly five-and-a-half to one. The well-filled-out frame is first emphasized through the shaping of the face. Fine-line drawing of the costume further makes the beautiful plumpness of the body stand out. In those days, the proportion between the upper and lower bodies does not seem to have been so much in consciousness as an indicator of physical charm. The bottom garment, pulled up extremely high over the chest, made it impossible to portray the lower limbs. Given the great emphasis on plumpness, the neck is nearly invisible, and the face is shaped like the full moon.

Figure 3.21. *Court Lady, a Silk Painting.* Tang. Museum of Xinjiang Uygur Autonomous Region. Source: *Museum of Xinjiang Uygur Autonomous Region.* Kōdansha, 1987, figure 146.

I would like to draw particular attention to the depiction of eyebrows. As evidenced in *The Goddess of the Luo Illustrated*, slim, long eyebrows were regarded as important from the old days as a characteristic of feminine beauty in portraits of women, and on this point basically correspond to references to eyebrows in literature. In this painting, however, eyebrows are far from being as long and thin as moth's feelers; they even come to an end before the outer halves are drawn.

Such eyebrows are even more exaggerated in *Court Ladies with Floral Hair Ornaments* (figure 3.22) ascribed to Zhou Fang. Or, maybe we should say that this painting presents different eyebrows from those in *Court Lady Holding a Fan*. Perhaps these two paintings were created with a fairly long temporal span between them. The short, thick eyebrows in *Court Ladies with Floral Hair Ornaments* are at an angle of roughly forty-five degrees, with eyes that are horizontal. Moreover, they are nearly oval-shaped. Judging from the realistic painting style, it is hard to consider such eyebrows to be a fabrication based on the painter's arbitrary imagination. Rather, he is likely to have drawn what he observed in reality. This sudden change in the eyebrow shape in art must have had something to do with the eyebrow makeup

Figure 3.22. Zhou Fang, *Court Ladies with Floral Hair Ornaments*. Tang. Liaoning Provincial Museum (Shenyang). *Source: Liaoning Provincial Museum.* Kōdansha, 1982, figure 84.

practice of those days, which I would like to cover in the next chapter. Here, I will simply discuss the divergence between beautiful figures in painting and literature.

Difference between Painting and Poetry

As stated before, Zhou Fang was an official in the Dali era and is conjectured to have painted from the mid to late eighth century. His paintings clearly captured the transformation in eyebrow makeup methods.

However, contemporary literature did not necessarily respond to this change as sensitively as did art. Poems in praise of "moth-feeler eyebrows" continued to be written.

Naturally, it was not that nobody noticed the change. Bo Juyi (772–846), who dexterously used the epic nature of verse, is one who did. In a poem titled "White-Haired Woman of the Shangyang Palace" ("Shangyang baifaren"), about a certain consort confined in one palace building, he describes her robes, ornaments, and makeup as follows:

Pointed shoes and tight-fitting clothes,
In blue ink, the eyebrows are thin and long
People at large do not see, or if they saw they would laugh—
The late Tianbao era's makeup fashion.[9]

As if they were human curios, court women in those days still adhered to the makeup practice of the Tang's Tianbao era (742–756). The same poem includes two lines that run, "First chosen to enter the court in the last year of Xuanzong / entering at age sixteen, now she is sixty." Emperor Xuanzong ruled from 712 to 756, which means that the poem refers to the sixteenth year of Zhenyuan (800) or around that time. During the past forty-four years the clothing and makeup had totally changed, but ladies-in-attendance secluded in the palace knew nothing of the situation and continued to don outdated costumes and ink their eyebrows long and thin.

As in *Court Lady Holding a Fan*, praise of a full body is also seen in *Court Ladies with Floral Hair Ornaments*. Strongly contrasted with the narrow eyes, small noses, and small mouths, the faces look all the rounder. The well-rounded bodies, just barely contained within their clothes, are also sensuously portrayed through thin garments. The depiction almost gives an impression that a slender body was already eliminated from the category of beauty. On that account, *Court Lady Holding a Fan* is even more thorough. Although the round bodies are covered by clothing, it is clear that they are now far from being thin-waisted.

Despite that, in the same period, the reference to a narrow waist continued to occur in literature as a metaphor for a beautiful woman. Yang Yan, who, like Zhou Fang, served the Tang court around the 780s, does not seem to have had any hesitation when he wrote, "The Chu waist, like a willow branch, does not withstand the spring"[10] in his poem "For Yuan Zai's Songstress."

The Prototype of the Image of a Beauty

Following the collapse of the Tang in 907, the nation was split for approximately seventy years. In 960, Zhao Kuangyin established the Song dynasty, and in 979 the country was unified. The era following the collapse of the Tang is called the Five Dynasties and Ten States period. During this period, due to wartime migration, the cultures of central China and of peripheral minority peoples intersected dramatically. It also affected paintings that often address everyday life situations, gradually bringing changes to the depiction.

Concerning Five Dynasties period paintings of court ladies, we must first cite *Han Xizai's Night Revels* (figure 3.23; also refer to figure 1.11). The painter, Gu Hongzhong (910–980), at that time served as Art Academy secretary with the responsibility to respond to the emperor's inquiries. At the order of Emperor Li Yu of the Southern Tang, the artist began making pictures of the luxurious life of Han Xizai, who was then chancellor. Han Xizai held parties at his private residence day and night, with musical performances and epicurean joys. Having directly witnessed those scenes, Gu's portrayal is said to be highly realistic.

Han Xizai's Evening Party holds deep significance in the formation of the image of a beauty. It is not too much to say that, with this piece, women appearing in paintings changed drastically. Moreover, its aesthetic taste constantly occupied a dominant status in the history of the following ten or so centuries.

What needs to be pointed out above all is that the faces of the women in this painting have become remarkably thinner. The full cheeks of Tang and earlier representations disappeared, replaced by the oval facial shape that later became considered the attribute of a beautiful woman.

The placement of the eyes and nose on the face is appropriate, indicating that the depiction was guided by an accurate observation. The nose in each face is straight, and moreover, unlike earlier line drawings, the skillful use of shading in color gives a strong three-dimensional sense to the nose and the face as a whole. In comparison with Tang and earlier painting styles, in which noses are line-drawn with bare simplicity, this painting captures

Figure 3.23. Gu Hongzhong, *Han Xizai's Night Revels*. Five Dynasties. Palace Museum (Beijing). *Source: Antiques Canon*, figure 11.

the characters' expressions far more accurately. This progress in technique allowed painters to portray the countenances of women more precisely than before.

Thin, long, and neatly curved eyebrows returned to those before the early Tang period. Such eyebrows, corresponding to "moth-feeler eyebrows" in literature, are central to portrayal here also as an important characteristic of feminine beauty. And yet they are not uniformly depicted in every woman. Rather, the differences in the distance between eyebrows and the way they curve richly convey individuality. In the light of Tang and pre-Tang representations of good-looking women, this painting makes the viewer feel the change of the times.

A similar change in aesthetics appears in the depiction of the eyes as well. Although the taste for finding elegance in long and narrow eyes is inherent here, in comparison with Tang and earlier representations of narrow eyes, *Han Xizai's Evening Party* differs in that interest is drawn to the size of the eyes and the expression that the irises convey. Here also we can glimpse delicate changes in the standards of appreciation and preferences of the times regarding beautiful eyes.

Depiction of Double Eyelids

Such changes in aesthetic taste from one age to another can be observed in later paintings as well. Passing through the Song period when landscape paintings flourished, Ming period paintings of women achieve further changes. Naturally, some painters seek ancient ideals through artistic activities, and they often became more absorbed in reproducing old paintings than in portraying women in real life—for which reason, we have to be quite careful when judging whether or not artworks portrayed attractive women of the times. On the other hand, there certainly were other artists who captured the spirit of the age by realistic methods and reproduced beauty from real life.

In particular, *Female Immortals* (see figure 3.3) by Chen Hongshou of the Ming period offers good material for considering the changing images of beautiful women. This painting portrays a goddess and her maid. Although supposedly immortal, no doubt both figures are modeled after women from real life. Clad in a roomy outer garment, the body shape of the immortal lady is somewhat unclear, but, partly from the proportion of the head to the body, we conjecture that she is slender. Such a physique, with the proportion of head and body being one to six-and-a-half, was barely found in ancient art. The size of the transition that occurred over a long period of historical development is striking.

The bottom part of the face is narrower than in the depiction in Gu Hongzhong's *Han Xizai's Night Revels*, contributing to forming an oval head shape. The eyebrows, unlike the short pairs in Zhou Fang's *Court Ladies with Floral Hair Ornaments* or the narrow, long pairs drawn by Gu Hongzhong, are somewhat thick and naturally shaped. While the preference for a straight nose is basically unchanged, the detailed sketch of the sides of the nose greatly differs from those in traditional portraits of beautiful women. One senses diversification of aesthetic sense in the Ming period.

Particularly notable is that double eyelids began to be depicted in paintings. It was generally considered that the view of double eyelids as beautiful was born in modern times under Western influence, but in fact it seems to have formed spontaneously within China. Because written sources do not refer to this, the significance of *Female Immortals* is all the greater. Even as the poet Wang Tingxiang of the Ming period repeated stock phrases resembling those from one thousand years ago when he wrote of "cloud-like knotted hair, moth-feeler eyebrows, a wind instrument shaped like a purple phoenix,"[11] a contemporary painting closer to real life was accurately expressing the shifts in aesthetic sensibility.

For a painting of a beautiful woman, *Female Immortals* used an unexpectedly large number of straight lines. If those bold touches are distinctive and exceptional in portraits of court ladies-in-attendance (*shinyü-hua*), the delicate style and supple line drawing in *Yinzhen Fei's Outing, a Screen* (figure 3.24) of the Qing period precisely recalls the tradition of the genre.

The imperial consort seated in a chair is clearly slender. She has an even thinner face than the figure in *Female Immortals* from the Ming period, and thin eyebrows somewhat shorter than those of the women in Gu Hongzhong's *Han Xizai's Night Revels*. Still, the careful drawing indicates that thin eyebrows were still an important characteristic for conveying the beauty of a woman.

The painter of *Yinzhen Fei's Outing* depicts her nose with skillful coloring and a masterful use of thin lines, with attention paid to details. He not only portrays its clean shape but also tries to ambitiously reproduce the consort's graceful dignity, presumably in order to respond to the demand of the times. Likewise, the slightly long mouth displays a different style from small mouths often seen in portraits of women until then. Although the thin, long eyes seem to resemble those in ancient portraits of court ladies, the depiction of the double eyelids here clearly reveals the change in aesthetic sense, as does *Female Immortals* from the Ming period.

So far, through a selection of characteristic paintings from the Han, Six Dynasties, Tang,

Figure 3.24. *Yinzhen Fei's Outing, a Screen.* Qing. Palace Museum (Beijing). *Source: Antiques Canon,* figure 11.

Five Dynasties, Ming, and Qing periods (some are later reproductions but they can be assumed to reproduce the composition and shaping), I have traced the changes in the imagery of beautiful women. As already observed, in the area of paintings, reality was grasped and reproduced with relative accuracy. Each art piece can be said to roughly reflect the aesthetic standards of its particular period.

There is not enough room here to discuss other portraits of court ladies. I wish to point out one thing, however. That is, in Ming and Qing period art, we occasionally encounter portraits in identical styles as in the Six Dynasty or Tang period. But those representations consciously imitate ancient artworks rather than reflect real life. In fact, Tang Yin, for one, attaches the phrase "After the Old" (*fang gu*) to the title of a number of his pieces, unhesitatingly admitting that they are imitations of ancient paintings. Aside from these exceptions, images of beauties in art can basically be considered to reflect reality.

Literature and art greatly differ in terms of mechanism of expression. In literature, at the same time that a work conveys meaning, it has autonomy as linguistic expression. Classical Chinese, in particular, profoundly emphasized the beauty of language itself like words, style, and meter. It is no wonder, therefore, that rifts or discords sometimes arise between the work and the object it attempts to give expression to. On the other hand, precisely because of such disparity, beauty portrayed in literary works all the more approaches universality. The immortal woman Fufei's beauty portrayed in *The Goddess of the Luo Illustrated* still today moves us thanks to Cao Zhi's dazzling literary style. In comparison, it must be said that the beauty of *The Goddess of the Luo Illustrated* has now come to retain only a historical meaning.

To probe the aesthetic sense of the past through the use of paintings is valid as one method. I do not intend to affirm that all ancient paintings reproduced reality as it was. Even if assuming that each piece graphically depicted reality, a question remains as to whether limited pictorial sources can indeed accurately reflect a dynamically changing aesthetic sense. Rather than the degree to which reality was reflected, what is more important is the manner in which conceptions of feminine beauty were expressed in formative art.

NOTES

1. An Lushan was a Tang military leader of foreign (perhaps Sogdian and Tujue) origin. Favored by Emperor Xuanzong, he wielded great military power in northeast China. His opposition to the imperial consort Yang Guifei's brother Yang Guozhong and others led to the An Lushan Rebellion. In the midst, Yang Guifei was forced to commit suicide, and An Lushan was assassinated by his own son.

2. Shiokawa Kyōko, *Women in Pictorial Representations: From Married Women in Picture Scrolls to Shōwa Paintings of Beautiful Women* (*Egakareta on'na tachi: emaki no shufu-zō kara Shōwa no bijinga made*) (Asahi Shinbunsha, 1999), 31.

3. Kitagawa Morisada, *Customs and Manners of the Recent Days: Morisada's Rambling Writings*, vol. 2 (*Kinsei fūzoku shi: Morisada mankō*), edited by Usami Hideki (Iwanami Bunko, 1997), 86.

4. Loc. cit.

5. Loc. cit.

6. Ibid., 79.

7. Chu-tsing Li (editor), James Cahill and Wai-kam Ho (coeditors), *Artists and Patrons: Some Social and Economic Aspects of Chinese Painting* (University of Washington Press, 1989).

8. Quotations from the translation by Burton Watson in John Minford and Joseph S. M. Lau (editors), *An Anthology of Translations: Classical Chinese Literature*, vol. 1, 315.

9. *Complete Tang Poetry* (*Quan Tangshi*) (Shanghai Guji Chubanshe, 1986). Takagi Shōichi (annotator), *Po Juyi*, vol. 1 (*Chūgoku Shijin Senshū* 12, Iwanami Shoten, 1968), 43.

10. Ibid.

11. Wang Tingxiang. "Court Lyric" ("Gongci"). *Selections from Ming Poetry* (*Mingshi-chao*), vol. 9, 31, in *Compilation in Four Categories, Continuation* (*Sibu congkan shupian*).

4

Beauty as a Construct

1. FLUCTUATING MEANINGS OF THE BEAUTIFUL FACE

Evaluation by the Other

The face belongs to its owner, but its aesthetic appreciation is a matter of others' judgment. What determines whether or not it looks beautiful is the perspective of the observer, independent of the owner's will or taste. Naturally, depending upon personal efforts, one can change one's "appearance" to a certain degree. Still, to the extent that "society's eye" provides the standard, those efforts must be directed to others' likes and dislikes rather than one's own taste.

When an aesthetic judgment is made, "the eye of the observer" is based on the sensibilities of the majority, not a specific individual's taste. In that sense, the determination of beauty or ugliness is always influenced by preferences of the general public. The point of view of observers differs with the climate and the era, and public taste also constantly changes. Representation of beauty too shifts dramatically with the passage of time.

Nor can the ideal face keep a fixed standard. Although a countenance may at a glance seem to be prenatally determined, depending upon how it approaches society's "standard," aesthetic evaluation of the same face is not necessarily immutable. As long as certain conditions are fulfilled, it is not impossible to artificially construct a beautiful countenance. Cosmetic surgery is an extreme example of this, but what is most frequently used in everyday life is makeup. Powder the face, apply lipstick, pencil eyebrows—humankind discovered this sort of basic makeup method from early on. Since obtaining this transformative magic, humans came to be able to "fabricate" beautiful looks to some extent. On the other hand, along with the discovery of makeup skills, a history of facial ordeals also began.

Makeup and countenance are interestingly related. While countenance is passive, makeup is an active behavior. One can only leave assessment of one's looks up to the gaze of others, but makeup is an act that works on that gaze. At a glance, makeup may seem to be intended to "make the face more beautiful," but it is essentially unrelated to beauty. The purpose is, while anticipating society's aesthetic eye, to show oneself according to its taste or expectation. Thus, makeup becomes meaningful only within the community. When drifting ashore alone on an uninhabited island, a woman would stop making up no matter how much she normally cares for her external appearance. There is the other that views, and there is the self that is viewed. Only when this basic relationship is formed does the act of makeup bear meaning.

Dual Characteristics of Makeup

If aesthetic judgment of appearance presupposes the relationship between the viewer and the viewed, makeup is an act that goes one step further. The reason is that makeup is a mode of communication that does not use words. Due to makeup, the face moves from the relationship between "viewing" and "being viewed" to that between "showing" and "being shown." In "Biographies of Assassins" ("Ceke liezhuan"), "Biographies" 26 of the *Records of the Grand Historian*, we find an expression, "women make up their faces for those who enjoy them." Makeup has a clear sense of purpose, and a different message can be conveyed depending upon its method or degree. In some cases, it is intended to attract a specific person's eyes, and in others to appeal to a large number of unspecified people.

Meanings attached to makeup vary with similarities and differences of cosmetic methods. Methods that are faithful to fashions convey, through similarity, a sense of ceremonial belonging to the community. On the other hand, makeup that differs from the practice of the surroundings and everyday life strongly asserts, through difference, various specific meanings such as confidence, ostentation, superiority, contempt, repulsion, and challenge.

Looked at historically, makeup went through gradual processes of going out from protected chambers to society. In those ages when women were forbidden to socialize, makeup was basically for one's husband or lord. Naturally, as with laments over an unvisited chamber, a specific male was not necessarily there, before a woman's eyes. Nevertheless, as with all other cases, the putting on of makeup assumed there was someone to show it to.

A courtesan's makeup was in principle subject to many gazes, but in reality it was seen exclusively within a specific time-space. In that sense, as representation, it had no greater public character than ordinary women's makeup.

Starting in modern times, along with the advance of women into society, makeup became exposed to general public view. In the process of moving from private to general spaces, the ceremonial aspect of makeup gradually grew more pronounced. In particular, in business and social arenas, makeup often turns out to be a code for demonstrating social courtesy. Clean appearance and moderate makeup show respect and at the same time suggest a proper distance from the viewer. In present-day society, along with clothing, behavior, speech, and so forth, makeup indicates social standing, occupation, education, and rank. In fact, the way and degree of makeup differ delicately in response to the environment like work, business talks, and socializing occasions, and they also vary by particular scenes such as partying, concertgoing, or dining together. It is social common sense to wear different makeup than usual for rites of passage like a wedding, birthday, and funeral.

On the other hand, the increase in the public nature of makeup brought forth diverse social meanings to this conduct. Side by side with the nature of the message in public spaces, private implications of makeup still remain in effect today. Or rather, its indicative nature can be said to have become stronger. In truth, when going out with a sweetheart or being near someone with whom one is secretly in love, one pays even greater attention to makeup than to clothing.

Counterfeit Beauty

As stated above, applying color to the face does not mean transforming the countenance but changing "how it looks." Whether done consciously or unconsciously, makeup flatters the gaze of the other and, at the same time, deceives it. At one glance, makeup may seem to be an indication of the intent of obedience, but in essence it is often aggressive. Makeup's aggressiveness is revealed in its clear purposefulness. Be it a public or a private purpose, when makeup is part of a planned act, the degree of aggressiveness is high. Although rare, exaggerated makeup is sometimes used as a sign of protest. For this reason, makeup not suited to the spatial and temporal context makes surrounding people uncomfortable. On the other hand, makeup as a message of love also assumes aggressiveness in a different sense, in that it too is intended to draw attention.

Given that beauty is favored, one attempts to compete by means of forging beauty—this is the hidden aspect of makeup. In this sense, makeup structurally resembles counterfeiting money. While pretending acceptance of male-chauvinist hierarchy, the act of applying makeup performs retaliation against cultural domination based on the gender gap.

Makeup for improving the countenance is a kind of self-expression. But at the same time it is self-expression that greatly restricts freedom. Putting aside cases where political intention or malice is present, makeup normally involves little preference for originality. When making up, while one is always aware of differences from others, there is no need to apply totally original makeup. In fact, nobody turns her own face into a canvass of modern art for the sake of creating "beauty" in an ordinary sense.

Makeup presupposes commonly shared images. Variations on those shared standards have added many different meanings to makeup. This is common to East and West throughout all ages. However, in modern times those standards of aesthetic judgment came to be greatly influenced by commercialism. Beautiful appearance in fashion is presented as an image that precedes reality, and permeates society through the media. Behind this, of course, consumption of the mode, accessories, and cosmetics is connected. Some faces gain popularity because they are beautiful; others look beautiful because they have gained popularity. In this manner, faces continue to ceaselessly drift on the rough waves of commercialism.

Fluctuating Meanings of Beauty

Such fluctuating standards for what is considered to be a beautiful face is not limited to modern times. Going back to ancient days, the art of makeup has, in the course of a long history, always been an important element affecting aesthetic judgment. Sometimes, makeup is emphasized even more than the countenance. Numerous praises of the proper makeup are found in literary works in history in the East and West. In those descriptions, attention goes to makeup in the same way as, or even more than, to the beauty of countenance itself.

Makeup is depicted not only in verse and prose but also in painting and drawing. Because aesthetic criteria change from age to age, makeup that represents fashion always provides a measure for distinguishing between the beautiful and the plain. The reason is that, as seen in today's examples, there are cases in which one becomes almost unrecognizably handsome by makeup alone.

Transition in makeup, which greatly changes external appearances and impressions given to others, is extremely important for gauging changes in aesthetic sense. As discussed in chapter 1, in the long course of history, favored body shapes were not constant. If plumpness was thought attractive in one age, in the next a slender physique was valued.

Compared to body shape, standards of good looks varied even more widely. Beautiful faces are often given stock expressions. Phrases like "moth-feeler eyebrows" and "bright irises" are typical examples. When we carefully examine those clichés, we find not a few that are related to, or show the results of, makeup. This was particularly the case in ancient times. For example, "snow-white skin" sometimes indicates the result of powdering, and "cherry-red lips" often presupposes the use of rouge. As a result, what is seen or depicted as beauty is not the actual face but beauty created by makeup.

Makeup can create many variants of countenance. The art of makeup sometimes changes as a result of internal factors within a culture, but it is not rare that, when plural cultures cross one another, criteria of beauty and methods of makeup change under the influence of foreign aesthetics.

In Chinese history, culture continued to change dynamically. Transitions in customs and manners were particularly intense. Amidst those changes, women's makeup did not remain the same. There are many reasons, but here I would like to explore the processes makeup went through as it changed from age to age.

2. TRANSMISSION OF SAFFLOWER

Cultural Politics of the Beautiful Woman

History books including the *Commentary of Zuo* and *Records of the Grand Historian* valued historical representations of the continuity and discontinuity of kingship. Because patriarchal society established itself early on in China, historical writings tended to be male-centered. Women's lives were hardly discussed seriously, and technical records concerning makeup are quite limited. The few materials remaining in historical books and notes are mostly fragmentary.

On the other hand, it was not rare that women became involved in battles fought for reinforcement or usurpation of kingship. Some politicians and historians also attempted to read omens of disasters and vicissitudes in changes in clothing and women's makeup. Further, there are countless examples of makeup methods or changes thereof being used as pretexts for power struggle. For such reasons, makeup, a private act within a chamber, came to be recorded as footnotes to political history. When adding modes of makeup and dressing depicted in literature as a supplementary line to makeup styles recorded in history books, we can to some extent resurrect the lost customs of the past.

Paintings from various ages also provide clues to changes in makeup practice. As we can see when comparing Gu Kaizhi's *The Goddess of the Luo Illustrated* (see figure 3.19) and the Qing dynasty screen of *Yinzhen Fei's Outing* (see figure 3.24), the image of the beauty greatly changed from age to age in physique, hairstyle, and clothing. The differing shapes of the eyebrows here also exemplify how the art of makeup changed a fair amount over the ages.

Various ethnic groups have lived on the Chinese continent from ancient times and through repeated power struggles. The Han were the majority in terms of population, and, culturally, exerted overwhelming influence. In military terms, however, they did not necessarily prevail. Following the collapse of the Han dynasty, war broke out frequently around supremacy over a unified empire. After cultural centers came to concentrate in urban areas, the military power of the Han gradually declined. Earlier, with their developed civilization and high degree of productive power, the Han were able to control peripheral minorities, but later they proved unable to compete with northern equestrians who had greater mobility.

As a result, central administration repeatedly passed to the hands of ethnic groups. While struggles for control evolved, cultures of different ethnicities began to collide with one another, incurring frequent expulsion, acceptance, and merger.

Founding of kingdoms by minority groups not only brought forth shifts of ruling groups but also gradually affected the culture and customs of the Han. Because gaining power also meant gaining wealth, clear hierarchical relations formed between the ruling people and the Han. In other words, during such periods, ruling minorities became "the higher" and the ruled Han "the lower." Value judgments regarding "the higher as beautiful and the lower as ugly" and "the affluent as beautiful and the poor as ugly" worked unconsciously in these cases as well. No wonder that Han women tried to emulate them when women of the ruling group appeared beautiful. It is also quite natural that they adopted the makeup methods of the ruling group. Thus, amidst confrontation and collision among diverse ethnic cultures, the criteria of beauty changed, and the face also constantly changed.

The most frequently used method for modeling oneself after women of different ethnicity is imitation of clothing and makeup. Yet, how good looks changed in Chinese history, and how ethnic cultures influenced women's aesthetic sense, makeup methods, cosmetic goods, and cosmetic tools, have rarely been discussed.[1]

Rouge That Came from the Western Region

Looked at from the perspective of hierarchical relationships in cultural power, there are two modes of acceptance of ethnic culture in makeup. One is the influence of higher culture on lower. The other is the reverse of this. Lower culture does not necessarily simply accept higher culture. Rather, it is closer to reality to say that intermingled cultures mutually exert influence. This also applies to the relationship between Han and peripheral peoples. In other words, when a minority group advanced to the core area of the continent and controlled the Han, the latter accepted the makeup method of the minority, but when the Han drove small minority groups to peripheral areas and gained predominance, they also adopted cosmetic goods and skills from the Western Regions and northern peoples. The reverse of this is also true, but first I would like to discuss the former.

In China, the introduction of cosmetic goods has profound relationships with cultural exchanges among ethnic groups. A typical example is the red pigment that is the material for rouge. It is called *yanzhi* in Chinese. It was not only used for lips but for cheeks as well. When women began using rouge in China is not yet clear. On reading old materials, we come upon a variety of theories. They can be divided into three large groups: one finds its origin in the Shang period, a second in the Zhou period, and a third in the introduction from outside in the Han period. In *Commentaries on Things Now and Old in the Central States* (*Zhonghua gujin zhu*) compiled by Ma Gao in the Five Dynasties period (907–960), we read:

> [The red pigment] existed since the age of King Zhou. *Yanzhi* is made by condensing safflower juice. It was called *yanzhi* (Yan oil) because it was produced in the State of Yan.

The Shang period, also called the Yin period, lasted from the seventeenth century to the eleventh century BCE. If we follow this statement, *yanzhi* was already produced three thousand to four thousand years ago. However, Li Shi of the Song period says in *Sequel to a Treatise on Curiosities* (*Xu Bowu-zhi*) that people "applied *yanzhi* made of gromwell roots starting in the Three Dynasties period, but came to use safflower starting in the Zhou dynasty." In other words, the compiler understands that the use of safflower began following the Three Dynasties; that is, Xia, Shang, and Zhou, or more precisely in the Zhou dynasty (1027–771 BEC). On the other hand, Zhang Hua of the State of Jin claims in *A Treatise on Curiosities* (*Bowu-zhi*) that the pigment was brought in from the Western Regions by Zhang Qian:

Zhang Qian, who went to the Western Regions as an emissary, brought back garlic, pomegranate, grape, bur clover, coriander, and safflower. Safflower can produce *yanzhi*.

In other words, safflower was brought in along with such vegetables as garlic and bur clover from the Western Regions in the Han period. Zhang Hua's view was supported by Cui Bao, also of the Jin period. He too states in *Commentaries on Things Now and Old* (*Gujin zhu*) that the original home of *yanzhi*, here written with a different character for *zhi*, is the Western Regions, and that northern peoples use it as a pigment:

> *Yanzhi*, with leaves resembling thistle and dandelion, hails from the Western Regions. Locals use it for dying, and call it *yanzhi*. The Chinese call it "crimson indigo" (*honglan*), use it to dye powder, and add hue to the face [with the dyed powder]. This is called "safflower powder" (*yanzhi-fen*).

The description of safflower in *A Treatise on Curiosities* is quite detailed, and the method of producing rouge from safflower is also introduced in detail. On the other hand, Cui Bao's *Commentaries on Things Now and Old* is also concrete, and can be trusted to a fair degree.

Zhang Hua, the author of *A Treatise on Curiosities*, held the office of secretary of internal affairs of the court (*zhongshu-ling*) in the era of Emperor Wu (236–290) of the State of Jin, which makes him approximately four hundred years junior to Zhang Qian. Cui Bao, slightly younger, held the high office of imperial advisor (*taifu*) during the reign of Emperor Hui (290–306) of Jin. Ma Gao, the author of *Commentaries on Things Now and Old in Central China* lived in the late Tang (923–936), postdating Zhang Hua and Cui Bao by approximately seven hundred years.

Zhang Hua's *A Treatise on Curiosities* and Cui Bao's *Commentaries on Things Now and Old* are not as accurate as history books. Yet, they are not fiction, either. Although some descriptions in them are simply absurd, the compilers assumed they were recording facts. Descriptions of safflower have little to do with the supernatural or hearsay, so it should be fine to basically trust them. It was between 138 and 126 BCE during the reign of Emperor Wu of the Han dynasty that Zhang Qian visited the Western Regions as a diplomatic emissary. If we follow Zhang Hua's claim, it turns out that the history of the use of safflower begins in the Han.

Regarding the origin of safflower, the description in the *Erya*, the oldest extant Chinese dictionary, is also helpful. According to the safflower entry (*Yancao*) in "On Herbs" ("Shi cao") in *Erya*, "safflower is not originally a product of China. It comes from the Western Regions." It further notes:

"In China, now it is called *honglan* (crimson-indigo) or *honghua* (crimson flower)." *Erya* is the compilation by early Han period scholars of documents from the Zhou to the Qin. It was widely used from long ago as a dictionary and is well reputed for its accuracy. Considering these factors, it is virtually certain that safflower and the use of rouge as a cosmetic have a deep connection with influence from the Western Regions.

Safflower not only served as raw material for cosmetics but was also widely used as a dye. In "Deposed Emperor, King Hailiang" in the "History of Qi" in *The History of Southern Dynasties (Nanshi)*, we read: "At the time of Emperor Wu, courtiers wore red robes [dyed] red with safflower." This indicates that in the Six Dynasties period, *yanzhi* was used for dyeing as well.

Safflower and the Huns

Crimson, or safflower red, called *yanzhi* in Chinese, is written with characters normally meaning "throat" and "fat." As seen in *A Treatise on Curiosities* and *Commentaries on Things Now and Old*, in olden days it was written with the character for "swallow" or "Yan" as in the State of Yan and the character for "branch," but later it changed to "Yan oil" or "swallow oil," then to the present form with some variations while the pronunciation remained the same.

Actually there was another old name for safflower red: *yanzhi* written phonetically with the character normally meaning "herein" or "wherefore" and another meaning "branch." This is said to be a word originally of the Xiongnu people (the Huns), derived from the name of the mountain by that name. The mountain was a producer of safflowers, the raw material for the crimson dye Hun women used for facial makeup from olden days. That is why, it is said, the crimson dye came to be called *yanzhi*. With respect to this, in his *Annotations on the Records of the Grand Historian (Shiji zheng'yi)*, Zhang Shoujie of the Tang period quotes the following, attributing the passage to *Geographical Compilation (Guadi zhi)*:

> Mount Yanzhi, also called Mount Shandan, is located 50 *li* southeast of Shandan prefecture in Ganzhou [in contemporary Gansu]. *Legends of the West River (Xihe gushi)* says that "when the Huns lost the two mountains, Qilian and Yanzhi, they sang: They robbed us of Mount Qilian, making our cattle unable to prosper. They deprived us of Mount Yanzhi making our women unable to do makeup." Thus [the Huns] regretted and lamented [the loss of the two mountains].

Legends of the West River is not extant, but it is quoted in *The Imperial Readings of the Taiping Era (Taiping yulan)* of the late tenth century. The same also appears, among others, in *Accounts of the Dressing Chamber* (*Zhuanglou ji*) by Zhang Mi of the Tang and *All about the North* (*Beibian duiyao*) by Cheng Dachang of the Song. From such references, we conjecture that *yanzhi* was a Hun expression. However, no direct proof of this can be found. Of the terms signifying rouge, *yanzhi* (with the character meaning the State of Yan or "swallow" and the character meaning "branch") is the oldest. But this is unlike usual Chinese words. Normally, one can read from a Chinese word some kind of original meaning. But the meaning *rouge* cannot be read into the word *yanzhi*. The term *yanzhi* may seem to be ideographic because of the character for "oil," but the fact that the combination "*yan* oil" postdates "*yan* branch" suggests that it was a result of a conscious change to make the latter into a term that better conveys the meaning. When we think of these things, it is highly possible that "*yan* branch" was a phonetic transcription of a word and that it was a foreign loan word.

3. WHITER SKIN, DARKER EYEBROWS

Original Powder

On earth, there is no such thing as "peculiar culture." When we talk about culture, words like *tradition* or *peculiar* are either fantasy or rhetoric.

In the first place, culture resembles a river. Even if the river itself does not change, the water that flows through it is never the same. Precisely because new water flows through it, the river is alive. The river may sometimes change course. As water spoils when the current of the river stops, culture, too, eventually declines unless it changes and develops. In historical imagination, the expression *peculiar culture* is only used rhetorically in its relationships with the surface of society that changes from day to day, moment to moment.

It is the same with the use of *tradition* when we talk about makeup. Namely, it is merely talked about with a nuance that the passage of time is relatively long, and its origin is no longer clear.

Among cosmetic goods used on the Chinese continent, rouge and white powder offer a good contrast. While rouge made of safflower is a result of interaction between China's periphery and core, powder is original. In that sense, powder can be called a "traditional" cosmetic.

Rice Powder and Lead Powder

Powder used from long ago was made of rice. It remained in use even after lead powder appeared on the stage.

We can think of many reasons for the coexistence of rice powder and lead powder. First, production technology differed depending upon the era and area, and probably rural areas, in particular, were able to produce only rice powder. Again, even in the same area, people of different classes did not necessarily use the same cosmetics. When considered as a commodity, lead powder, which required somewhat complex processing, is likely to have been higher priced than rice powder. *Essential Skills for Commoners (Jimin yaoshu)*, volume 5, introduces the production method of cosmetic powder called *zifen* ("purple powder"). According to that source, *zifen* was made by combining three parts of powder made of refined rice and one part of "Hu powder" (*hufen*, so called because it was transmitted from the regions where Hu people lived). The reason, it points out, is that rice powder does not stay on the face unless "Hu powder" is added. The proportion of the "Hu powder," superior to rice powder as a cosmetic material, was kept low presumably because the cost was higher.

"Rice" (*mi*) in ancient Chinese does not necessarily refer to rice from rice plants. All edible grains, including common millet and foxtail millet, were called *mi*. This applies to "rice" used as the raw material for facial powder. *Essential Skills for Commoners*, volume 5, describes how to prepare "powder" (*fen*) for "making up the body." Regarding how to choose materials, it states:

> *Liangmi* is the best, followed by *sumi*. [It is crucial to use just one kind alone without mixing.] Prepare with great care. [Throw out cracked grains.] Selectively use just one kind of grain, avoiding mixing with other kinds. [The kind made by mixing (millet), rice, sticky rice, wheat, any variety of millet, and so forth is not of good quality.][2]

Liangmi means "good grain," and it does not originally refer to a specific variety of grain. Here it probably indicates sticky rice. Unmistakably, *sumi* simply refers to *su*, or foxtail millet. This description suggests that, long ago, not just rice but various kinds of millet and wheat were also used as materials for facial powder.

The Spread of Powder

Records of Light and Dark (*Youming lu*) contains a story called "Powder Girl." A wealthy man's son fell in love at first sight with a powder seller in the street because of her lovely looks. Puzzled by his buying powder every day, the girl asked him the reason and he confessed his inner thoughts. They instantly became sweethearts, and the man invited her to his house. But when she visited for a tryst, from extreme excitement he suddenly fell down and died. Because more than one hundred packs of powder were discovered in his room the following morning, the girl was hurried to court. With the permission of the magistrate, she went to see the dead man. When she began wailing before the corpse, the man, thought dead until then, came back to life. The two were united as man and wife.

Because the *Records of Light and Dark* is a work by Liu Yiqing (404–444) of the Six Dynasties period, we can conjecture that around the fifth century, white powder was mass produced to the extent that it was sold in the market. Also, the man was considered suspicious because he went to buy some daily, not because a man bought powder. Men may have still used powder as late as in the Six Dynasties period.

It is not clear how long the habit of men applying powder lasted. However, hardly any mention of it is found in Tang texts. Aside from stage makeup in drama, men must have stopped using powder in everyday lives, at the latest in the Song period.

Among cosmetic powder, there was the kind called "scented powder" (*xiangfen*). It not only whitened the skin but functioned as perfume. *Essential Skills for Commoners* introduces the production method of "scented powder" as follows:

> Just put a large amount of clove in a case of white powder, then it spontaneously produces fragrance. [There is also a method of pounding clove till it becomes powdery, then mixing it with white powder after screening through silk. Another method is to soak clove in water, and mix the juice into white powder. In either case, the color deteriorates, and moreover large amounts of clove are necessary.][3]

Powder in the market was not simply used but seems to have been further processed, depending upon the purchaser, to suit a variety of usages.

Painting Eyebrows

In China, the history of drawing eyebrows is as old as that of using powder. According to literary and historical texts, it began earlier than rouge. The phrase *powdered white, eyebrows dark, with rich luster* from "The Great Summons" ("Dazhao") in the aforementioned *Songs of the South*, for example, is proof of that. The cosmetic method involving drawing eyebrows already existed at the latest by the Spring and Autumn period.

According to Liu Xi's *Etymological Dictionary of Names*, eyebrow makeup is not done over the eyebrows, but refers to shaving them off and replacing them with drawn eyebrows. In many cases, the drawing was black, but there were also "blue eyebrows" (or blue-green eyebrows, *qingdai*). According to *Accounts of the Dressing Table* (*Zhuangtai ji*) from the Tang period, Emperor Wu of the State of Wei ordered his consorts to draw blue eyebrows. Again, during the Zhenyuan era (785–805), blue eyebrows were drawn at court.

The shape of eyebrows varies depending upon the times. Emperor Wu of Han had court ladies wear drooping eyebrows, and at the time of Emperor Wu of Wei of the Three Kingdoms, long eyebrows that formed a straight line were in fashion in the rear palace. The latter, called "immortal moth makeup" (*xian'e zhuang*), remained popular in the Qi and Liang periods (479–502, 502–557) (*Accounts of the Dressing Table*). Emperor Wu of the state of Wei refers to Cao Cao, a warlord and penultimate chancellor of the Eastern Han dynasty. He did not accede to the throne during his life. But after his death, his son Cao Pi became emperor, so Cao Cao was posthumously titled Emperor Wu of Wei. He was born in 155 and died in 220, which means that straight-line eyebrows began to be fashionable starting in the second century.

Accounts of the Dressing Table gives ten names for eyebrow makeup. Because those names use rhetorical expressions, it is hard to know the precise eyebrow shapes. Nor can we confirm them by extant representational materials. However, there is no doubt that a variety of ways to wear eyebrow makeup were practiced.

In China, narrow, long eyebrows were traditionally regarded as beautiful. But a large change occurred in the Tang period. As referred to in chapter 3, the eyebrows of the beauties portrayed in *Court Ladies with Floral Hair Ornaments* are abnormally thick and short. Although the use of eyebrow makeup can be confirmed by paintings, in reality many more ways of drawing them must have existed as recorded in *Accounts of the Dressing Table*.

Few poems refer to the change in eyebrow makeup, but it is not that there is none at all. As mentioned in chapter 3, Bo Juyi touched upon the sudden change in "White-Haired Woman of the Shangyang Palace." According to that, in the Zhen'yuan era (785–805), court women were still drawing narrow, long eyebrows like those of the late Tianbao era (742–755). The reason is that court women were sequestered, unaware of the change of fashion. In fact, there were some changes in eyebrow makeup even before the Tianbao era.

In 1960, the tomb of Princess Yongtai of the Tang period was excavated in Gan prefecture in Shaanxi province. A procession of court women is portrayed on the east wall of the front room of the tomb (figure 4.1). Their eyebrows are relatively thick, or at least they are not long, narrow "moth-feeler eyebrows." Princess Yongtai, whose personal name was Li Xianxun, was a daughter of Li Xian, Emperor Zhongzong of Tang. According to the *New Book of Tang*, volume 83, Biographies 8, she was executed because she went

Figure 4.1. A Mural Painting in the Tomb of Princess Yongtai. Tang Period. Liaoning Provincial Museum. *Source: Liaoning Provincial Museum,* figure 173.

against Zhang Yizhi and his brother, favorite vassals of her grandmother, Empress Consort Wu Zetian. Princess Yongtai was reburied in 706, the second year of the Shenlong era after Emperor Zhongzong, once banished by his mother, was restored to the throne. The eyebrows of court women in the mural painting probably reflect the fashion of the early eighth century when the reburial occurred.

The "Late Tianbao era" mentioned in Bo Juyi's "White-Haired Woman of the Shangyang Palace" is considered to be around 754 or 755. Within half a century, thick eyebrows as in the mural painting of Princess Yongtai's tomb declined, and thin eyebrows became fashionable. In another half a century, the narrow, long eyebrows changed to short, thick eyebrows, as in *Court Ladies with Floral Hair Ornaments*.

Lip Makeup

When rouge began to be used for lip makeup is unclear. But in the Tang period, not only was rouge made of safflower used but lip makeup methods developed to a fair degree.

Accounts of the Dressing Table lists sixteen different names for lip makeup. The author of the book is Yuwen Shiji of the Tang period, about whom little is known. But the date of his death, the sixteenth year of Zhenguan (642), appears in the *Old Book of Tang*, volume 63. Thus, those sixteen makeup methods belong to early Tang.

The same description occurs also in "Rouge Products" in the *Record Clarifying Different Names (Qing'yi lu)* by Tao Gu. According to it, at the time of Xizong and Zhaozong of Tang, women competed with one another in lip makeup. Methods were minutely differentiated, it says, each with its own name. The names given here are roughly the same as those found in *Accounts of the Dressing Table*. Xizong of Tang reigned in 873–889, and Zhaozong in 888–904. The author, Tao Gu, born in 903, could not have witnessed it directly. But given chronological proximity, there may have been a fair amount of evidence. In other words, the sixteen types of eyebrow makeup enumerated in *Accounts of the Dressing Table* continued without break for two or three hundred years.

The question is, rather, how lipstick makeup was done. Regrettably, the real image of it is still unclear because no conclusive proof can be obtained as yet from pictorial representations. In order to clarify the whole picture, we have to wait for the emergence of new materials, including archeological finds.

There are other lip cosmetics. One is "lip oil" (*chunzhi*), introduced in *Essential Skills for Commoners* along with "facial oil" (*mianzhi*). It states:

> How to make facial oil: Use cow's marrow. [If the supply of cow's marrow is limited, it is fine to mix cow's fat.] When there is no marrow oil, it is fine to use just fat. Soak in warm wine two items: clove buds and *huoxiang* plant. [The method of soaking is the same as when soaking material for hair oil.] The method of boiling is the same as when combining hair oil. Likewise, add mugwort for color. Filter the material through silk floss, and gel the liquid in a container either of unglazed pottery or lacquer. If making lip oil, add "heated vermilion"(*shouzhu*), then cover it with "blue oil" (*qingyou*).[4]

This cosmetic method is mostly intended for protecting the skin and is like today's lip cream. However, neither "blue oil" nor "heated vermilion" is known, and the amounts to be mixed are not specified. Because mugwort is also added for coloring, there is no knowing what kind of color was ultimately produced.

Since safflower came to be cultivated and used as pigment, rouge has long prevailed in the field of cosmetics as well. Down into the Qing period, its position was unshaken. Regarding this, we find an interesting description in *A Dream of Red Mansions*, installment 44.

The rouge too, in its small white-jade box, she observed, was not in the usual sheets but looked more like rose salve.

"The rouge sold in the market isn't clean, and the colour's faint," explained Baoyu. "This is made from the essence of the very best safflower, which is steamed after all impurities have been extracted and attar added. You need only take a little on a pin, rub it on the palm of your hand, then dilute it with a drop of water and apply it to your lips. What's left on your palm will be enough for your cheeks."

Pinger carried out his instructions and did indeed find the rouge extraordinarily vivid and fragrant.[5]

Even in the nineteenth century, water-based rouge was used for lips in China. Moreover, the preparation was roughly the same as what is described in *Essential Skills for Commoners*, with the exception that the step of distilling was added.

4. MAKEUP METHODS FROM ETHNIC GROUPS

Why the Image of the Beautiful Woman Changes

When comparing historical Western and Eastern images of beautiful women, one remarkable fact surfaces. In the West, beautiful women in ancient Greek sculptures and Roman stone images like Venus and Aphrodite are still beautiful by today's standards. In contrast, in the East, the ideal image of beautiful women changed greatly. Not to speak of the Han and Tang period, the majority of beauties appearing in Ming and Qing portraits of ladies-in-attendance cannot be thought of as beautiful today. This is the case in Japan as well. The images of beauties in *The Tale of Genji* picture scrolls and *ukiyo-e* products are hardly accepted as such nowadays.

It is certain that, in modern times, Western sense of beauty permeated the East, Westernizing Easterners' aesthetics. However, despite the fact that China before the Opium War had not received European influence, the image of a beauty greatly differed from era to era.

Figures 4.2, 4.3, and 4.4 represent a Tang, Ming, and Qing beauty respectively. Figure 4.2 is *Ladies-in-Attendance Playing Go* (*Yiqi shinü tu*, portion) from the Tang period, figure 4.3 *The Han Palace at Spring Dawn* (*Hangong chunxiao*, portion) by Qiu Ying of the Ming period, and figure 4.4 *Stealing Immortals' Herb* (*Dao xiancao tu*, portion) from the Qing period. As comparison makes clear, the beauty in China differs much depending upon the era. Likewise, beauties represented the Qing period in Japanese pictures also differ from age to age. Why are there differences in views of beauty between West and East?

Figure 4.2. From *Ladies-in-Attendance Playing Go*. Tang Period. Museum of Xinjiang Uyghur Autonomous Region. *Source: Museum of Xinjiang Uyghur Autonomous Region*, figure 151.

Figure 4.3. Qiu Ying, *The Han Palace at Spring Dawn.* Ming Period. The National Palace Museum (Taipei). *Source: Glimpses,* 36.

Figure 4.4. *Stealing Immortals' Herb*. Qing Dynasty. Tianjin Art Museum. Source: *Tianjin Art Museum*, figure 259.

When limiting our view to China, crosscurrents of different cultures can be given as the first cause. As a result of Han culture incorporating cultural influences of minority groups that entered central China in the Yellow River basin, changes occurred in the images of the beautiful woman. Because a different minority group held ruling power in each period, the influence was multilayered.

Under the influence of a different culture, a people may directly adopt its sense of beauty, or a mixture of a variety of aesthetics may inspire diversification of artistic expressions.

Persian Eyebrows

Gleanings of the Daye Era (*Daye shiyi ji*) of the Tang period records the following episode. When Emperor Yang of Sui was making a tour of inspection in Jiangnan, the area to the south of the Long River, he chanced, when getting on a boat, to put his hand on the shoulder of a woman by the name of Wu Jiangxian, who was towing a boat. As she turned around, he noticed her beauty and fell in love with her. Wu Jiangxian was skilled at eyebrow makeup, and always painted long eyebrows. Because Emperor Yang of Sui became so fond of them, other women in the rear palace came to paint long eyebrows. So, Emperor Yang of Sui ordered that those women be provided daily with five hu^6 of "conch ink" (*luozi dai*). It was produced in Persia, and cost ten gold pieces each. Later the supply from Persia was halted, so they began to mix in copper ink before distribution.

There was a cosmetic called "blue eyebrow ink" (*qingdai*) in the Sui period. According to volume 83 of the "Book of Sui," it was a special product of the "State of Cao." Cao was an ancient kingdom in the Western Regions, located in the northwestern part of today's Samarkand in Central Asia.

Some believe that "blue eyebrow ink" was a product of Persia. *Compendium of Materia Medica* (*Bencao gangmu*) by Li Shizhen of the late Ming period states that "the blue eyebrow ink is an indigo pigment from Persia, but when it is not available, Chinese indigo can also be used." It is not clear whether it was indeed a special product of Persia, or it was so misunderstood because it was imported through Persian merchants. Either way, "conch ink" was still imported in the Ming period. Moreover, the description in the *Compendium of Materia Medica* suggests that it was expensive and not easily available.

Contemporaneous Makeup

Memorabilia of the Kaiyuan and Tianbao Eras (*Kaiyuan Tianbao yishi*) introduces a method called "tear-stained makeup" (*leizhuang*): "Consorts at court apply plain powder on both cheeks and cry together to turn that into 'tear makeup.'" In other words, consorts in the rear palace shed tears on their whitened cheeks with the result that their makeup became tear-sodden. Knowledgeable people of those days considered this an ill omen, and sure enough, it says, the rebellion of An Lushan occurred. However, what exactly "tear makeup" was is not detailed.

Somewhat later, Bo Juyi depicted such a makeup style in a poem titled "Contemporary Makeup" ("Shishi zhuang").

Contemporary makeup, contemporary makeup—
Out from the city it spread in all four directions.
Contemporary fashion has no sense of far or near:
No rouge on the lips, no powder on the face,
Black oil on the lips so lips resemble dirt,
The two eyebrows slant to make the character for "eight."
Fair or ugly, black or white, all lose original form,
Once makeup is done, everyone looks as if with sad sobs.
The chignon, with no ado on the sides of the head, is topknot-like,
Diagonal brushing of rouge, not gradated, produces a ruddy face.
Long ago I hear there was one in Yichuan with unkempt hair,
Xin You saw him and knew barbaric culture would soon prevail there.
Keep in memory this makeup of the Yuanhe era today,
Neither topknot nor red face is Chinese in style.[7]

"Once makeup is done, everyone looks as if with sad sobs" in line 8 probably refers to "sob makeup" (*tizhuang*), the kind of makeup suggestive of a crying face. "Tear makeup" in the *Memorabilia of the Kaiyuan and Tianbao Eras* used "plain powder"; that is, white powder, but in the case of "Contemporary Makeup," neither lip rouge nor white powder was used as the fourth line indicates: "No rouge on the lips, no powder on the face."

In the first place, the *Memorabilia of the Kaiyuan and Tianbao Eras* and Bo Juyi's "Contemporary Makeup" refer to different makeup methods. The former records the practice of the Kaiyuan (713–741) and Tianbao (742–755) eras, so this was right before the An Lushan incident. It was in the fourteenth year of the Tianbao era, or 755, that An Lushan rose in rebellion. We can assume that "tear makeup" probably came into fashion in the early eighth century.

Bo Juyi, born in 772, did not witness the An Lushan Rebellion. What his "Contemporary Makeup" describes is the practice of the Yuanhe period (806–821). In other words, even if "sob makeup" may seem to fall together with "tear makeup," it is not the same as the "tear makeup" recorded in the *Memorabilia of the Kaiyuan and Tianbao Eras*. However, it is possible that Tianbao era fashion, even as it went through changes, may have revived in the Yuanhe era. At least, the "sob makeup" Po Juyi depicted may bear some relationship with "tear makeup."

Figure 4.5. Image That Seems to Represent "Sob Makeup." *Source:* Gao Chunming and Zhou Xun, *Zhongguo lidai funü zhaungshi* (Chinese Women's Makeup of Successive Dynasties). Xuelin Publishing House, 1988, figure 173.

Makeup Methods of Ethnic Groups

In fact, "makeup suggestive of crying" existed long before. According to Memoirs 13, the Five Elements Part I, in the *Book of the Later Han*, women in the capital wore at the time of Emperor Huan of Han "sad eyebrows" (*choumei*) and "sob makeup." Thus, the history of "cry makeup" traces back to 146–167. The *Book of the Later Han* also introduces cosmetic methods in concrete terms. According to the description, "sad eyebrows" refers to "thin and curved" eyebrows and "sob makeup" to a method of lightly wiping under the eyes to make a trace of having cried.

The "tear makeup" of *Memorabilia of the Kaiyuan and Tianbao Eras* and "sob makeup" of "Contemporary Makeup" may not necessarily be identical to the Later Han "sob makeup" (see figure 4.5). However, both try to convey the appearance of "being in tears." In particular, the "tear makeup" recorded in the *Memorabilia*, which used white powder, may be close to the "sob makeup" of the *Book of the Later Han*. On the other hand, the "character eight eyebrows," or drooping eyebrows, mentioned in Bo Juyi's "Contemporary Makeup" coincides with "sad eyebrows," thin and curved, in the *Book of the Later Han*.

What is most worthy of note is the "barbarian" makeup method pointed out in "Contemporary Makeup." The line that goes "The chignon, with no ado on the sides of the head, is topknot-like," refers to a combed-back hairstyle with a bun, and "Diagonal brushing of rouge across the cheeks, not gradated, produces a ruddy face" alludes to the more traditional method of shading off the rouge on the cheeks. What makeup did "ruddy face" (*zhemian*, literally "red-clay face") refer to? According to the *Old Book of Tang*, in 641 Taizong of the Tang married a daughter, Princess Wencheng, to the king of Tufan (now Tibet) by the name of Sungcan Gangbu. There was the custom of "ruddy face" makeup in Tufan then. Because the princess did not like it, the king issued an order to suspend it throughout the country.

It is not clear whether the "ruddy face" in "Contemporary Makeup" is identical to the Tibetan "ruddy face." Yet the term used was identical. Bo Juyi probably had his own reason when he asserted that it was not "Chinese in style." The Tang dynasty enthusiastically adopted the cultures of different ethnic groups, and at court there were even many military officers of different ethnic origins called "barbarian officers" (*fanjiang*). In that tolerant cultural atmosphere, it is not at all surprising that hairdo and makeup from different ethnicities were in fashion in Chang'an, its capital.

NOTES

1. Harada Yoshito (1885-1974) made a detailed study of Tang makeup practice. However, he does not discuss how changes in the art of makeup related to the influx of ethnic cultures. Harada Yoshito, "On Tang Period Women's Makeup" in *Shigaku zasshi*, April 21-24, 1910; reproduced in *Tōa kobunka kenkyū* (Zayūhō Kankōkai, 1940).

2. Jia Sixie, compiler, Nishiyama Takeichi and Kumashiro Yukio, translators. *Saimin yōjutsu* (Ajia Keizai Shuppankai, 1969). The bracketed statements are original notes.

3. Ibid.

4. Ibid.

5. Yang Xianyi and Gladys Yang (trs.), *A Dream of Red Mansions*, vol. 3 (Foreign Languages Press, 2003), 1249.

6. One *hu* corresponds to today's twenty liters.

7. Takagi Shōichi (annotator), *Bo Juyi*, vol. 1 (*Chūgoku Shijin Senshū* 12, Iwanami Shoten, 1968), 163-65.

5

Beauties in Chinese Verse and Prose, Beauties in Japanese Literature

1. IMAGES OF BEAUTIFUL WOMEN IN SUGAWARA NO MICHIZANE'S CHINESE VERSE

Language and Imagery

Beautiful women are portrayed not only in pictures and sculptures but also in poetry and fiction. While images of beauty in literature inspire imagination, they do not directly represent attractive looks in visual terms. In contrast, pictures and sculptures not only appeal to the visual sense through concretization and individualization of beautiful appearance, but also create standards of beauty. Such standards give feedback to everyday life, contributing to the formation of aesthetic sense in the culture it belongs to. This is why the conception of beauty among those who grew up seeing Greek sculpture differs from that held by those who only know picture scrolls of *The Tale of Genji*.

To begin with, there can be no artwork that successfully depicts absolute beauty. However superior a portrait or sculpture of a beautiful woman, it is no more than an aggregate of colors and shapes. It is recognized as "beauty" because meaning is produced around that image. There are two connotations regarding production of meaning. One is interpretation by the viewer, and the other is a series of discourses revolving around images. The latter plays a more important role. Discourses define the gaze of the viewer and greatly affect the viewer's imaginative power. If not for the discourse on the beauty of representations of Venus, she would have become neither the incarnation of beauty nor the criterion for judging beauty. The reason that Venus and Yang Guifei entered the "canon" of feminine beauty rests heavily upon discourse construction. Suppose there had been no writings discussing the beauty of Venus or verse and prose repeatedly extolling the "Four Great Beauties," including Yang Guifei. Their beauty would not have been exaggerated into fables nor been viewed as something absolute.

However, discourse has an extremely complex relationship with visual representation of beauty, and it is not as simple as saying that discourse creates the beautiful woman. Nor is it rare that discourse is created by the representation of beauty. Examples of the former are a variety of art theories. Typical examples of the latter would be images of goddesses created on the basis of Greek myths, or by *The Goddess of the Luo Illustrated* based on the rhyme-prose "The Goddess of the Luo" and *The Tale of Genji* picture scrolls. As evident from such artworks, not a few beautiful images in pictorial representations are produced as an extension of discourse. Through interpretation and evaluation, discourse over images has restricted the meaning of pictorial representations. In that sense, discourse has played a more important role than images in the production and distribution of images of beauties.

Again, through vehicles like poetry, prose, and drama, linguistic expressions have directly contributed to establishing the "canon" of beauty. From ancient times until today, how did the image of beauty change in literature? Very interesting questions surface when we compare Japan and China on this issue.

In premodern Chinese culture, the formation of the image of beauty was basically controlled by various elements on the continent itself. In considering Japanese culture, however, we must bring into the field of vision its relation with Chinese culture. The Chinese concept of the beautiful woman can be considered to have entered Japan primarily through two routes. One is literature and art, and the other cosmetic culture. As for paintings from the Nara and Heian periods of Japan, few materials are extant. In comparison, many literary sources remain by which we can trace the spread of aesthetic sense. Literature exerted influence for a longer period of time than paintings. When we think of this, examination of images of beauties appearing in Japanese verse and prose written in literary Chinese becomes indispensable. There is also the problem of the lack of sources related to cosmetic practice. However, mention of cosmetic goods and makeup practice occurs in verse and prose, so we can trace certain aspects through those literary pieces.

Differences in Expression between Literary Chinese and Literary Japanese in Japanese Literature

An example from the *Record of Ancient Matters* (*Kojiki*, 712), a text predating the development of the Japanese phonetic script (*kana*) and written in Chinese characters (*kanji*), can be pointed to as the oldest description of personal appearance in Japan: "face and figure being extremely beautiful" (*yōshi tanrei*). This four Chinese-character phrase, which appears in a passage introducing a maiden named Hiketabe no Akaiko in the section on Emperor Yūryaku, reads in literary Japanese *katachi ito uruwashikariki* (her appearance was extremely lovely). But the expression itself originally comes from Chinese.

This expression points to a number of possible interpretations. First, expressions related to appearances in continental literature had already been transmitted, enabling similar Chinese expressions to appear in Japanese writings. Equivalent expressions, such as *katachi ito uruwashikariki*, undoubtedly already existed in Japanese.

As is well known, Heian literature can be largely divided into Chinese verse and prose (*kanshi kanbun*, normally adapted to Japanese pronunciation and grammar), and Japanese verse and prose (*waka wabun*). Despite the fact that the former influenced the latter, fundamentally they are totally heterogeneous in expression. Some authors wrote in both categories, but because the languages used were of different nature, the texts produced by the same author substantially differed. Even when the identical scene is portrayed, there are clear differences in the approach to the depiction between Chinese and Japanese, and the impressions the reader receives also greatly differ.

When considering images of beauties appearing in Japanese literature written in Chinese, we must take into account another element; that is, its relationship with Chinese literature. Whether a portrayal of beauty truly reflects aesthetic consciousness of those days in Japan, or it represents mere imitation of poetic diction and attempts in rhetorical competition—this should first be diagnosed. If the text is influenced by Chinese literature, it is necessary to clarify by which author of which period. Further, we need to examine whether new aesthetic consciousness had already been accepted in Japan then and was commonly recognized, or if it remained within the world of literature with nearly no influence on real life.

Because traditional Japanese poetry is brief in addition to being nearly devoid of epic character, it offers little description of personal appearances in today's sense. In contrast, we can find numerous examples in Japanese narrative literature, as demonstrated in Yuhara Miyoko's research on the aesthetics of physical appearance in the Heian period.[1] Through detailed statistics and analyses, Yuhara clearly outlines descriptions of appearances; but the problem is that she never brings into her field of vision Japanese literature in Chinese. Writers and readers of narrative literature were capable of reading literature written in Chinese. Not a few readers were able to write in Chinese themselves. Descriptions in narrative literature written in native Japanese unmistakably assumed such readers. In other words, word play and literary allusions lurked behind narrative literature: "If I write this way, it will evoke that Chinese poetic phrase" or "The reader would know that this description is based on so-and-so's Chinese verse." Thus, unless we bring into view descriptions in Chinese verse and prose, an overall image will not be visible.

In this chapter, drawing on predecessors' researches, I would like to consider images of beautiful women in Heian literature. I will first examine how they are portrayed in Heian verse and prose, and how such descriptions are related to images of beauty in Chinese literature. Then I will probe such issues as whether Japanese and Chinese images are identical or different, and, if different, how they differ, as well as which more precisely reflected the aesthetic sense of those days.

Spread of Aesthetic Sense

In considering Heian period verse in Chinese, naturally the name of the representative poet Sugawara no Michizane (845–903) should be mentioned. In those days, reading and writing verse and prose in Chinese were part of the basic aristocrat culture. In particular, *The Bo Collection* (*Bozhi wenji*, a collection of writings by the Tang poet Bo Juyi), known for his accessible style, and *The Grotto of Immortals* (*Youxian ku*), which contained some vulgar expressions, were widely read, for one thing because of the ease of comprehension. Aristocrats in those days must have learned that white skin was a prerequisite for beauty from the line, "Her eyelids resemble peony, her chest resembles a jewel" from Bo Juyi's "White-Haired Woman of the Shangyang Palace." From "Peony is like her face, willow like her eyebrows" found in the same poet's "The Song of Lasting Regret," they must have known full well that narrow, long eyebrows like willow leaves were regarded as beautiful.

In fact, court poets who composed in Chinese not only knew such aesthetic sense and portrayal of beauty as part of their cultural upbringing but also themselves depicted ideal visages with the use of similar rhetoric. In a section called "Ō Shōkun" (in Chinese "Wang Zhaojun") in the *Collection of Chinese and Japanese Poems for Singing* (*Wakan rōreishū*, early eleventh century) there is a Chinese expression, "Blue eyebrows, rouged cheeks, decked in brocade," which mentions facial makeup. Again, a section called "Courtesans" quotes two lines from "Pulling a Silver Jug from the Bottom of a Well," a poem contained in *The Bo Collection*: "The charming hair on both sides are wings of an autumn cicada / the slowly curving pair of moth feelers are the color of a distant mountain."

When Heian period poets writing in Chinese portrayed beauty, did they simply copy modes of expression found in Chinese poetry, or did they, having mastered the technique of composition, express a Japanese sense of beauty through that literary genre?

Let's look at "On Breaking a Willow Branch" ("Setsuyōryū . . ."):

A tear likens itself to a dewdrop on a branch
Her makeup is mistaken for the snow amidst willow flowers
Her delicate fingers nip a tender cluster
Her knit eyebrows are darkly painted
Leaves shade her face, disturbing her chignon
The threadlike branch snaps, her heart also broken.[2]

It is not clear who the beautiful person is in this poem, but it would be almost meaningless to question that. What is crucial is, rather, how her beauty is portrayed. In the above lines, the willow and the person are mingled in ways that each is a metaphor for the other. From such treatment, we can roughly grasp what sort of visage was considered beautiful. Judging from the fact that white powder, slim fingers, and dark eyebrows characterize this person, it is clear that the greatest attention went to skin, fingers, and eyebrows in evaluating appearance.

Impressionistic Descriptions Abound

Another example would be "Also on 'Languid Spring Beauties' at the Jijū Hall on the Occasion of an Early Spring Court Banquet, with an Introduction" ("Sōshun no naien . . .") from *Sugawara Poems* (*Kanke bunsō*, probably 900).

Let's first observe a passage related to the portrayal of physical appearance from the introduction:

> At this point, the dressing chamber selects talented dancers, and powdered women proceed to their service. Their delicate hands and narrow waists are gifts from their parents; soft clouds of their hair and ripe peaches of their skin they have by birth.[3]

The poem is about women dancers at a court banquet. The introduction again emphasizes slim fingers and slender torsos as indications of beauty. Rich hair, which does not appear in "On Breaking a Willow Branch" above, is here extolled as "soft [spring] clouds."

The verse that follows expresses the beauty of dancing girls from a different angle:

Why do your white-silk figures barely withstand the robe's weight?
In jest they reply: we heavily don the hue of spring around our waists.
Some makeup still left, they are too languid to open their jewelry caskets,
Short steps outside the mud walls toward their quarters stir melancholy.
Their enticing eyes send ripples, and a breeze is about to stir,
Their dancing figures resemble whirls of snow still flying after the sky clears.
Amidst flowers the day dusks as the sound of wind instruments fades away,
Viewing the faint clouds in a distance, they retreat inside their grotto.[4]

To paraphrase, the poet questions the women why even thin dancing robes appear heavy on their skin. They reply on a whim that they wear spring around their middle. The dance is over, their makeup is somewhat faded, and their hands, opening accessory boxes, are lazy. As they walk in small steps to exit the inner palace gate, they feel drawn back. Their charming, twinkling eyes resemble white caps of repeatedly pounding waves or winds blowing enticingly. The lingering images of their airborne dances suggest snowflakes still dancing in the air after the snowfall. The spring day dusks, and the sounds of the wind instrument, *sheng*, also vanish. Just as Wang Ziqiao returned to the immortals' cave on a white crane playing his *sheng* and viewing the clouds over the distant mountain peak, the dancers retreat to their sequestered quarters, leaving lingering thoughts behind.

Unlike in the prose introduction, this eight-line "regulated verse" (*lüshi*) with seven characters in each line hardly refers to concrete appearances of the dancing girls. Instead, it vividly portrays their light dancing, lovely gestures, enchantingly expressive eyes, deep sentiments revealed in their gentle, feminine movements, and so forth. The only exception is "white-silk figures." This expression suggests that fairness of the skin denoted beauty.

In a separate verse in the same collection, called "In Early Spring, Observing a Banquet Given to Courtiers" ("Sōshun en wo . . ."), Michizane focuses on hairstyle as characterizing beauty in a couplet quoted in *Collection of Chinese and Japanese Poems for Singing*: "Twin hair-loops freshly tied up, spring clouds are soft." *Neatly finished hairdo* is also a synonym for beauty. As seen from a line such as "Her makeup is mistaken for the snow amidst willow flowers" or a phrase such as "white-silk figures," aesthetic sense viewing white skin as beautiful had been accepted in the Heian period through Chinese literature, at least conceptually.

2. RECEPTION AND REJECTION OF CONTINENTAL AESTHETIC SENSE

The Grotto of Immortals as Background

Smooth, white skin; slender fingers; richly lustrous hair; thin and long crescent eyebrows; neatly combed hair—these constituted the image of the beauty appearing in Sugawara no Michizane's Chinese-language verse.

Now, how does his image relate to Chinese literature? As long as he uses the same language and the same style of literary expression found in the Chinese tradition, it is unavoidable to conclude that he is influenced by continental literature. Moreover, in Chinese prosody there is a rule that the composer uses literary sources. To consciously quote phrases from literary predecessors in terms of diction and rhetoric was never to be held in contempt. Far from it; rather, it was an indispensable rhetorical device. Thus, it is quite normal that similarities, derivatives, or reversals occur between sources and later products. In fact, Sugawara no Michizane's portrayals quote conventional phrases from Chinese poetry and demonstrate direct influence in rhetoric as well.

Chinese verse and prose in the Heian period in Japan are said to have been heavily influenced by Chinese literature of the Six Dynasties and Tang periods. First, *The Grotto of Immortals* by Zhang Wencheng can be quoted as a source of major influence. Naturally, Michizane was no exception. The date of composition of *The Grotto of Immortals* is unclear, but judging from the fact that the author passed the government examination in 679, it would be reasonable to think it was written around 700. Michizane was born in the twelfth year of Jōwa (845) and died in the third year of Engi (903). The premodern Chinese literature scholar Yoshikawa Kōjirō once stated that at that time it took roughly fifty to one hundred years for literature of the Chinese continent to be transmitted to Japan. If we follow this guideline, the date of the transmission of *The Grotto of Immortals* overlaps the period when Michizane was composing Chinese poems.

Because *The Grotto of Immortals* is a romance, its style is close to the vernacular. It would be fine to consider it to have been a relatively easy-to-understand piece of "popular" literature at that time. The main characters being women, the work naturally abounds with descriptions of feminine beauty. Comparison with Michizane's poetry reveals a fair amount of commonality shared by both.

In the first place, Michizane's poem quoted above, "Also on 'Languid Spring Beauties'" can be said to have been composed with *The Grotto of Immortals* in mind. The last line, "Viewing the faint clouds in the distance, they retreat inside their grotto," clearly suggests that he locates the court dancers' abode within a grotto because he is likening them to the female immortals in the Chinese work.

Descriptions of physical appearances also include what seems to demonstrate direct or indirect influence. For example, the surpassing beauty Shiniang is described as follows in *The Grotto of Immortals*:

> Her floral visage is tenderly beautiful beyond compare even in the celestial domain; her jewel-like body is gracefully pliant, rarely paralleled in the human world. Her radiant face is so delicate that a finger's pluck might pierce it; her slender waist is so delicate that an embrace might cause it to fall apart. Han E, the singer of the Warring States period, and Song Yu, the beau of the Chu period, would feel melancholy if they saw her; Jiang Shu, the beautiful consort of the State of Wei, and Qing Chin, the ancient divine woman, would have chosen death if they faced her. Her thousand charms and hundred appeals are impossible to readily find metaphors for; her fragile physique and weightless essence can be recounted but not exhaustively.[5]

In terms of diction, the passage exerts no direct influence on Michizane's poem. The reason is easy to surmise. *The Grotto of Immortals* gained reputation the moment it was transmitted to Japan, and at one point it was quite widely read. If Michizane were to imitate poetic diction and rhetorical device everyone was familiar with, his reputation as a first-class poet composing in Chinese would be questioned. In using rhetorical sources, he would be better evaluated if he quoted from obscure texts. The distance in diction between his poem and *The Grotto of Immortals* demonstrates Michizane's rich learning, while at the same time conveying his consciousness of the work. In fact, judged from the content, aesthetic sense demonstrated in *The Grotto of Immortals* is nearly fully shared by Michizane's Chinese poem. Expressions used differ, but the pieces closely resemble one another in emphasizing tender, white skin and slender torso.

The Shadow of *The Bo Collection*

In terms of diction, Michizane's poems are somewhat closer, rather, to *The Bo Collection*. His poem "In Early Spring, Observing the Imperial Banquet

Given for Courtiers, Likewise on Makeup" contains a couplet partially quoted above:

Twin hair-loops just tied up, spring clouds are soft
One eyebrow barely drawn, the dawn moon is slim.

As with "white silk skin," these are, originally, conventional expressions used in Chinese poetry. Likening a beautiful woman's hair to clouds is an often-seen rhetorical device. For example, when Bo Juyi described the beautiful countenance of Yang Guifei in "The Song of Lasting Regret," he likened rich hair to clouds in such expressions as "Cloud-swept tresses, flowery features, quivering hair-pendants of gold," and "With her cloud-chignon half-mussed to one side, nearly awakened from sleep."[6] Further, the poetic expression *double loops* is probably based on such usages as in "A graceful woman with double hair-loops, she is like a jewel both in appearance and virtue" in Bo Juyi's "Ten Poems in the Old Style, a Sequel" ("Xu gushi shishou"). The expression *dawn moon* appears in the line that goes, "Dawn moon originates in the cloud's light, the setting sun follows the vermilion direction" in "On Composing a Poem under the Tomb of King Luling" by Xie Lingyun. A narrow, long eyebrow is likened to a crescent moon in, for example, a tune called "Water Reflections" by Fan Jing's Wife, Surname Shen: "Light hair at the temples learn from floating clouds, the twin moth feelers imitate the early moon."

Michizane Does Not Extoll "Lustrous Teeth"

What is interesting is that Sugawara no Michizane did not uncritically imitate continental literature. When comparing images of beauties in his Chinese poems and those in China, along with common points, clear differences also emerge.

As stated earlier, Michizane's poetry depicts as feminine beauty white skin, soft and slender hands, slender torso, hair like spring clouds, and thin, long eyebrows. These are exactly as in Chinese poetry. However, other specifics in Chinese poetry are not at all referred to in Michizane's. For example, in Chinese literature, bright eyes (*mingmou*), red lips (*danchun*), and lustrously white teeth (*haochi*) often appear as requisites for a beauty. These hardly appear in Michizane's poetry. White teeth, especially, are never mentioned.

Viewed from the perspective of versification and the art of depiction, it is not at all difficult to portray such facial characteristics. Had Michizane wished to adopt such expressions as part of poetic diction, he could have easily done so. The fact that he, with his profound knowledge of Chinese verse and prose, did not do so seems to indicate that he consciously avoided doing so.

Why did Michizane not portray a woman in that manner? The only reason that suggests itself is that "white teeth" were not a standard for beauty in Japan in those days. He would not have used a description totally contrary to Japanese reality just because it was found in Chinese literature.

On the other hand, while the expression *red lips* does not appear in Michizane's poetry, a description related to rouge does. The term *cream powder* (in Chinese *zhifen*, Japanese *shifun*) occurs in the introductory prose section in the piece, quoted above, titled "In Early Spring, Observing a Banquet Given for Courtiers, Likewise on Makeup." In Chinese poetry, the term *zhifen* refers to both rouge and white powder. It is said that rouge had, as a product of continental culture, already entered Japan by the Heian period. Not only did Michizane know the term, but it is probable that he had seen the actual thing.

Intrinsically, if the purpose is mere rhetorical imitation, it is not impossible for Japanese poets to use in their Chinese-language verse or prose a Chinese image that is not found in reality. In fact, many such cases exist. For example, Ōe no Asatsuna's rhyme-prose titled "Nuptial Song for Man and Woman" ("Danjo kon'in fu") introduces rouge as part of a favorable appearance along with white hands, ink (clearly drawn eyebrows), and white skin.[7] The expression there, *applying rouge to her lips*, probably simply echoes a phrase from Chinese verse rather than records a fact.

In comparison, Michizane is far more careful. That he did not extol white teeth as beautiful may mean that he felt uncomfortable about including what did not exist in real life in Japan. Conversely, the very absence of mention allows us to see one side of his literary view.

There is one other thing that concerns me about Michizane's poem titled "On Breaking a Willow Branch." A phrase goes: "Slanting eyebrows are brushed with dark eyebrow ink." At first glance, this seems to be no more than common description, but the use of the words *slanting eyebrows*, suggestive of the beautiful woman's melancholy frown, points to the fact that Michizane closely read *The Bo Collection*. Bo Juyi's poem called "Contemporary Makeup" ("Shishi zhuang") contains a phrase: "The two eyebrows slant to make the character for 'eight'" (八). The poet laments that eyebrow makeup rapidly changed with the passage of time, and that, while in the old days thin lines were drawn, the number-eight eyebrows are now in fashion. Probably having learned the latest information on makeup from this poem, Michizane introduced it in poetic form. His words *slanting eyebrows* recalls Bo Juyi's mention of "eyebrows slant to make the character for eight." It is unclear as to whether eyebrows were drawn in the same manner in Japan around that time, when it was common to shave them off in favor of lightly painted brows higher on the forehead. It is more likely that such makeup did not exist. In other words, "Slanting eyebrows are brushed with dark eyebrow ink" could have been intended to show off his knowledge rather than to convey an actual sight.

Through this sort of shrewd description with the use of wit and cunning, sometimes Michizane offered fictitious portrayals while displaying his erudition in Chinese literature, while at other times he reproduced with precision things of the Heian period.

3. DESCRIPTIONS OF BEAUTIFUL WOMEN IN JAPANESE PROSE

Japanese Prose as a Frame of Reference

As seen above, descriptions of women in Sugawara no Michizane's Chinese-language poems are influenced by Chinese literature, but they are no mere unconditional imitations; rather, at times he consciously rejects Chinese views of beauty.

Now, did Michizane's image of feminine beauty accurately reflect Heian period aesthetic sense? If so, it would follow that Japanese and Chinese views of beauty were fairly similar. The reason is that, with few exceptions like "red lips" and "white teeth," his portrayal of beauty shares a fair amount in common with Chinese literary representations.

Did the Japanese of the Heian period have the same view of beauty as that of the Chinese? Or did Michizane's description diverge somewhat from reality? If the latter is the case, Michizane did not portray reality as it was, but presented fictitious portrayals in order to adopt the continental sense of beauty.

Unlike Chinese-language verse and prose, narrative prose literature of the Heian period was a form of expression that used native Japanese (*Yamato kotoba*). Naturally, there were some points of contact between Japanese and Chinese literatures, such as assimilation and application of grammar or imitation of rhetoric. Moreover, the authors of narrative literature had profound knowledge of Chinese verse and prose, which were in their daily view. In other words, Japanese narrative literature was created in the situation in which Chinese verse and prose dominated written expression. But due to the difference in linguistic form between Chinese and Japanese, narrative literature written in Japanese has basically different linguistic logic, expression of emotions, and rhetorical structure from that of Chinese. While Chinese literature is one frame of reference, obviously Japanese authors need not always respect its standard. As long as it is a frame of reference, the distance, difference, conflict, and reversal, too, offered the possibility to use them as technique.

In Japanese narrative literature created with awareness of Chinese literary products, which its authors must have kept close by their writing desks, how was feminine beauty portrayed? Was it the same as the image of beauty appearing in Chinese verse and prose, or was it different? If different, which is closer to Japanese reality? By examining such questions, we can approach the Heian sense of beauty from a different angle.

Because Japanese and Chinese are significantly different forms of expression, it is difficult to confirm influences on the basis of similarities in vocabulary and descriptive methods. Still, due to the fact that Japanese narrative literature uses totally heterogeneous expressions from Chinese verse and prose, it is possible to discover elements therein that are absent in Chinese literature.

White Teeth Are Not Beautiful

As stated before, we find no expression in Michizane's Chinese poems that praises white teeth as an element of a winning countenance. What about narrative literature?

In works like *The Tale of Genji*, likewise we find no reference to white teeth as attractive. On the contrary, black teeth are regarded as beautiful. A description in the "Safflower" chapter can serve as a basis for saying so:

> In deference to her grandmother's old-fashioned manners her teeth had not yet received any blacking, but he had had her made up, and the sharp line of her eyebrows was very attractive.[8]

It must be because there was the custom of teeth blackening in those days that black teeth were valued above natural teeth. In the Edo period, married women blackened their teeth, but in the Heian period unmarried women too wore black teeth. In a culture in which blackened teeth were thought beautiful, aesthetic sense finding white teeth as an attribute of a beautiful woman is hard to accept. Unless there is a dramatic change in the social system, aesthetic sense cannot be expected to easily turn around.

In the age when people regarded black teeth as a symbol of feminine sexuality, those who did not apply blacking were handled as deviants. That is evident if we observe how people around her treat the main character in

"The Lady Who Loved Caterpillars" in *The Tales of the Riverside Middle Counselor* (*Tsutsumi Chūnagon monogatari*, 1055).

> She never plucked her eyebrows. She didn't apply teeth blacking, saying "It's bothersome, unclean." Smiles exposing her white teeth, she poured her love on these worms morning and evening. . . . When she glared under her black eyebrows, it was extremely bewildering.[9]

Far from beautiful, white-toothed smiles must have been uncanny in the eyes of people around her. Given her strange taste for insects and caterpillars, her dark eyebrows seem to have appeared dreadful, beyond ugliness. Intrinsically, it appears she was not at all bad-looking.

> She wore her robe with its lapel pulled up to the head, and the way her bangs hung down looked pure, but perhaps because she was not well kempt, they looked disorderly. Her eyebrows were very dark, glorious and striking, and cool looking. Her mouth was also charming and clean, but because she didn't black her teeth, somehow she seemed aloof to the ways of the world. "If she made up, she would look nicer. Too bad," people thought.[10]

This passage somewhat contradicts the previous quotation about her eyebrows, but both passages concur about not blacking the teeth as appearing uncanny. There are two theories about the time of the compilation of the collection: the Heian and Kamakura periods. Either way, in the Heian period, teeth blacking was a makeup that could be called a symbol of womanhood rather than feminine beauty. It is not at all strange that in real life the Chinese aesthetic of "white teeth" was rejected.

Interestingly, it is the case with Sugawara no Michizane's Chinese verse and prose. As everyone knows, "white teeth" was, in China, a condition for beauty. Michizane, as a poet writing in Chinese, knew this well. However, he did not, just for that reason, bring in the same sense of beauty into Japan by extolling white teeth. Even if fictitious description were allowed rhetorically, Michizane perhaps did not wish to write what was too far apart from prevailing Japanese conceptions of beauty. It was not just Michizane; other contemporary Japanese poets writing in Chinese did not praise white teeth as a feature of a beautiful countenance. For example, the expression *lustrous teeth* (*haochi*; Japanese *kōshi*), meaning pearly white teeth, nowhere appears in the following five anthologies: *Yearnings for the Ancient Chinese Style* (*Kaifūsō*, late Nara), *A Collection from Above the Clouds* (*Ryōunshū*, early ninth century), *Glories and Graces* (*Bunka shūreishū*, early Heian), *Collection of National Polity* (*Keikokushū*, early Heian), and *Literary Gems of Japan* (*Honchō reisō*, around 1010). References to teeth, such as "fine teeth" (*sōshi*) in *Collection of National Polity*, exclusively occur in descriptions of men. Red lips are not found in any of these five anthologies.

In contrast, the slender lower torso, referred to as "delicate waist" (Japanese *senyō*) or "Chu waist" (Japanese *Soyō*), and thin, white hands, expressed as "jewel-like hands" (Japanese *gyokushu*) or "delicate hands" (Japanese *senshu*), are depicted as symbols of feminine beauty with relative frequency. On this point, the above five anthologies more or less concur with Sugawara no Michizane's Chinese poems.

Possibly because of writing in a foreign language, Heian period Chinese poems in Japan on the whole contain limited physical descriptions. Among them are some expressions that occur relatively frequently; others whose examples of usage are infrequent; and still others that are conventional in China but never used in Heian Japan. Chinese descriptions of feminine beauty were not simplistically imitated in Japan; during the process of acceptance, conscious and unconscious selection is likely to have occurred.

In comparison with Chinese-language verse and prose, it can be said that narrative literature is nearly indifferent to "teeth." According to Yuhara Miyoko, the word *teeth* (*ha*) or its honorific form (*o-on-ha*) occurs only three times in *The Tale of Genji*: the plain form once in "Trefoil Knots," and the honorific form once each in "The Green Branch" and "The Flute." In "The Green Branch," the pertinent sentence comments on the child heir apparent: "Mild decay affected his teeth, darkening the inside of his mouth and giving him a smile so winsome that she [Her Highness, his mother] would gladly have seen such beauty in a girl."[11]

Is White Skin Beautiful?

Another issue is white skin. Heian period Chinese-language verse and prose often refer to white skin as a requisite for a beauty. How does this appear in narrative literature? Did Japanese people in those days actually consider white skin beautiful? Many researchers offer affirmative views on this question.[12]

The "Young Murasaki" chapter of *The Tale of Genji* contains a passage in which Genji, who is suffering from a recurrent fever, visits an ascetic at a temple in the Northern Hills to receive his healing rite. While at the temple, Genji discovers by chance young Murasaki, and meets the graceful nun caring for the child. The nun is described as follows:

> She was leaning against a pillar, with her scripture text on her armrest before her and chanting with obvious difficulty, and she was plainly of no common

distinction. Past forty and very thin, with elegantly white skin, she nonetheless still had a roundness to her cheeks, fine eyes, and hair so neatly cut that to Genji it seemed much more pleasingly modern in style than if it had been long.[13]

As such expressions as *neatly* (*utsukushigeni*) indicate, the narrator favorably depicts the nun's looks as giving a good impression.

This is not the only example. "Spring Shoots II" introduces Murasaki, whose illness was then in a state of remission:

> His love, whom the heat troubled, had had her hair washed and was feeling somewhat refreshed. It was slow to dry, since she lay with it spread out all around her, but not a strand was tangled or out of place, and it had a beautifully supple richness; meanwhile, despite her pallor, her skin was so exquisitely white as to seem almost transparent, and she made an utterly enchanting sight.[14]

The combination of the words *white* and *exquisitely* makes it unmistakable that Murasaki's white skin is portrayed as beautiful.

In "The Cicada Shell," a passage goes: "Tall, very fair-skinned and nicely rounded, striking in head and forehead and with a delicious mouth and eyes, she made an arresting sight."[15] This also clearly asserts that white skin is beautiful.

Because *The Tale of Genji* is fiction, it is hard to readily judge whether such passages represent realistic or purely fictitious situations. Fortunately, its author, Murasaki Shikibu, left a diary. We need, then, to look at it and ascertain whether there are differences between diary and fiction.

In *The Diary of Murasaki Shikibu* (*Murasaki Shikibu nikki*, 1008–1010), the appearance of a lady-in-waiting is described as follows:

> Miya no Naishi is also very attractive. She is just the right height so that when seated she has a most imposing, stylish air about her. Although not the kind of woman whose attractiveness can be ascribed to any one feature, there is a freshness in her countenance and an air of distinction in her face; the contrast between her pale skin and her black hair sets her apart from the rest. Everything, the shape of her head, her hair, her forehead, surprises with its beauty and yet gives an impression of openness and candour.[16]

Because the lady's countenance makes a viewer think "how pretty," white skin, after all, seems to have been regarded as a sign of beauty.

Ugly White Skin

At a glance, as with Chinese-language verse and prose, narrative literature also seems to regard white skin as beautiful. In other words, whether under the influence of Chinese literature or reflecting a native Japanese sense of beauty, it seems that, in Heian Japan, as in China, white skin was considered beautiful.

On the other hand, however, we find evidence that makes this hypothesis untenable. *The Tale of Genji* contains statements holding white skin not as beautiful but even ugly. "Safflower" has the following portrayal:

> In color she was whiter than snow, in fact slightly bluish, and her forehead was strikingly broad, although below it her face seemed to go on and on for an extraordinarily long way. She was thin to the point of being pitifully bony, and even through her gown he could see the excruciating angularity of her shoulders.[17]

Here the image of white skin is totally different from the earlier examples. In the first place, this passage is intended to describe an ugly appearance. Because "white skin" is mentioned in it, it goes without saying that "white skin" here is supposedly viewed negatively.

According to Yuhara Miyoko, *The Tale of Genji* contains nineteen examples of white facial skin, fifteen of which handle it as a beautiful characteristic.[18] Undoubtedly, white skin was in many cases favorably evaluated, but it is also a fact that it was sometimes viewed as ugly.

The view of white skin as less than beautiful is found in the description of Hyōbu no Shō (junior assistant head of the Ministry of War) in *The Tale of Ochikubo* (*Ochikubo monogatari*, mid-Heian period):

> His smiling face was snow white. His neck extremely long, his visage was simply like a horse, with an endlessly angular nose. He looked as much as to say hee-haw and move away. Those facing him would not be able to refrain from laughing.[19]

This is a well-known description of an ugly face.

However, even if we suppose that the view is derived from *The Tale of Ochikubo*, the question remains unresolved. Murasaki Shikibu bases herself upon the line, "The lotuses of Grand Inchor Pool, the willows by the Night-Is-Young Palace,"[20] when she refers to Yang Guifei (Japanese Yōkihi) in *The Tale of Genji*: "A superb artist had done the paintings of Yōkihi, but the brush can convey only so much, and her picture lacked the breath of life. The face, so like the lotuses in the Taieki Lake or the willows by the Miō Palace. . . ."[21] Judging from this, she knew well "The Song of Lasting Regret." If so, she must have been aware of the line, "Whose snow-white skin and flower-like features appeared to resemble hers,"[22] and the rhetoric of "snow-white skin." However, we find in *The Tale of Genji* no rhetoric that likens the whiteness of the skin to the snow and presents it as beautiful. On the contrary, the tale carries on the aesthetic sense of *The Tale of Ochikubo*, which regards "the skin white as snow" as ugly.

Why was white skin ugly?

No Associative Relations Yet

There is a view that, against expectations, overly white skin can appear ugly.[23] However, once the aesthetic sense of viewing white skin as beautiful establishes itself, being too white never should be problematic. The reason is that, if the concept that white skin means beauty becomes set, it creates a connotation that simply equates "white" with beauty. Then, white skin itself comes to be never viewed as ugly. In fact, we find no example in descriptions of countenances in Chinese literature in which white skin is portrayed as ugly.

When a woman looks white because of illness, lack of health, or excessive bleeding, the word *white* is not applied to her. In such cases, the expressions used are "sickly complexioned," "pale," "blanched," "drained of color," and so forth. Even today, when wheat-colored skin is regarded as beautiful in Japan, there are hardly any examples of character description in which "white skin" is presented as ugly.

Some may suspect that his white skin was ugly because Hyōbu no Shō was male. But there is hardly any possibility of that. The reason is that, once white skin came to be highly evaluated, it was considered attractive not only with women but also with men. We find supporting evidence in an episode from year 890 in "The Construction of the Outer Palace; Also the Sacred Hall" in chapter 12 of *The Chronicle of the Great Peace* (*Taiheiki*, fourteenth century; the first twelve of the forty chapters are known as *The Taiheiki: A Chronicle of Medieval Japan* in Helen McCullough's translation):

> So he thought, and put a bow with practice arrows in front of the Kan minister of state, saying, "Since it is the beginning of spring, amuse yourself awhile."
> The Kan minister of state did not draw back, but joined himself to a side. He bared his snowy skin to the waist, raised up and pulled down, steadied the bow for a while, and let go an arrow.[24]

Miyako no Yoshika, the host of the party on the day, assumed the Kan minister of state, as Sugawara no Michizane was known, was learned but weak at martial arts. Thus, Yoshika thought of having him shoot an arrow and laugh when he failed. The above quotation describes how Michizane behaved after accepting the bow and arrow. As understood from the expression "his snowy skin," white skin was a marker of handsomeness for males as well. Written in Japan's South and North Courts period (1336–1392), *The Chronicle of the Great Peace* postdates *The Tale of Genji* by over three hundred years, but if there had been a gender difference in terms of skin color, it should have been apparent here as well.

In China too, when women's white skin was beautiful, men's white skin was handsome. I referred in chapter 1 to an example in "Attitude" in *A New Account of Tales of the World*. In vernacular fiction from the Ming and Qing periods on as well, white-skinned men were considered handsome. Installment 15 of *A Dream of Red Mansions* describes a young man titled the Prince of Beijing: "His face like a beautiful jewel, his eyes resembling bright stars, he was truly an outstandingly beautiful figure."[25] Even in the eighteenth century, white-skinned men were considered handsome.

Differentiation between Beautiful and Plain

Despite the fact that, in Japan, white skin was regarded as beautiful in Heian period Chinese-language verse and prose, why do we find contradictory descriptions in narrative literature?

The reason can probably be found in the fact that white skin had not yet been fully established as an aesthetic criterion. Thus, white skin appears in portrayals of both beautiful and plain characters. In cases of attractive women and lovely children, white skin is described as beautiful, but it is ridiculed in association with villains and clowns. The way of thinking differed from that of today: white skin was not unconditionally regarded as beautiful, but it was deemed beautiful if possessed by beautiful people. Conversely, ugly people were seen as ugly even if they were white-skinned.

That is easy to grasp if we refer to present-day Japanese "brown hair" (*chapatsu*). In nineteenth-century English literature, "golden hair" by itself meant "a beautiful person." Plain-looking people were not described as possessing "golden hair" even if they were in fact fair-haired. In Chinese literature, too, "bright irises, lustrous teeth" meant a beautiful person. No matter how white, a plain-looking woman's teeth were not described as "lustrous." The reason is that, in both cases, the connotation equating golden hair and white teeth with a beautiful woman was already set.

Before the establishment of this convention, such association was hardly constant. To take brown hair mentioned above for example, for Japanese people brown hair itself is not a criterion for beauty or plainness. Brown hair on a beautiful person is lovely, but a plain person is plain even if brown-haired. In modern fiction and nonfiction, if a character dyes his or her hair gold, the author would describe it as such. At least, the author does not consciously avoid referring to it. Because there is no implication that "gold hair" means a beautiful person, there is no fear of misunderstanding.

The notion of white skin in the Heian period was probably likewise. The continental aesthetic sense that held white skin to be attractive had been transmitted. However, the connotation of white skin as marking beauty had not yet been established. That should be the reason that contradictory depictions appeared in the same text.

4. BEAUTIFUL WOMEN IN JAPANESE NARRATIVE LITERATURE

Plump Is Beautiful

Sugawara no Michizane, writing in Chinese, depicts a slender torso as beautiful in his verse. On this point, he totally concurs with continental literature. But how was it in narrative literature in the Japanese language?

What is interesting is that *The Tale of Genji* includes no descriptions suggesting that a slender torso is beautiful. Not only that; here and there we encounter portrayals favoring gently rounded shapes as more beautiful. In "Young Murasaki," from which I quoted earlier, is an expression, "very thin ... she nonetheless had a roundness to her cheeks."[26] This probably refers to a facial shape known as *shimobukure*, rounder toward the bottom. In other words, the expression implies that a round face looking somewhat plump is attractive. As the conjunction between "very thin" and "nonetheless had roundness to her cheeks" indicates, a slender physique was rather negatively evaluated.

The same is the case with *The Diary of Murasaki Shikibu*, in which the same author seems to have recorded facts with fair accuracy. In a passage describing the beauty of Dainagon no Kimi, is an expression *round and plump* (*tsubutsubu to koetaru*). Judging from the context, plumpness, far from being ugly, is presented as a beautiful body shape. Plumpness was probably associated with affluence, social standing, and nobility.

A typical example occurs in the diary where the author refers to Miya no Naishi's sister: "Lady Shikibu, her younger sister, is chubby—fat even. . . . I remember her plump little figure as being really most charming."[27] Despite her conspicuous plumpness, the younger sister was thought quite beautiful.

On this point, picture scrolls from those days provide supporting evidence. They present round faces and fairly plump body forms as characteristics of beautiful women. Conversely, we see no beauties with a slender torso.

To begin with, in narrative literature no attention goes to the middle of the body. The expression *the way one carries the center of the body* (*koshitsuki*) refers to the impression of a posture rather than a physique. We find two examples in *The Tale of Genji*.[28] One is the description of Chūjō no Kimi in the "Twilight Beauty" chapter.

> Chūjō accompanied him [Genji] toward the gallery. Silk gauze train neatly tied at her waist, over an aster layering perfect for the season, she carried herself with delicious grace. He glanced back and sat her down by the railing at the corner of the building.[29]

Genji finds gracefulness in Chūjō's *koshitsuki*, or the way "she carried herself." To begin with, loose clothing in the Heian period does not show the bodyline around the waist. One could only guess a woman's physique from the way she walked or sat. Moreover, what is described here does not concern whether the torso was thin but how it moved. In Japanese narrative literature, we find few descriptions of the torso. That *The Tale of Genji* contains only two references to *koshitsuki* is probably because the objective condition of clothing placed restrictions. As long as women wear clothing that does not show how the body narrows around the middle, an aesthetic that favors the "willow waist" does not come into existence.

Truth or Falsehood of Descriptions of Body Shape

We can conjecture the body shape of beautiful women in those days to some extent from descriptions of their faces. We encounter beautiful women with a tenderly plump face in *The Tale of Genji*. A woman with a plump face is, in most cases, fairly full-bodied as we can easily conjecture from today's common sense. Thus, when a plump face is considered beautiful, its owner will normally not have a slender middle.

This suggests that aesthetics of body shape totally differs between Chinese-language writings and Japanese-language narrative literature in Heian period Japan. While beautiful women in Chinese-language verse and prose are slender, those in Japanese-language tales are of a well-rounded build.

Which type was closer to conveying the actual taste of the times? Using descriptions of teeth, eyebrows, and skin as references, we can surmise that narrative literature was closer to reality. In other words, well-rounded women were regarded as beautiful among Heian aristocrats, and narrative literature reflected it without modification. Poets writing in Chinese paid little attention to the reality, and devotedly continued to refer to the "willow waist" as beautiful.³⁰ Here too, we clearly see the difference between Chinese-language poetry and narrative literature.

This is not to say that all descriptions in narrative literature are realistic. In fact, *The Tale of Genji* adopts various elements from Chinese literature. Let me give an example from "Spring Shoots II," where Genji peered past the curtain at Her Highness, the Third Princess,

> and saw an unusually small, pretty figure who seemed to be all clothes. She still lacked any womanly appeal, but she offered instead the charming grace of new willow fronds halfway through the second month, frail enough to tangle in the breeze from a warbler's wing. Her hair spilled left and right over her cherry blossom long dress and it, too, recalled willow fronds.³¹

It has long been pointed out that this description echoes Bo Juyi's "Willow Branches" ("Yangliuzhi ci"). However, unlike Chinese-language poems of Japan, the passage does not merely render the original into Japanese or follow Chinese expressions concerning feminine beauty. While partially adopting poetic expressions of Chinese poetry, it incorporates bold changes as well. For example, aesthetic preference for the petite body came from China, and likening it to a willow branch is a rhetorical device often found in Chinese poetry. While *willow* is a Chinese metaphor for a narrow waist and slender body, in the above quotation *willow* does not work as a metaphor for the waist. In order to express a beautiful girl's delicate gracefulness, *willow* is used as an image of the entire body. The plant no longer serves as a trope for the lower torso as in Chinese poetry. If so, where such an intention exists, it is not impossible to use it as a metaphor even when describing a well-rounded body. The above quotation does not clarify whether the Third Princess was plump or slender, but even if it portrays a full physique, there is no contradiction. This can be considered an ingenious rhetorical application, not restricted by the "willow waist" metaphor in Chinese literature.

Hands and Eyebrows Slighted

It is the same with slender fingers and white hands. As we can tell from Michizane's Chinese poems, such physical characteristics are often portrayed as a metaphor for a beautiful woman. However, Heian narrative literature never refers to them. In *The Tale of Genji*, the word *hand* almost always refers to handwriting and rarely to a hand itself. There is no mention of fingers at all.³²

Then, which better reflects actual Japanese taste? There is no decisive proof, but judging from the difference between the two genres found in the treatment of "white teeth" and "white skin," it is likely that narrative literature is closer to reality. The reason is that Chinese-language verse and prose, profoundly related to continental literature, cannot completely ignore Chinese modes of expression. In comparison, narrative literature has greater freedom.

The world of Chinese-language verse and prose accepted aesthetics of the continent emphasizing fingers and hands as indicators of physical beauty. But such a view was no more than a "concept" from across the sea, which had not necessarily permeated actual taste. Thus, people probably were not very interested in whether the waist and fingers were narrow or hands were white.

Depiction of eyebrows also differs between Japan's Chinese-language poetry and Japanese narrative literature. As mentioned earlier, Michizane extolled slender eyebrows despite the custom in the Heian period of unmarried women shaving off their eyebrows.

Not so at all in *The Tale of Genji* and other narrative literature. *The Tale of Genji* refers to eyebrows only twice.[33] The "Young Murasaki" chapter refers to the child's brow: "somewhat hazy around the eyebrows," or in Royall Tyler's translation, "the faint arc of eyebrows."[34] This describes lovely eyebrows, but the author does not indicate their precise shape.

The "Safflower" chapter, mentioned above, also describes Murasaki's eyebrows: "the sharp line of her eyebrows was very attractive."[35] This refers to painted lines after eyebrows have been plucked, but here too there is no reference to the shape of the painted eyebrows; far less is there mention of whether they were long and thin.

Of course, it is not that Murasaki Shikibu was unfamiliar with "moth-feeler eyebrows" in Chinese literature. Well versed in Chinese writings, she knew that thin eyebrows like willow leaves were favored in the Tang. In fact there is a reference in *The Tale of Genji* that testifies to it. It is the famous passage referring to Yang Guifei in "The Paulownia Pavilion" chapter:

> The face, so like the lotuses in the Taieki Lake or the willows by the Miō Palace, was no doubt strikingly beautiful in its Chinese way, but when he remembered how sweet and dear his love had been, he found himself unable to compare her to flowers or birdsong.[36]

The references to the Taieki Lake and the Miō Palace are based on "The lotuses of Grand Ichor Pool, the willows by the Night-Is-Young Palace" from "The Song of Lasting Regret."[37]

If narrow and long eyebrows had been thought beautiful, Murasaki Shikibu surely would have written so in *The Tale of Genji*. Moreover, should she have wished to Japanize a Chinese expression like "moth-feeler eyebrows," she could have easily done so, given her literary talent. We can only think that the reason she chose not to depict long, narrow eyebrows as a characteristic of a beautiful woman is simply that there was no such aesthetic sense in reality. As an author of a tale, a genre regarded many levels lower than Chinese-language verse and prose in those days, there was no reason for her to fabricate things quite distant from reality. In addition, in a situation in which written Japanese was closer to spoken Japanese than was written Chinese, the author had to keep the readers' ear in mind to a certain degree. This must have been one reason that facial descriptions in narrative literature were closer to reality than in literary works written in Chinese.

The Common Image of the Beautiful Woman

We find similar portrayals of beautiful women in other narrative literature produced around that time. I referred mostly to *The Tale of Genji* above because this long fiction is characteristic of this genre. In fact, nearly identical trends can be pointed out from *The Tale of the Hollow Tree* (*Utsuho monogatari*, early Heian) and *The Tale of Ochikubo* (*Ochikubo monogatari*, perhaps late tenth century), both written prior to *The Tale of Genji*, and *The Tale of Sagoromo* (*Sagoromo monogatari*, late Heian) and other stories written later.

The *Tales of Yamato* (*Yamato monogatari*, probably mid-tenth century) uses terms such as *face* and *appearance*, but it grasps the overall image of a person impressionistically, as we find in such expressions as "with a pure-looking appearance and long hair, she was a nice young person" (section 103). Aside from the hair, we find no descriptions of the eyes and nose or the body shape.[38] This also applies to *The Tale of the Hollow Tree*. While "missing expressions that indicate what portion of the body is beautiful in which way, what the protagonist is doing under what circumstance is first described" and conveys that "the way she appears then is graceful and beautiful as a whole."[39] *The Tale of Ochikubo* also often expresses Ochikubo's beauty with such words as *lovely, elegant, beautiful*, and *pure-looking*. In most cases, physical beauty is depicted through elegance demonstrated by attitude, gestures, and manners, and is presented as impressions received by the viewer.

The Tale of Sagoromo, which appeared nearly half a century after *The Tale of Genji*, is influenced by *Genji* but embodies elaborate variations. In descriptions of appearances, however, we note certain similarities between them.

In the clear summer's sunlight, as Sagoromo's eyes meet her radiantly beautiful face, she feels embarrassed and pretends to be reading this book. As she does so, her gesture, the look of her eyes, loose hair at the temples, and the way her face appears are indescribably lovely.[40]

In narrative literature, beauty is represented, rather than through facial features, through the gracefulness demonstrated by gestures, deportment, speech, and gorgeous clothing. The same tendency is observed in *The Tale of Sagoromo*. The above quotation mentions eyes, temples, hair, and face, but offers no detailed descriptions of their shapes. This is neither because authors of narrative literature were inept at detailed description, nor because such portrayals were not desirable. Although the criteria might have been loose, it is not that there was no means of judging what facial features were appealing in those days. However, impressions on the viewer seem to have received greater emphasis than concrete details. Judgment related to social status and moral values is also considered to have been important in determining a person's beauty. In many cases in premodern literature, we find owners of beautiful countenances presented as good-natured and of superior character. Conversely, good-natured, noble, and refined women were probably regarded as beautiful. When considering that clothing and makeup can change appearance to some degree, rigid "standard measures" may not, in narrative literature, have been necessary in describing facial features. As stated earlier, this may be the reason that aristocratic women's average features were vaguely demonstrated in terms of, say, tenderly round and with richly flowing hair.

Ambiguity Maintains Universality

Physical beauty depicted in *The Tale of Genji* and other Heian literature is said to be not a matter of graphic, detailed description of physical beauty, but of expressing beauty through spirituality.[41] Such an approach to expression is also said to be "peculiar" to Japanese literature.[42]

In the first place, character portrayal in literature can be roughly divided into physical description and internal description. The former is, literally, description of physical features, the latter of the character's facial expression, emotion, manners, speech, or psychology. What the so-called spirituality refers to is somewhat unclear, and we can think of the following two categories.

One is that "spirituality" can be considered to refer to the depiction of appearances through the impression the viewer receives. But such viewpoint and descriptive method are not merely characteristic of the Heian period;

rather, they are fairly universal in the depiction of characters and are seen in the literature of every nationality.

In Chinese literature too, in the Han period and earlier, verse and prose provided only impressionistic sketches of personal appearances. In the Six Dynasties period, ornate style combined with brilliant rhetoric. In the genre called *rhyme-prose* (*fu*), literary writings gradually began to make detailed references to appearances. Still, in most cases literary pieces simply recorded impressions of viewers rather than offering concrete descriptions of physical features like eyes, nose, mouth, eyebrows, shoulders, and waist.

In prose, tales of the strange in the Six Dynasties period hardly depict facial features but simply give general descriptions such as "good-looking" and "graceful."

There are many such examples in Western literature, but I will not give specific examples here. At any rate, description of beauty through the impact on the viewer is the most frequently used convention.

We may also note that the phrase *expressing physical beauty through spirituality* points to description of the facial expression, emotional expression, manners, language, and psychology of a character. However, such "spirituality" is not limited to narrative literature. It is widely used in literature of all ages, West and East, as a most important method of character portrayal.

Of course, descriptions of facial features are not abundant in Heian narrative literature. But that is not a peculiar phenomenon. The quality of portrayal of beautiful women in literature is determined by whether or not it can surpass preceding works. In this sense, portrayal must not be a mere repetition of what precedes. However, an original expression is not easy to create. In China too, Tang dynasty verse and prose do not necessarily abound with descriptions of facial features. Those that are found simply use rhetorical comparisons to flowers and buds. Such eloquent descriptions as seen in rhyme-prose pieces of the Six Dynasty period mostly disappeared after *The Grotto of Immortals*. In fact, the image of Yang Guifei in "The Song of Lasting Regret" is merely presented impressionistically, with the abundant use of metaphors.

Descriptions of appearances found in *The Tale of Genji* after all reflect the cultural consciousness of the Heian period, and it would not do to suggest that they represent the essence of Japanese culture. The reason is that, if lack of interest in concrete portrayals of facial features is characteristic of Japanese culture and of narrative literature in a period notable for the predominant use of *kana*, then concrete descriptions of facial features in *kana* literature of later periods cannot be explained. I would like to discuss it in detail later, but in the Edo period prose literature in Japanese not modeled after Chinese writing, descriptions of facial characteristics relating to such things as eyes and nose began to appear. While still different from realistic depictions in modern literature, in comparison with Heian period narrative literature, it offers relatively detailed depictions of facial features.

NOTES

1. Yuhara Miyoko, *Inquiry into the Aesthetics of Physical Appearances in Heian Narrative Literature* (*Ōchō monogatari bungaku ni okeru yōshibi no kenkyū*) (Yūseidō, 1988). See also Saeki Junko, "Women of Light" ("Hikari no on'na") in *Iconography of the Beautiful Woman* (*Bijo no zuzōgaku*) (Shibunsha, 1994).
2. Kawaguchi Hisao (annotator), *The Sugawara Poems and a Later Sugawara Collection* (*Kanke bunsō, Kanke goshū*) in *Nihon Koten Bungaku Taikei* (hereafter NKBT, Iwanami, 1966), 112.
3. Ibid., 221.
4. Ibid., 221–22.
5. See Yagisawa Gen (annotator), *Fully Annotated Grotto of Immortals* (*Yūsenkutsu zenkō*) (Meiji Shoin, 1967).
6. From the translation by Paul W. Knoll, in Victor Mair (ed.), *The Columbia Anthology of Traditional Chinese Literature* (Columbia University Press, 1994), pages 479 and 484.
7. See Ōsone Shōsuke, Kinpara Tadashi, and Gotō Akio (annotators), *Japanese Literary Essence* (*Honchō monzui*) in *Shin Nihon Koten Bungaku Taikei* (hereafter SNKBT) 27 (Iwanami, 1992), 131.
8. Royall Tyler (tr.), *The Tale of Genji*, vol. 1 (Viking, 2001), 130.
9. Matsuo Satoshi (annotator), *The Tale of Ochikubo, The Tale of the Riverbank Middle Counselor* (*Ochikubo monogatari, Tsusumi Chūnagon monogatari*) in NKBT (Iwanami, [1957] 1977), 376.
10. Ibid., 381.
11. Tyler, *op. cit.*, 205. It is not that similar aesthetic sense never existed in China. The biography of Liang Ji in the *History of Later Han* refers to his wife Sun Shu's "decayed teeth smile," finding charm in a smile that displays cavities.
12. Kozakai Toshiaki, *The Paradox of Reception of Foreign Culture* (*Ibunka juyō no paradokkusu*) (Asahi Shinbun Press, 1996). As the author points out, mention of white skin as beautiful is found in *The Record of Ancient Matters*. However, considering the influence of Chinese historical writings at the time of its compilation, it would be problematic to determine merely from that reference that such aesthetics existed in reality.
13. Tyler, vol. 1, 86.
14. Ibid., vol. 2, 657.
15. Ibid., vol. 1, 48.
16. Richard Bowring, *The Diary of Lady Murasaki* (Penguin Classics, [1996] 2005), 48.

17. Tyler, vol. 1, 124.
18. See note 1.
19. *The Tale of Ochikubo* (NKBT), 129.
20. From the translation by Paul W. Kroll in Victor Mair (ed.), *The Columbia Anthology of Traditional Chinese Literature* (Columbia University Press, 1996), 482.
21. Tyler, vol. 1, 11.
22. Kroll in *The Columbia Anthology of Traditional Chinese Literature*, 483.
23. See note 1.
24. Helen McCullough (tr.), *The Taiheiki: A Chronicle of Medieval Japan* (Charles E. Tuttle Company, 1979), 352.
25. "With his face fair as fade, his eyes bright as stars, he was truly a handsome figure." *A Dream of Red Mansions*, vol. 1, translated by Yang Xianyi and Gladys Yang, 377.
26. Tyler, vol. 1, 86.
27. Bowring, 48.
28. Yuhara, *op. cit.*
29. Tyler, vol. 1, 60.
30. Here is something we have to be careful about. In the Tang period too, aesthetics changed by the era. At one time a slender body was thought beautiful, but at another a plump shape was seen as attractive. A slender physique was favored in Chinese-language poetry in the Heian period, probably because Heian poets were more conscious of the former type. Whether or not the well-rounded appearance popular in an era of the Tang had anything to do with plump feminine beauty in Japanese narrative literature is yet to be examined.
31. Tyler, 640.
32. Yuhara, *op. cit.*
33. Ibid.
34. Tyler, 86–87.
35. Ibid., 130.
36. Ibid., 10.
37. *The Columbia Anthology of Traditional Chinese Literature*, 48.
38. See note 1.
39. See note 1.
40. Komachiya Teruhiko and Gotō Shōko (annotators and translators), *The Tale of Sagoromo*, vol. 29 (*Sagoromo monogatari*) in *Shinpen Nihon Koten Bungaku Zenshū* (Shōgakukan, 1999).
41. See note 1.
42. See note 1.

6

Resonance of Aesthetic Views

1. HEIAN ARISTOCRATIC WOMEN

Double Standards of Beauty

The aesthetics of the Heian period were profoundly influenced by continental culture. However, even as the Japanese imitated Tang culture, they also maintained their own aesthetic values. Culture is grounded in multiple factors including social priorities, geography, and even climate; it does not change overnight. For example, teeth blacking among Heian aristocrats did not come about merely for cosmetic reasons. It was part of a symbolic system for distinguishing social standing and age. With its contribution to strengthening the teeth, it also achieved a certain hygienic role. The combination of cosmetic methods such as this and aesthetic sense based on them cannot suddenly change with the fashion overseas.

The influence of foreign cosmetic methods can also be greatly affected by the productive capabilities of the importing country. When, as in the Heian period, the use of rouge and powder remains within the aristocracy, the potential for their domestic mass production as commodities is low. At best, it takes time before such items are widely used and taken up by commoners. Considering these factors, it is impossible to imagine that continental aesthetics suddenly spread and rapidly took root in daily life in Heian Japan.

However, in the era when *The Tale of Genji* was written, aesthetics must have been in flux. Although continental culture could not have been wholly adopted, foreign aesthetics were undoubtedly a stimulant. It is common that, when one culture encounters another, it borrows from it while new and old lifestyles and aesthetics coexist. Absorption of another culture gradually proceeds over a protracted period.

In Heian narrative literature, we often encounter multiple or even contradictory judgments. While a plump woman is here portrayed as beautiful, elsewhere a slender woman may be regarded as attractive. In the case of narrative literature, we must keep in mind that descriptions may be fictitious; but the same is evidenced in diaries, which should be relatively close to real life. *The Diary of Murasaki Shikibu* contains a passage in which the author comments on court ladies. She finds beauty equally in "full-figure" Lady Saishō, "a little plump" Dainagon no Kimi, and "plump but compact" Lady Saishō of the Kitano. Not only that, she praises Lady Shikibu, "chubby—fat even," saying that she remembers "her plump little figure as being really most charming." On the other hand, she regards Lady Senji, "very slim," and Miya no Naishi, "very pure-looking and slender," as likewise beautiful.[1]

It is the same with height. Both Lady Saishō and Miya no Naishi are described as "just the right height," which indicates that a height neither too tall nor too short was thought attractive. However, Lady Senji, "on the petite side," and Lady Dainagon, "petite, one might almost say small," are equally held to be beautiful.

At a glance, this seems contradictory, but presumably it reflects the aesthetic sense of those days. When foreign culture is introduced, an exclusive choice is not necessarily made between traditional standards and new, foreign criteria. At first, people retain old aesthetics, while adopting new values. As a result, aesthetic standards become less strict than before. As with white skin discussed in the previous chapter, perhaps a single standard of height or physique did not yet prevail.

Today too, similar phenomena can be observed. Until modern times, a small mouth was regarded as appealing in East Asia. In the West, however, the size of the mouth is not a measure for distinguishing between beautiful and plain women. Under the influence of this, at present, while a small mouth remains beautiful, a large mouth is almost never thought unseemly except when it is exceptionally large.

Center-Prominent Face and Tall Nose

Few descriptions of the nose appear in Heian narrative literature.[2] Not only that, the nose is rarely referred to as a characteristic of beauty. A passage in the "Cicada Shell" chapter of *The Tale of Genji* refers to the nose of a plain-looking woman: "With her perhaps somewhat puffy eyes and a nose vague enough in form to age her, she had no looks."³ The "Wind in the Pines" chapter also of *The Tale of Genji* contains a reference to an unpleasing male face: "a defiant look and a reddening nose."⁴ Both are described as flawed. However, *The Diary of Murasaki Shikibu* comments on Miya no Naishi: "There is . . . an air of distinction in her face; the contrast between her pale skin and her black hair sets her apart from the rest."⁵ The "air of distinction in her face" (*nakadakaki kao*, literally, a face lofty around the center) is generally interpreted to refer to a straight nose. If this is the meaning here, it follows that the aesthetic standard is no different from that of today.

Chapter 1 of *The Tale of Sagoromo* (*Sagoromo monogatari*, late eleventh century) includes a scene in which Sagoromo's father conjectures about his daughter's rival, the cherished daughter of the Minister of the Right: "High nosed, she is probably striking looking." After a few more lines of guessing, a sentence follows that explains the thinking of Sagoromo, who espied her once by candlelight: "Although it didn't seem so much as a flaw in a white gem, he has guessed right about her high nose—recollecting her sight, he smiled a little." Judging from the context, being "high nosed"⁶ (*hanataka*) seems to be regarded as a flaw. However, how that "high nose" was shaped is not made clear.

We find a reference to a tall nose as ugly in the "Safflower" chapter of *The Tale of Genji*: "Next came the real disaster: her nose. He noted it instantly. She resembled the mount of the Bodhisattva Fugen. Long and lofty toward the end, and with at the tip a blush of red—a real horror."⁷ The mount of the Bodhisattva Fugen being a white elephant, that her nose was "lofty" would mean it was quite long and its tip was pointed. Possibly the "high nosed" in *The Tale of Sagoromo* is used in the same sense.

Voice, Air, the Way a Person Is

Descriptions of facial features in the Heian period differ from author to author and work to work. Some authors enjoyed portraying them, while others were hardly interested. This applies to diaries and memoirs as well. *The Tosa Diary* by Ki no Tsurayuki (*Tosa nikki*, ca. 935) contains nothing that resembles depictions of physical appearances. Nor does *The Diary of Izumi Shikibu* (*Izumi Shikibu nikki*, date unknown, attributed to Izumi Shikibu) go beyond such general sketches as "graceful unlike all others."

In comparison, Murasaki Shikibu seems to have closely observed human appearances. However, she places greater importance on portraying the carriage of a character than on describing facial features. This characteristic is handed down to later narrative literature.

The third chapter of *Awake at Night* (*Yoru no nezame*, also *Yowa no nezame*, author unknown, mid-eleventh century) contains a passage in a scene where the emperor is invited to eavesdrop by the empress mother on the central female character, Lady Nezame:

> She looked petite and lovely, unparalleled in the bright candlelight. The Emperor felt awakened to her beauty, thinking that the gem said to glisten at night might be just like this, and beheld her fondly. Both the way she faced the Empress Mother and the way she gently laughed as she talked to her was beyond description. She looked wonderfully youthful and charming, so much so that listeners were induced to smile, and it was as if radiance suddenly filled the space. Her beauty and gracefulness were beyond words.[8]

Awake at Night, written approximately half a century after *The Tale of Genji*, abounds with descriptions of physical features. This tale, as is well known, draws inspiration from *The Tale of Genji*. The above quotation is not directly based on the source tale. However, the depiction that focuses on the posture, gesture, and atmosphere of a character rather than facial features and physical shape certainly resembles the predecessor's. In *Awake at Night*, words like *voice*, *air*, and *the way a person is* are often used to express beauty. Things like cultivation and manners, we can surmise, played an important role in judging beauty. For this reason, in portrayals of characters, gestures, rather than physical appearances, often convey beauty, charm, and youth. In particular, descriptions of bodily movements expressive of shyness, like hiding the face behind a fan or a sleeve, are intended to convey feminine beauty. A passage in "Two Minor Captains Misidentified" in *The Tales of the Riverside Middle Counselor* depicts exactly that kind of beauty: "As he added a poem [on the sheet of paper on which he saw one she had written] and showed it to her, she was so embarrassed that she hid her face behind a sleeve, looking graceful and childlike."[9]

Sartorial Metaphor

The Tale of Genji often uses the method of suggesting, or causing the reader to imagine, beautiful looks through glamorous clothing. This is not limited to Japan; it is a convention observed in Western and Chinese literature as well. Because clothing differed in different cultures, however, expressions are dissimilar. Japanese narrative literature expresses feminine beauty through unique sartorial descriptions. The approach continues to be used after *The Tale of Genji*. Let me quote another example from the same scene in volume 3 of *Awake at Night*:

> Looking quite shy, [Lady Nezame] raised her fan to her face. It would be foolish to mention how clean and lovely the part that remained uncovered appeared. She wore an outer garment of the "cherry" combination, pale on the outside with a deep hued lining, but did not use ordinarily expected colors to go with it. She donned underneath a single-layer robe of the "birch cherry" combination with an appropriately deep shade matched with pale blue. Still underneath was a mixture of deep and pale blue, with a layer in between of the "blossoming cherry" combination of rich pink lined with nicely pale pink. Altogether, she wore five robes, each in three layers. Under these robes, she wore a divided skirt made of a cloth dyed grape-red, mixed with red. Her divided skirt was also layered, one layer being of the "willow" combination of pale and deep green with willow branches woven in relief. A five-layered bottom, the Emperor thought, but in fact it was hard to clearly see at night. She seemed as if to wear colors perfectly gradating from the deeper to the paler, with an outer skirt of twilled Chinese silk fabric donned just as a gesture. One might have expected to see this and that less perfect, ordinary aspects.[10]

The passage presents unparalleled beauty through portraying the hues of the clothing and the physical appearance highlighted by them. With vivid details of the Heian Japanese garments and the way they are worn, the description of the character's habiliment and that of her physical appearance become inseparable.

Long, Black Hair

Black hair was repeatedly emphasized as a symbol of feminine beauty in Japanese poetry and narrative literature. Although Chinese verse and prose abounds with descriptions in praise of coiffed hair, hardly any examples exist of regarding naturally let-down hair as beautiful. Unlike such practice in continental literature, Japanese literature, including *The Tale of Genji*, presents many examples of straight hair. It was conventional to express a woman's attractiveness through hair cascading over the shoulders and back. *Awake at Night* is no exception. In a passage in chapter 1, where the beauty of Lady Nezame's older sister is described, her hair occupies the center.

> She is particularly refined, graceful, and pure. Her hair, jet-black and glossy, in fine strands and refreshingly clean, gently streams to the hems of her divided skirts.[11]

Black and long, glossy and rich—this is the hallmark of beautiful hair and also a characteristic of a beautiful woman. The hair should not be tied into a knot but let down naturally over the clothing. Reaching the hems of divided skirts as in the above case, it can be extremely long. And it has to be properly cared for. The phrase *in fine strands and refreshingly clean* refers to a well-kempt, flowing state with no entanglement. At first glance, it appears simply natural, but in fact minute care is required. To conceal "culture" behind "naturalness," it could be said, is Heian aesthetics.

Chapter 5 of *Awake at Night* regards the hair as the most important prerequisite for beauty, and repeatedly describes it in passages portraying attractive women. Lady Nezame's father, when first seeing her young daughter, notices the child's hair:

> Of lovely appearance and shape, her hair is full of luster, gently swaying and rich without spaces or loose strands, except that it is slightly short of her height.[12]

Here again, being "rich" and "glossy" receives emphasis. Additionally, "gently swaying" also defines beautiful hair. Naturally, in the same way as in the above quotation from chapter 1, this passage alludes to how clean and well-cared-for the girl's hair is.

Such a hairstyle, long and requiring daily care to keep clean, must have been possible only for aristocratic women. Outfits and daily lives, it is easy to imagine, were heavily restricted by class. From another perspective, precisely because of its scarcity value, it was regarded as an aspect of feminine beauty.

In daily lives, in *Awake at Night*, women do not bind their hair, or only bundle it loosely partway down in back (*hikiyuu*, chapter 2). However, for formal occasions, sometimes the hair was tied up above the head and pinned with a hair ornament. Presumably this was a hairstyle after the Tang fashion. Chapter 1 of *Awake at Night* introduces a dream Lady Nezame had as a child, in which she learned how to play a four-stringed instrument from a heavenly being: "In the little princess's dream, a very attractive and serene person, with her hair done up neatly and looking like a character in a Chinese painting, brought a pipa." *The Diary of Murasaki Shikibu* also contains references to "upping" or "upped" hair and "stylists to do the hair up" (*kami age, kami agetaru, kamiage*). Arguably, the author of *Awake at Night* could have had this and other preceding works in mind.

Handling long hair as a symbol of beauty was a fairly general technique. Similar descriptions are seen, for example, in *The Great Mirror* (*Ōkagami*, also known as *Yotsugi monogatari*, ca. 1119). In the "Minister of the Left Moromasa" section under the category of Heaven is a passage that exaggerates the length of hair:

> The imperial consort at the Sen'yō Palace at the time of Emperor Murakami looked charming and beautiful. On her way to the Inner Palace, when she proceeded to the carriage, she herself got on it, but the tip of her hair remained at the

foot of a pillar in the main house. When one part was laid on a sheet of Michinoku rice paper, it is said that it left no white space. The way her eyes slanted somewhat was very lovely.[13]

The Great Mirror often introduces a woman in simple terms as "looking very beautiful" (Prime Minister Kaneie in the "Earth" section) or "quite lovely" (Prime Minister Michinaga in "Miscellaneous Tales" in the "Humanity" section), rarely offering detailed descriptions. The above quotation is an example of those few cases. What is most emphasized there is the consort's beautiful black hair.

2. BEAUTY OF AN EMACIATED LOOK

Charm of Emaciation

Traditional Chinese literature has a long history of regarding a slender body as a characteristic of feminine beauty. A related image of fragility, as discussed in chapter 2, was depicted as sexually attractive. We can trace this back to the *Book of Later Han* of ancient times, but it also came to be extolled in rhyme-prose in the Six Dynasties period. Wang Can's "Seven Explications" contains a phrase, "rich skin and beautiful surface, weak bones and delicate shape." Smooth, glossy skin, slender physique, and tender carriage—these defined a beautiful woman. The same aesthetic sense exists in Tang dynasty poetry and prose. In *The Grotto of Immortals* we find a statement: "Her fragile physique and light body could be talked of but were impossible to completely describe."

As discussed above, Murasaki Shikibu's depiction of beautiful physique differs from case to case. However, pre-Kamakura Japanese literature more often than not presents an opulent physique as being beautiful. A tenderly round body shape, favored as ideal feminine beauty over a slender shape, can be exemplified by one of the items stored in the Shōsōin, the treasure house that belongs to Tōdaiji in Nara: *Standing Female Figures with Bird Feather Ornaments, a Screen*, listed in the registry of offerings of the eighth year of the Tenpyō Shōhō era (756) in the Nara period (figure 6.1). As mentioned earlier, a similar fashion prevailed temporarily in the Tang period as well. That Chinese aesthetic sense may have reached Japan after a certain time lag and continued on into the Heian period.

By the time of *Awake at Night*, slender types had gradually increased. Not that a slender body is directly mentioned, but we see many descriptions of a woman in ill health, her face somewhat thinner than usual, and all the lovelier looking. Lady Nezame, ill in bed, is described as follows:

Figure 6.1. From *Standing Female Figures with Bird Feather Ornaments, a Screen.* Nara Period. Shōsōin. *Source:* Ōkawa Naomi et al., eds. *Shōsōin to jōdai kaiga* (*Shōsōin and Early Japanese Paintings*), Comprehensive Collection of Japanese Art, vol. 3. Kōdansha, 1992, figure 127.

Her flowing hair was straight with no disarray, dense and glossy, and her face, now very much thinner, appeared inexpressively lovely, with a fragrant charm ready to pour out. (chapter 2)[14]

The passage does not necessarily say that a thin face is beautiful; it means she looks emaciated. Still, that an ill, or at least unhealthy, state rather than a healthy appearance is portrayed as beautiful or attractive may be said to result from a delicate change in aesthetic views.

Drawn Face Symbolizes Sensitivity

However, the idea of the attractiveness of an emaciated look on a face (*omoyase*) goes back to *The Tale of Genji*. The "Twilight Beauty" chapter describes Genji: "He was extremely thin, it is true, but for that very reason his beauty had acquired a new and special grace."[15] Having recovered from his illness, his face was thinner, but he looked all the more attractive. In the "Bracken Shoots" chapter, the younger daughter of the Eighth Prince is described: "Lovely as she already was in the full bloom of youth, her cares had drawn her features a little, giving her a nobler grace that made her resemble the sister she had lost."[16] In this case, too, the character looks more graceful because she is drawn. The implication is that she looks thin and drawn because of her sensitivity. We find a similar description also in *The Diary of Murasaki Shikibu*: "[Her Majesty] was reclining listlessly and looked pale and drawn, even more fragile, young and beautiful than ever, I thought."[17] Each of these passages finds charm in an emaciated look. However, whether it is *The Tale of Genji* or *The Diary of Murasaki Shikibu*, such scenes are on the whole few. In comparison, we find a strikingly larger number of descriptions of a drawn face in *Awake at Night*.

Among them are cases in which thinness of the face (*omoyase*) does not refer to thinning away but simply to natural slenderness. Volume 1 of *Awake at Night* contains a scene in which Lady Nezame appears as beautiful as before despite becoming quite slender because of her illness:

> She was elegantly and charmingly clad in a light green outer garment over eight or so layers of plum blossom color underlined with dark red cloth, with attention to the opening of the sleeves and the hems of the robes [where inner layers show]. But her face that had been so radiant having so thinned away, she looked all the more graceful if poignant to behold.[18]

Becoming ill and looking therefore thin was not in the beginning regarded as constituting physical beauty. Yet, it is worthy of note that thinness is portrayed in connection with beauty. Moreover, similar descriptions recur. Chapter 5 of *Awake at Night* depicts Kan no Kimi, a palace attendant and daughter of the former Minister of the Left, who is pregnant. Of particular interest is the reference to her body shape.

> Quite slender and fragile to begin with, she now looks all the more troubled and drawn. While she does not really look radiant, she looks all the more elegant and charming, as Lady Nezame observed with painful thoughts.[19]

Again, it is not that the emaciated look itself is regarded as beautiful. However, a change worthy of note here is that the narrator has in mind that Kan no Kimi was slender to begin with. Moreover, similar descriptions also appear here and there in the piece. Chapter 1, for example, introduces an episode in which the Middle Counselor eavesdrops on three women, including Lady Nezame. What first enters his eyes is Tai no Kimi, Nezame's cousin and the daughter of the former Minister of the Left, playing a Japanese zither by the railing on the porch. "Her head and body are slender, supple, and pure-looking," it goes, "and her glossy hair flows gently down." This passage also portrays a "slender" physique as beautiful.

"Eyebrow Ink" in *The Tales of a Riverside Middle Counselor* also refers to an emaciated look: "The graceful and childlike person appeared somewhat thinner around the face from her recent days of worry, and it moved his heart." Although this gives an impression of elegance, the drawn face is not directly presented as beauty or depicted in connection with beautiful looks. In passing, it is conjectured that "Eyebrow Ink" was written approximately two centuries after *Awake at Night*.

Needless to say, these descriptions do not allow us to readily affirm that aesthetic sense changed 180 degrees. In fact, as I will discuss later, opulent physique continued to be associated with feminine beauty, for example in *The Confessions of Lady Nijō* (*Towazugatari*, around 1307). Literary works do not necessarily reflect real life. Intertextual resonance and reproduced rhetoric are important elements that affect the manner of character portrayal. However, it is a fact that *Awake at Night* ended in reinforcing the image of slender beauty even while it followed the aesthetics of *The Tale of Genji*. In that process, plumpness went out of fashion as slender body shape gradually became established as a factor of feminine beauty.

Metaphorical Relationship between Snow and Skin

Awake at Night rarely presents white skin as beautiful. Only two or three examples can be found there. The following is a quotation from chapter 5:

> In striking contrast against the deep hue of her unlined red robe, her white skin was unclouded as though snow was rolled into shape. Her side hair fell along her cheeks like braided threads gently down to her sleeves. Between strands of hair, the white skin of her cheeks showed charmingly, and she appeared different from how she used to appear to the accustomed eye.[20]

Here again, glamorous clothing is emphasized as emblematic of physical beauty, or as a background for casting feminine beauty into relief. The only specific features of the body mentioned are hair and skin. The white skin looks all the whiter against the red robe, and is also contrasted against the jet-black hair. As we can see from the expression, *as though snow was rolled into shape*, the rhetorical relationship between white skin and white snow was already established.

Skin that is not just white but fine and nearly translucent remained an object of admiration. Chapter 1 of *Awake at Night* introduces the third daughter of the governor of Tajima province, as the Middle Counselor saw:

> in a garment in safflower red or perhaps safflower-indigo double dye, a likable person, white to the extent of translucency, slid down to the verandah, and leaning toward the horizontal bar, looked out toward the garden. Then she bent over her four-stringed zither and played on it. The moment he heard the sound,

he was also struck by the person's carriage and appearance that were quite outstanding with an air of affection and gracefulness. Underneath her parted hair let down from the forehead along the cheeks, white skin showed in a lovely manner. She appeared truly elegant.[21]

This passage shares in common the depiction of a woman with translucent, white skin with *The Tale of Genji*. In addition, the white skin showing between spaces of the side hair is also emphasized. It may be that the white-skin-is-beautiful connotation may have already been established around then. *Awake at Night* includes absolutely no instance of describing white skin as ugly. Of particular interest is the following passage from chapter 2 of the same:

> Her complexion was endlessly white and clean as though snow or something was rolled into a shape. Her cheeks, expressing pain, looked ruddy. As she lay unable to do otherwise, her face looked beautifully clear.[22]

This describes Lady Nezame lying ill in bed. Noteworthy is the expression, *endlessly white*. Once the connotation establishes itself of white skin belonging to a beautiful woman, it becomes impossible to view excessively white skin as ugly. I have already discussed this above, but this passage would serve as added support. For Lady Nezame is portrayed as "clean," in other words beautiful, even as she is "endlessly white."

The Sarashina Diary (*Sarashina nikki*) by the late Heian diarist Sugawara no Takasue's daughter, approximately dating from the same period as *Awake at Night*, likewise only refers to long hair and white skin in praise of a courtesan she encountered in Mount Ashigara: "Her hair was quite long, nicely falling from her forehead along her cheeks, while her complexion was white with no hint of lack of cleanliness."

The time around which *Awake at Night* appeared seems to have been the crossroads. In fact, the absence of reference to white skin as ugly is not limited to *Awake at Night*. Neither in *The Confessions of Lady Nijō* nor in later tales of war like *The Tale of the Heike* or *The Taiheiki*, do we find any examples of portrayal of white skin as ugly.

In addition, along with the transmission of Buddhism, the beauty of the Buddha began to be accepted. He was considered to be equipped with thirty-two superior outstanding external features. This later came to be applied to symbolizing feminine beauty under the name of "thirty-two aspects." An example of this expression occurs as early as the first part of chapter 4 of *The Tale of Sagoromo*. In chapter 3 of *Awake at Night*, we also find expressions like "possessed with all thirty-two aspects," "twenty-eight or nine, or thirty aspects, would be sufficient."

"Brilliance" and "Shine" That Were Handed Down

Intrinsically, there is a limit to accurately conveying the image of beauty of ancient times through descriptions of countenances appearing in literature. Literary expressions do not precisely reproduce visual impressions, nor does the author intend that. Rather, literature presents aesthetic emotion that cannot be expressed through pictorial representations, or evokes aesthetics that go beyond visual appeal. Such a description lacks mechanical precision. However, through language, it conveys an ideal image. Moreover, such an image of beauty creates an aesthetic norm and greatly affects aesthetic sense of future eras.

However, differences in literary works are large, with a sense of beauty varying from author to author. Thus, it is no wonder that methods of expression also differ. Again, how a literary work inherits methods of expression used in preceding narrative literature also differs greatly by author and by work. For example, *Awake at Night* contains numerous descriptions of beautiful looks, while these are quite limited in *The Tale of the Matsura Palace* (*Matsura no miya monogatari*, perhaps late twelfth century), which appeared approximately 120 years later. Concrete descriptions are thoroughly avoided, and we find no example of reference to black hair, which is otherwise frequent in narrative literature. There are even fewer references to facial features, skin color, and body shape. Instead, beautiful appearances are conveyed indirectly through perception of light and sense of smell as in "brightly shines" and "fragrant."

> Appearing more ineffable than usual, it was as though her shape radiated light and awakened the onlooker's eyes. With no sign of her feeling hot, she was as spotlessly pure as the beams of the clear moon rising in the blue sky. Startled, he thought to himself for wont of any other words, "How can there be such beauty in this world." Her usual fragrance, hard to tell whether it was aloe or boxwood, coolly reached him, drifting on the wind. She appeared no different from that woman performing on the *sheng* he had seen earlier, but he thought he could be wrong. He felt as if he were in the land of the Buddha, and though lacking in piety, perhaps it was like "eyes not lifted even a moment." Forgetting fear, he beheld her, as tears kept collecting in his eyes.[23]

This passage portrays the beauty of Empress Mother Deng of the Tang, viewed by Tachibana Ujitada, the main character of *The Tale of Matsura* in section 43 titled "The Proof of the Peony." Although this tale was completed in the early years of the Kamakura period (1185–1333), it is one of the so-called pseudo-classical tales (*giko-monogatari*), or tales written after the manner of Heian narratives. The description of visual beauty through nonvisual perceptions like "fragrant" and "shining" simply follows the approach of earlier works.

3. BEAUTIFUL WOMEN IN TALES OF WAR

Changes in Height

With the advent of the Kamakura period, how did the ideal image of a beautiful woman change in Japanese literature? And how did it relate to Chinese literature? These questions are indispensable in charting the shifts in the concept of beauty.

In considering the processes through which Chinese ideas of beauty were accepted in Japan, examination of literary works by age is an effective method. How did beautiful appearances depicted in *The Tale of Genji* change later? Not all literary works contain portrayals of beautiful women. For example, *Stories Gleaned at Uji* (*Uji shūi monogatari*, ca. 1190–1242) merely describes good looks with such words as *an attractive, sensual lady-in-attendance, an exceptionally beautiful person, of beautiful complexion, ineffably beautiful looking,* and *beautiful beyond words*.

As in the Heian period, in the Kamakura period Japanese language was often used in private areas of life. The genre of narrative literature came to adopt literary Chinese diction, and men began to participate in creative activities. On the other hand, as before, diaries by women were still written in native Japanese free of Chinese influence.

In observing changes in the images of beauty, *The Confessions of Lady Nijō* is worthy of attention. We can cull much information from its limited descriptions. The following portrayal found in chapter 2 is extremely interesting in considering the question of the idea of beauty.

> She appeared uncomfortable in her stiff costume, which consisted of a gown embroidered with huge fans, two undergowns lined in green, and crimson pleated trousers. From the back she looked bulky, her collar drawn up as high as a priest's. But she was without question a beautiful woman—her face delicate, her nose finely molded, her eyes vivid—despite the fact that she was obviously not of aristocratic birth. She was a well-developed girl with a fair complexion and had the advantage of being both tall and plump; had she been a member of the court in fact, she would have been perfect in the principal female role at a formal ceremony of state, carrying the sword, with her hair done up formally.[24]

Although this passage does not detail the shape of eyes and nose, it conveys the beauty of her well-rounded body and white skin. *The Confessions of Lady Nijō* was written in the early fourteenth century approximately three hundred years after *The Tale of Genji*, but the images of beautiful women in both works coincide on many points. The above quotation is striking in that it indicates how a palace attendant would tie her long, black hair up for ritual occasions instead of letting it fall over her shoulders and back. It is also interesting that the author regards being tall as an element of feminine beauty.

As stated earlier, Heian narrative literature regards women of middle or petite build as beautiful. This does not change in late Heian. The narrator of "The Lady Who Loved Caterpillars" in *The Tales of the Riverside Middle Counselor* finds beauty in a height neither tall nor short: "Her height was just right with her hair, which was very full and long enough to reach the bottom of her divided skirt." "Eyebrow Ink" in the same collection provides an example of a petite build as beautiful: "In the bright moonlight was her figure, very petite with glossy, beautiful hair that matched her height." Descriptions differ by the story, character, and scene, but there is no Heian example in which tallness was praised as a feature of feminine beauty. *The Confessions of Lady Nijō*, however, says outright that tallness is beautiful. In this sense, the above quotation is worthy of note. *The Confessions of Lady Nijō* was completed approximately 250 years after *The Tales of the Riverside Middle Counselor*. During that interval, some changes might have occurred in views of women. How universal the aesthetic sense finding tallness as representing feminine beauty was, however, is uncertain.

The beauty of white skin is also emphasized here. Unlike in *The Tale of Genji*, this aesthetic sense seems to have settled in the Kamakura period. In fact, warriors' tales like *The Tale of the Heike* totally share the positive view of white skin.

The Look of Peach and Plum

In examining the images of beauty in the Kamakura period, *The Tale of the Heike* is an important work. By combining Chinese and Japanese linguistic elements it played an important role in the history of the development of the Japanese language. It can be said that the work created a criterion for later literature in terms of content and character portrayals.

Because *The Tale of the Heike* depicts the battles between the Genji and the Heike, it does not contain many portraits of beautiful women. Women do enter the stage, but, being side characters, there is little detailed description of their personalities and appearances. When a beautiful woman appears, she may be "the number one beauty under heaven" (chapter 1, "Empress for the Second Time"), "an exceptionally beautiful lady-in-attendance" (chapter 9, "Kozaishō Plunges Herself"), or "the top beauty in the place" (ibid.), often with no mention of any concrete external looks. Naturally, it is not totally devoid of relatively detailed descriptions:

He was just entering the bath when the door of the bathhouse opened and there appeared an exquisitely graceful lady of some twenty years. Her complexion was pure and white. She was clad in an unlined tie-dyed silk robe and a blue patterned overwrap.[25]

After being captured by Genji, when Taira no Shigehira was given a chance to bathe, this woman appeared. She is introduced only as white-skinned. Most portrayals of good looks in *The Tale of the Heike* are quite concise. Details are mostly absent, as we see in such general descriptions as "starting with her hair and countenance, she was beautifully shaped with a lovely voice and a skilled way of carrying a melody" (chapter 1, "Giō") and "being beautifully shaped and gracefully natured" (chapter 11, "The Affair of the Documents"). The reason that white skin is mentioned in the above quotation is probably that the color of skin was particularly noticeable. In fact, this is the only concrete description throughout the entire tale.

Besides white skin, we also find a description of black hair in *The Tale of the Heike*. However, it relates not to a beautiful woman, but to a child emperor. "The Former Emperor Plunges Himself" in chapter 11 refers to the young Antoku in the following passage:

> The emperor was then eight years old but looked much older. He was so handsome that it was as if an aura of light glowed around his head. His long raven locks flowed loosely down his back.[26]

It may be that, in tales of war, white skin may have become a more important indicator in Heian narrative literature of personal appearances than black hair.

When considering that the prototype of *The Tale of the Heike* was the promptbooks used for folk performances, it is natural that it is relatively sparse in portrayals of appearances using glamorous rhetoric. However, sections that seem to have been edited by literati do include slightly more detailed descriptions:

> This year she turned twenty-nine years of age. Her appearance of peach and plum was still delicate, and her countenance of lotus had not yet waned; but even if she wore a head ornament of jade, her fate would be unchangeable. Thus, in the end she changed her form into that of a nun.[27]

This passage from "The Initiates' Book" describes how beautiful Kenreimon'in, the mother of the child emperor Antoku, was. This sort of style that reflects Chinese verse and prose did not exist in vernacular Japanese. As the diction and rhetoric suggest, it draws heavily on Cao Zhi's "Miscellaneous Poems" ("Zashi") and Bo Juyi's "The Song of Lasting Regret."

Ornate Figurative Speech

A look at its descriptive method makes clear that *The Tale of the Heike* is richly influenced by Chinese verse and prose. Neither Cao Zhi in his "Miscellaneous Poems" nor Bo Juyi in his "The Song of Lasting Regret" realistically portrays facial features. Likewise *The Tale of the Heike* adheres to figurative expressions. Such a descriptive approach is repeated in later tales of war as well. The section on "Band of Roisterers and Gen'e's Discourses on Literature" in *The Chronicle of the Great Peace*, or *The Taiheiki*, introduces young women serving wine:

> The wine was served by more than twenty maidens of sixteen or seventeen years, clear-skinned and superior in face and figure, through whose unlined robes of raw silk the snowy skin gleamed fresh as lotus blossoms newly risen from the waters of T'ai-i.[28]

The general description like "superior in face and figure" and the rhetorical reference to "The Song of Lasting Regret" concur with *The Tale of the Heike*. This passage once again holds white skin to be the key point for beautiful women, making no mention of other physical features.

The Taiheiki contains many other examples of snow-white skin symbolizing feminine beauty. "Kakuichi and Shinjō Narrate a Passage from *The Tale of the Heike*" in chapter 21, which describes how, after Minamoto no Yorimasa killed the monster bird that had disturbed the emperor's sleep, the emperor bestows on him a beautiful woman by the name of Lady Ayame ("Iris") from the rear palace, whom Yorimasa had a longing for. The emperor chooses twelve court ladies including her, clad all alike, and has them sit in the gloom, challenging Yorimasa to correctly spot the right person. Before his eyes evolves the following scene:

> Sixteen or seventeen years of age, all were elegant and enchanting, ornamented in gold and emerald, vying for snowy complexion and trying to look their best. The fragrances from their sleeves of red flowers and green leaves made Yorimasa feel as if he had been touched by orchid and musk, making sweet even the invisible breezes on which they waft. The entire area shone, and their unparalleled beauty was like cherry trees of Arashiyama or Yoshino, where blossoms and clouds are difficult to distinguish. His eyes shifting from lady to lady, he was unable to tell which one was Lady Ayame, the right iris to pull.[29]

As in Chinese rhyme-prose, flowery rhetoric abounds. However, the gaze is exclusively on the glamorous attire and white skin. This indicates that the equation of white skin with beauty had already been established by the Kamakura period.

It is an abundantly used rhetorical approach in describing beautiful features to quote from Chinese prose and poetry from China and Heian Japan or compare them to those of historical beauties. Moreover, free from the stiffness found in Chinese prose and poetry, Chinese expressions are here skillfully woven into the Japanese language. Chapter 15 of *The Taiheiki* portrays the daughter of a newly appointed Kamo Shrine official:

> Since the days when she was nurtured in an inner chamber, she was unusually lovely like white flowers of young *murasaki*, and with the disorder after sleep of her hair, first tied with her coming of age, would have affected the viewer with the thought of how she might turn out when she matures. Having already reached the age of sixteen, she recalled the image in the Emperor Hui's dream of the immortal woman of Mount Wu, and retained the springtime charms of Yang Guifei outside the Taizhen residence where she received the visit of a Daoist sent by Emperor Xuanzong. She was not just delicately beautiful in appearance beyond compare, but learned the path of poetry that Ono no Komachi enjoyed and followed the trace of music that the Imperial Layman Priest enjoyed, so that she plucked her pipa before the moon beckoning it back as it began to descend, and composed poems under cherry blossoms regretting their fading hue. Thus, everyone who heard about her refined taste and saw her countenance felt restless at heart.[30]

This passage uses not only Chinese sources such as "The Rhyme-Prose on Gao-Tang" from the *Literary Selections* (*Wen xuan*, ca. 520) and Bo Juyi's "The Song of Lasting Regret," but also the Japanese *The Tale of Genji*. Moreover, Chinese and Japanese expressions are skillfully juxtaposed. It is also noteworthy that the representative Japanese woman poet Ono no Komachi is mentioned along with Yang Guifei of the Tang. In addition to appearance, cultural backgrounds like playing a Chinese string instrument and composing Japanese poetry are regarded as conditions for a beautiful woman.

Interestingly, detailed observations of a woman's appearance occur at an unexpected place. "On Onimaru and Onikiri," about the two swords thus named, chapter 32 of *The Taiheiki* records how Watanabe no Gengo Tsuna, at the order of the lord of Settsu province Minamoto no Yorimitsu, defeats a monster that haunts the woods in Uda county. Afraid of Tsuna's prowess, the monster does not appear readily. Tsuna disguises himself as a woman in order to put him off guard. The disguise provides some clues to the sense of beauty around the time when the tenth-century episode was retrospectively narrated:

> Thinking that he would then disguise himself to trick the monster, he let his hair down in disarray, wore a wig, blacked his teeth, drew thick eyebrows, and wearing a thin robe, he went out and walked under the tree shade of the woods at dawn under a hazy moon.[31]

176   Chapter 6

Although this is a passage recounting a past incident, aesthetics of the fourteenth century is expressed fairly strongly therein. Tsuna must have tried to make himself look as feminine as possible. Blacked teeth and thick eyebrows appear to have been striking features of makeup along with white skin.

4. YANG GUIFEI AND THE IMAGE OF BEAUTY

Yang Guifei Frequently Appears in Japanese Tales of War

The image of ideal beauty is often described using a proper noun. A beautiful woman does not become an eternal woman without "legends." Rather than her looks, how she enchants men stirs interest. In China, images of beauty like Xi Shi and Mao Qiang of the Spring and Autumn period entered the stage early on. As time passed, Wang Zhaojun, Lady Li (or Li Furen, consort of Emperor Wu of Han), and others were added. Yang Guifei is one of those later emergences.

I have already noted that *The Tale of Genji* refers to Yang Guifei as an idealized image of beauty. The same practice continues into the Kamakura period. As mentioned earlier, "The Initiates' Book" chapter of *The Tale of the Heike* refers to Kenreimon'in: "Her appearance of peach and plum was still delicate, and her countenance of lotus." Needless to say, "her countenance of lotus" is based upon the line from "The Song of Lasting Regret," which runs in Paul W. Knoll's translation: "The lotus blossoms resemble her face, the willow branches her eyebrows."[32] About the great imperial favor bestowed upon her, the same passage mentions, now playing on, now directly following, the expressions from "The Song of Lasting Regret": "staying close to the monarch's side, she assisted with his morning administrative work and in the evening she concentrated on her evening duties."

In the history of representations of beauty in Japan, Yang Guifei is worthy of particular mention. Not only were her life episodes and physical appearance repeatedly handled in literature, but Bo Juyi's literary style exerted great influence on the portrayals of women of later times. Lady Li and others are often mentioned alongside her, but Yang Guifei's presence is overwhelming.

She also frequently appears in Japanese tales of war postdating *The Tale of the Heike*. *The Taiheiki* alone introduces her six times. If one looks for a model for a beautiful woman, an immediate association would be Ono no Komachi of Heian Japan and Yang Guifei of Tang China, but in Japanese tales of war, mention of Yang Guifei is overwhelmingly more frequent. Naturally, it is not simply because of her beauty, but because tales of war draw on Chinese history as sources of moral instruction. Yang Guifei, who triggered the An Lushan Rebellion, is indeed a model of "nation-toppling women" (*jingguo*) who cause the state to perish. However, portrayed against the backdrop of political occurrences, she was as a result passed down as an image of beauty. For example, Yang Guifei in "Yang Guifei; Yang Guozhong" in chapter 36 of *The Taiheiki* is described as follows:

> A ruddy face and blue-green eyebrows are, to begin with, things that heaven creates. Why should we necessarily be concerned with the more transitory fine powder and golden ointment? The painter who made a portrait of Lady Li of the Han would doubt that his brush would be sufficient in reproducing Yang Guifei in a painting, while Song Yu who composed a rhyme-prose on the immortal woman of Mount Wu would be ashamed of his humble diction if he were to compose a eulogy about her. It would be bewildering just to hear her speak. Far more so when seeing her beautiful figure.... As she decorated her already outstandingly beautiful countenance with gold and jade ornaments and sprinkled fragrant incense, she was no different from Lady Shezhi in the shade of blossoms in the Garden of Joy, dressed up and harmonizing with the spring.... As Yang Guifei bathed with orchid-scented ointment on her beautiful, white skin, he [Emperor Xuanzong] wondered if this were not just, as the couplet went: "In Mount Lantian the sun is warm as beads of water sprinkle like tears; in Mount Yuling the snow thaws as plum blossoms exhale fragrance."[33]

This passage can be said to offer a model of how to apply, in describing feminine beauty, such rhetorical methods as figurative speech, quotation, and contrast. In comparison with Ono no Komachi, Yang Guifei comes with many more literary precedents that could serve as sources. It does not necessarily have to be "The Song of Lasting Regret"; any description whatsoever of a beautiful woman in Chinese literature can be used in references to Yang Guifei. We may find one reason here for more frequent references in Japanese tales of war to Yang Guifei than to Ono no Komachi.

Descriptive Approach after the Manner of "The Song of Lasting Regret"

Not only did descriptions of Yang Guifei portray her, but figurative speech used therein was widely applied to beautiful Japanese women. For example, "Kakuichi and Shinjō Narrate a Passage Together from the *Tale of the Heike*" in chapter 21 of *The Taiheiki* contains the following passage:

> In her exquisite appearance of gold skin and bones of jewels, she seemed unable to bear even the weight of her thin robe. With her listless hands she languidly stroked her wet hair, rich in disarray. Her eyes looked comely as she gazed vaguely at the candlelight through the falling strands of her hair. Her face that covered the mirror recalled a large flower blooming out of water. Jewels from

Mount Lantian, when shining in the sun, must have been just as she appeared. He [Kō no Moronao] thought that the one [Yang Guifei] who was extolled even though wearing neither rouge nor powder might have been just like this lady.[34]

This passage does not describe Yang Guifei but the warrior En'ya Hōgan's wife, whom Kō no Moronao, the shōgun's deputy, espied through a slit between screen doors as she just finished her bath. Despite the fact that a descriptive approach after the fashion of "The Song of Lasting Regret" is used, nothing jars here. This is because the Yang Guifei–style of portrayal had already become assimilated into Japanese context and settled within Japanese modes of expression. The establishment of such rhetoric in Japanese literary writing is quite significant. For, by the fusion of Chinese vocabulary and rhetoric with Japanese writing, the scope of Japanese-language expression expanded by leaps.

In Chinese literature, as is seen in "The Song of Lasting Regret," descriptions of appearances frequently use ornate rhetorical speech rather than realistic observations. This, originally, was absent in Japanese-language literature in Japan. In the age of the *Taiheiki*, a literary style that accepts such rhetoric was finally discovered.

From Yang Guifei to Ono no Komachi

The Taiheiki, The Rise and Fall of the Minamoto and the Taira (*Genpei jōsuiki*), *The Tale of the Heiji War* (*Heiji monogatari*), and *The Tale of the Hōgen War* (*Hōgen monogatari*) introduce many Chinese historical characters. Of the top twenty-three characters referenced, Yang Guifei is the only woman. Moreover, she is referred to as many as seventeen times in these four works collectively, proudly gaining third place. In passing, first place goes to Xiang Yu, the prominent military leader of Chu in the late Qin dynasty period, second to Liu Bang, founder of the Han dynasty, who defeated Xiang Yu in the long struggle known as the Han-Chu contention.[35] Zhuge Liang, the great strategist of the Three Kingdoms period, still extremely popular in Japan, occupies twenty-first place. In painting, too, we find the theme of Yang Guifei (figure 6.2). These are indicative of her popularity in medieval Japan.

Yang Guifei played an extremely important role in the process of transmitting literary Chinese descriptions of beautiful women into the Japanese-language context. Her name was quoted from the Muromachi to the early Edo period. In shorter narratives called "companion tales" (*otogizōshi*) flourishing then, rhetoric in the lines of "The Song of Lasting Regret" is still repeated, and Yang Guifei frequently appears as a synonym for a beautiful

Figure 6.2. From Kanō Sansetsu, *The Song of Lasting Regret in Two Scrolls* (*Chōgonka gakan*), early Edo period. The Chester Beatty Library. *Source:* Hirayama Ikuo and Kobayashi Tadashi (editors), *Comprehensive Treasury of Japanese Art*, vol. 5. Kōdansha, 1993, figures 43–44.

woman. For example, "The Fox of Kowata" ("Kowata-gitsune") compares the beauty of the ancient fox's daughter to Yang Guifei: "As the Middle Captain saw this princess, he was not certain if he was dreaming or awake. Her countenance was beyond words. One would think her a Yang Guifei, the consort of Emperor Xuanzong, or Lady Li if this were in the era of Emperor Wu of the Han."[36]

On the other hand, expressions indicating that a character is more beautiful than Yang Guifei also began to stand out. "The Bowl Wearer" ("Hachikazuki") says that the girl who wore a bowl on her head "was such a beautiful person that her surroundings shone. Everyone found it miraculous and could not utter a word. How would Yang Guifei and Lady Li of the Han have surpassed her?" Again, "The Tale of Bunshō" ("Bunshō sōshi") contains this passage: "The princess's appearance was such that Lady Li of the Han and

Yang Guifei would not surpass her." In both cases, beauty beyond that of Lady Li and Yang Guifei is emphasized.

Besides Lady Li and Yang Guifei, *otogizōshi* tales also introduce Japanese beauties like the Heian poet Ono no Komachi and the legendary Sotōrihime. Sometimes all four are brought together: "Oh, such a beautiful lady. We have heard of Lady Li, Yang Guifei, Sotōrihime, and Ono no Komachi, but how would they surpass this person" ("Saiki"). At other times Chinese and Japanese beauties are referred to separately. Moreover, Ono no Komachi and Sotōrihime can be said to be images of beauty created with Yang Guifei in mind. There is no doubt that behind the Japanese version of ideal beauty was the model of Yang Guifei with stories of her life and descriptions of her looks.

Appearance Onstage of Narrow Eyebrows

Otogizōshi tales use much figurative speech, with few concrete descriptions.

To put together the descriptions in literary pieces starting with *The Taiheiki*, images of beautiful women in the Kamakura period can be summarized into the following elements: long, black hair; smooth, white skin; thickly penciled eyebrows; and blackened teeth. Regardless of how these matched reality, in literature beautiful women were described more or less in this manner.

In the Muromachi period (1336–1573), some change occurred. The beautiful woman who appears in "Lady Shizuka Visits Wakamiya Hachimangū" in chapter 6 of *The Story of Yoshitsune* (*Gikeiki*) differs significantly from the beauties in the aforementioned tales of war. There is a scene in chapter 6 in which the captive Lady Shizuka, brought before the warrior Minamoto no Yoritomo and forced to dance, boldly sings a song expressing her love of Yoshitsune, his half brother and now his enemy.

> Shizuka's outfit on that day included a white inner robe with small sleeve openings, a robe of brocade, a white divided skirt long enough for her to step on, a white outer robe with broad sleeve openings woven with decorative diamond patterns. She wore her height-long hair neatly tied, looking slender-faced from her recent grief, with light makeup and thin eyebrows. Opening her red folded fan, she stood facing the treasure hall. Perhaps she felt nervous because she was to dance before nobody else but Yoritomo, the Kamakura Lord, she hesitated for a while, unable to start dancing.[37]

The greatest difference is in the eyebrows. Those thickly painted in *The Taiheiki* have now become long and thin.

In those days, not only women but young boys wore similar makeup. Chapter 2 of *The Story of Yoshitsune* (*Gikeiki*) describes a young boy: "Extremely white of skin, with teeth blackened, only a light application of makeup with eyebrows thinly drawn, loosely covering his head in a woman's robe [to conceal his identity]. He looked almost like Sayohime of Matsura, who waved her scarf [seeing off her husband sailing off] for years atop the mountain, and whose smudged eyebrows, seen through her hair somewhat in disarray after sleep, were ready to be affected by a breeze stirred by a warbler's wings."[38]

This indicates that young boys' makeup was nearly the same as that of women excepting the length of the hair. It is not just a matter of a change in eyebrow makeup. A change in aesthetics, it can be said, had already occurred.

That narrow eyebrows were regarded as beautiful can be confirmed in art as well (figure 6.3). A portrait from approximately the same era, however, represents a different pair of eyebrows (figure 6.4). It is unclear why there is such a large difference between the two portraits. In any case, there were many variants depending upon the status, age, or makeup method.

Figure 6.3. *Reportedly: Portrait of Lady Yodo.* Momoyama Period (late sixteenth century). Nara Prefectural Museum. *Source:* The Agency of Cultural Affairs (supervisor), *Nihon no bijutsu (Japanese Fine Arts)*, no. 384 (May 15, 1998), "Josei no shōzō" ("Portraits of Women"), figure 11.

Figure 6.4. *Portrait of Lady Asai Nagamasa.* Momoyama Period. Jimyōin Temple. *Source:* The Agency of Cultural Affairs (supervisor), *Nihon no bijutsu (Japanese Fine Arts)*, no. 384 (May 15, 1998), "Josei no shōzō" ("Portraits of Women"), figure 14.

NOTES

1. The quotations, except the last one, in this paragraph are from Richard Bowring, *The Diary of Lady Murasaki* (Penguin Books, 1996). The description of Miya no Naishi as "very pure-looking and slender" follows the version in *Shinpen Nihon Koten Bungaku Zenshū* (hereafter SNKBZ), 25.
2. Yuhara Miyoko, *Inquiry into the Aesthetics of Physical Appearances in Heian Narrative Literature* (*Ōchō monogatari bungaku ni okeru yōshibi no kenkyū*) (Yūseidō, 1988).
3. Royall Tyler (tr.), *The Tale of Genji*, vol. 1 (Viking, 2001), 49.
4. Ibid., 334.
5. Bowring, *op. cit.*, 48.
6. Mitani Eiichi and Sekine Keiko (annotators), *Sagoromo monogtari*. *Nihon Koten Bungaku Taikei* (hereafter NKBT, Iwanami, [1965] 1977) 79, 59.
7. Tyler, *op. cit.*, 124.
8. Sakakura Atsuyoshi (annotator), *Yoru no nezame* (NKBT 78, [1964] 1976), 204. Cf. Suzuki Kazuo (annotator and translator), *Yoru no nezame* (SNKBZ 34, Shōgakukan, 1996).
9. Teramoto Naohiko (annotator), *Riverside Chūnagon monogatari* (NKBT 13, [1957] 1977), 404.
10. *Yoru no nezame* (NKBT), 204.
11. Ibid., 89.
12. Ibid., 352.
13. Tachibana Kenji and Katō Shizuko (annotators and translators), *Ōkagami* (SNKBZ 34, 1996). Reference omitted for the following quotations from the same work.
14. *Yoru no nezame*, 168.
15. Tyler, *op. cit.*, 68.
16. Ibid., 918.
17. Bowring, *op. cit.*, 20.
18. *Yoru no nezame*, 89.
19. Ibid., 383.
20. Ibid., 397.
21. Ibid., 54.
22. Ibid., 125.
23. Higuchi Yoshimaro (annotator and translator), *Matsuura monogatari* (SNKBZ 40, 1994–1998).
24. Karen Brazell (tr.), *The Confessions of Lady Nijō* (A Doubleday Anchor Original, 1973), 84–85.
25. Kitagawa Hiroshi and Bruce Tsuchida (trs.), *The Tale of the Heike* (University of Tokyo Press, 1975), vol. 2, book 10, "Senju no Mae," 604–5, modified by Kyoko Selden.
26. Ibid., book 11, "Drowning of the Emperor," 676.

27. Or, in the Kitagawa-Tsuchida translation: "Now at the age of twenty-nine, she was still beautiful, as beautiful as peach or apricot blossoms. Her elegant form was like a lotus flower. But what was the use of keeping her raven locks, as lustrous as jade? [new paragraph] At last she renounced this fleeting world and became a nun." (Epilogue, 764)

28. Helen McCullough (tr.), *The Taiheiki: A Chronicle of Medieval Japan* (Charles E. Tuttle Company, 1979), 14-15.

29. Hasegawa Tadashi (annotator and translator), *Taiheiki* (SNKBZ 54-57, 1994-1-98). Corresponds to "En'ya Hōgan Dies Because of a False Charge" in Gotō Tanji and Kamata Kisaburō (annotators), *Taiheiki*, vol. 2 (NKBT 34-36, [1961] 1977), 350. Cf. Hiroaki Sato's translation in *Legends of the Samurai* (The Overbook Press, 1995, 190) of the pertinent passage based on the NKBT edition: "Yorimasa, who was standing with his hands on the edge of the large floor of the Seiryō palace, became visibly confused as he looked from one woman to another, utterly incapable of hitting upon the right iris to pull. All the ladies were about sixteen years old, each with facial features so exquisite that no painter's brush would have been able to reproduce a semblance of them, all wearing necklaces of gold and green, radiating coquetry as peaches in their ripeness might."

30. *Taiheiki* (NKBT), vol. 2, 118.

31. Ibid., vol. 3, 227.

32. Paul W. Knoll, in Victor Mair (ed.), *The Columbia Anthology of Traditional Chinese Literature* (Columbia University Press, 1994), 481.

33. *Taiheiki*, vol. 4 (SNKBZ 57), chapter 36. The passage corresponds to *Taiheiki* (NKBT 36), vol. 3, chapter 37, 387-88.

34. *Taiheiki* (NKBT 35), vol. 2, 357.

35. Masuda Motomu, *A Comparative Study of* The Taiheiki *("Taiheiki" no hikakubungakuteki kenkyū)* (Kadokawa Shoten, 1996).

36. Ichiko Teiji (annotator), *Otogi-zōshi* (NKBT 38, [1958] 1977), 151.

37. Kajiwara Masaaki (annotator and translator), *Gikeiki* (SNKBZ 62, 2000).

38. Okami Masao (annotator), *Gikeiki* (NKBT 37, [1959] 1977), 61.

7

Edo Culture as a Filter

1. "ADAPTATIONS" OF THE IMAGE OF BEAUTY

Importing Images

In the Edo period, there was a boom of "translating" Chinese literature. The milieu was *kana*-based Japanese studded with Chinese-style expressions. This was a revolutionary change in the history of reading Chinese verse and prose simply by means of *kundoku* or *yomikuashi*, which keeps the Chinese intact but uses Japanese pronunciation and grammar.

However, rather than genuine "translations," what first appeared were "adaptations," in which details in original texts were ignored. One of the earliest attempts is *The Protective Doll* (*Otogibōko*, 1666) by Asai Ryōi, author of short narratives of the type known as *kanazōshi* (books in vulgar script), written mostly in kana and primarily intended for children, women, and the modestly lettered. "The Peony Lantern" ("Botan no tōrō"; popularly known as "Botan dōro") in that collection includes a scene in which Hagiwara Shinnojō by chance encounters a lovely woman on the roadside on the night of the fifteenth day of the seventh month:

> One beautiful woman, seemingly about twenty years of age, slowly passed by with a fourteen- or fifteen-year-old maid who carried a peony lantern. The woman's slanting eyes of lotus petals were clear, and her body shape of willow was delicate. Her eyebrow ink of katsura and hair of green sheen were lovely beyond expression.[1]

The Japanese "The Peony Lantern" is an adaptation from "The Account of the Peony Lantern" in the late fourteenth-century Chinese collection called *New Lamp-Wick Trimming Stories* (*Jiandeng xinhua*). The Chinese source describes the same scene as follows:

> Qiao saw a maid walk ahead holding a double-headed peony lantern, and a beautiful woman following her. The woman was about seventeen or eighteen years old. In a red skirt and green sleeves, looking lovely and demure, she passed gently by toward the west. As he saw her under the moon, she was a true beauty with a resonant face and a youthful set of teeth.[2]

The original Chinese wording *lovely and demure* (*tingting niaoniao*) is a set phrase describing a beautiful appearance. *Resonant face* (*shaoyan*) denotes a young, lovely countenance. *Tender teeth* (*zhichi*) also stands for youthfulness. In other words, the original text merely provides an impressionistic description with no reference to facial features or body shape.

In comparison, the description in *The Protective Doll* introduces such details not in the original, as cool-looking eyes like lotus blossoms, beautiful eyebrows like katsura (a tree that was reputed to grow in the moon), and dark hair. The descriptions are not perhaps true to life, but do refer to concrete parts of the character's face and body.

"Hair of green sheen" (*midori no kami*) is a direct quote from the Chinese expression "green hair" (*lüfa*), found, for example, in "Tian Zhu Encounters Xue Tao and Joins in a Linked Verse" in *Supplementary Lamp-Wick Trimming Stories*. Other than that, each added description reflects the author-translator's hand. Metaphors like *lotus flower* and *willow* go back to "The Song of Lasting Regret," but they are also often seen in literary Chinese fiction like *New Lamp-Wick Trimming Stories*. Seeing that we find expressions like *her waist and legs are a willow without the wind* in that collection, it is not at all strange that such an expression as *her body shape of willow was delicate* surfaced in this Japanese story. In contrast, the origin of the phrase *eyes of lotus petals* is unclear. Perhaps this expression is not a direct borrowing but something derived from such usages as *the lotus skin, green cloud chignon* ("An Account of Plucking on the Zither on a Moonlit Night," *Supplementary Lamp-Wick Trimming Stories*, vol. 1). However, it is unclear whether Asai Ryōi quoted directly from a Chinese source or drew from an earlier Japanese work.

The source of the expression *eyebrow ink of katsura* is unknown. Because katsura is a tree that legendarily grows in the moon, it signifies "moon" by extension. Thus, *eyebrow ink of katsura*, which refers to eyebrows that are drawn like a crescent moon, is not a totally unexpected metaphor. A piece called "Saiki" of the genre called *otogizōshi* (companion tales, late Muromachi to early Edo period) also refers to "dark eyebrow ink of katsura, beautiful lips of red fruit."

Later, this became a set format handed down to authors of "reading books" (*yomihon*, didactic long fiction popular from the mid-eighteenth to mid-nineteenth century). The passage found in Santō Kyōden's *The Tale of Udumbara Flowers* (*Udonge monogatari*, 1804), volume 2, section 3, can be called a case of direct borrowing rather than an adaptation: "She looked about twice eight years of age, graceful with eyes of lotus petals and a figure of willow, and with striking eyebrows of katsura and hair of green hue."

How Old Is the Beautiful Woman?

There is an expression, *ideal age* (Chinese *miaoling*; Japanese *myōrei*). In Japan it exclusively refers to women's tender youth, but in China it was originally applied to men as well. Like "sixteen" (Chinese *erba*; Japanese *nihachi*, both meaning "twice eight"), it does not refer to a specific age. Besides meaning "tender youth," it carries the nuance of "being beautiful."

The concept of "sixteen = beautiful" no longer exists today. While the term *ideal age* is not completely obsolete, it seems to refer to a somewhat older age than sixteen.

If so, what about "tenderly young" (*urawakai*) or "young" (*wakai*)? Today, some may think of eighteen or twenty; others would find youth in people in their thirties and forties. In premodern literature, however, there was a correlation between age and beauty. Particularly in descriptions of beautiful women in literature, the age carried a kind of symbolic character.

Fu Liqing in "The Account of the Peony Lantern" in *New Lamp-Wick Trimming Stories* is "seventeen or eighteen years of age." In "The Peony Lantern" in the Japanese *The Protective Doll*, this changed to "about twenty years of age." Why did the translator-author Asai Ryōi make the change?

In "companion tales" we encounter unmarried women "fifteen or sixteen years of age" ("The Bowl Wearer") and "about twenty" ("Saiki"). Married women's ages also vary: "age twenty-two," "age twenty," "age eighteen" (the last in "The Bowl Wearer"). Intrinsically, Asai Ryōi had no reason to change "seventeen or eighteen years of age" to "about twenty years of age."

As discussed earlier, the correlation between age and beauty had not yet been established in *The Tale of Genji*. A woman of twenty-nine, possibly viewed as middle-aged in those days, is also portrayed as beautiful. As a whole, Heian narrative literature tends to share this judgment.

"Empress of Two Emperors" in chapter 1 of *The Tale of the Heike* describes the empress of the retired emperor Konoe: "But at the time in the

Eiryaku era, she was still only twenty-three years old, barely past her prime."[3] Even while calling her "the top beauty under heaven," there are indications that the author views age twenty-three as past the peak of womanhood. "The Letters" in chapter 11 refers to a twenty-three-year-old princess as beautiful looking "although somewhat mature in terms of age," in short, a little older than ideal.

The Tale of the Heike does not clearly indicate what age is desirable. "Kozaishō Plunges Herself" in chapter 9 introduces the second daughter of Fujiwara no Norikata. "Top beauty of the court," she chanced to meet Courtier Michimori "in the spring of the Angen era when she was sixteen." Michimori "fell in love with her at first sight." The passage carries a nuance that sixteen is an optimal age. This an aesthetic common in eras when marriage at an early age was customary. However, in literature, "sixteen = beautiful" was not necessarily an established standard. The "Lady Senju" section in chapter 10 refers to her as a "court lady about twenty years of age." Twenty was also beautiful.

The expression *twice eight* came to be used relatively late as a metaphor for a beautiful woman. In China, it recurs in *New Songs from a Jade Terrace* (*Yutai xin'yong*, the North and South period) and Bo Juyi's poems. It does not merely represent age, but bears the nuance of "beautiful" and "unmarried." In Japan, it was used early on in Chinese-language poetry as exemplified by lines like "When I was twice eight years of gracefully charming age" in *Glories and Graces* (*Bunka shūreishū*, 818) and "Enchantress at twice eight in the east wing of the main residence" in *Collection of National Polity* (*Keikokushū*, 827). It began to be used apparently in the Kamakura and Muromachi periods in texts in native Japanese (*wabun*) or those in a mixed style of Japanese and Sino-Japanese (*wakan konkōbun*). For example, "The Nomination of a Consort" in chapter 1 of *The Taiheiki* refers to the aristocrat Saionji Sanekane's daughter as "already twice eight." The newly appointed principal official's daughter is "already twice eight" in "Replacing the Kamo Shrine's Head Priest" in chapter 15. "Kōtō no Naishi, Nitta Yoshisada's Beloved Consort" in chapter 20 contains a phrase, "since the spring when she was twice eight." By the time of *The Taiheiki*, the expression had perfectly merged into the Japanese context. In that context, the ascription of "age seventeen or eighteen" is also used as a metaphor for a beautiful woman.

As stated earlier, "The Peony Lantern" in *The Protective Doll* says, "a beautiful woman, with a fourteen- or fifteen-year-old maidservant carrying a beautiful peony lantern, passes by quite leisurely," attributing to its main character an age different from the Chinese original. Probably this was written with a passage from "Lady Senju" in chapter 10 of *The Tale of the Heike* in mind: "A lady of about twenty years of age . . . a girl servant aged about fourteen or fifteen. . . ." That Chinese descriptions of beautiful women, including "twice eight," were smoothly adapted into the genre of "reading books" (*yomihon*) owes much to tales of war written in a mixed Japanese-Chinese style.

From "reading books" the idea of "twice eight" came to denote a beautiful young woman. In the "reading books" of Takizawa Bakin (1767–1848), in particular, "about twice eight years of age" was nearly a set phrase for portrayals of beautiful women. References to ages eighteen or twenty are not totally absent, but "twice eight" recurs far more often. Another thing we cannot ignore is the acceptance in Japan of the "Three Words and Two Slaps" and *Outlaws of the Marsh*. For "twice eight" had completely settled as a metaphor for a beautiful countenance in Chinese fiction in the vernacular.

The situation somewhat differs in cases like "books of human feeling" (*ninjōbon*), narratives of love from the Edo period. For example, we spot fourteen- or fifteen-year-olds as well as girls of sixteen, seventeen, eighteen, and nineteen years of age in Tamenaga Shunsui's *The Love-Tinted Plum Calendar* (*Shunshoku umegoyomi*, 1832–1833). When the woman is sixteen, the cliché "twice eight" is not used. Shunsui must have deliberately avoided it with Bakin's usage of it in mind.

Compression of Forms

"Books of the vulgar script" do not as a whole spend much ink on descriptions of characters. That is the case with adaptations from Chinese literature like *The Protective Doll* as well. "The Peony Lantern" mentioned above can be called an exception. To begin with, given its topics, such Japanese short fiction in the vernacular contains few descriptions of good looks. In addition, because it is written in native Japanese, it is somewhat difficult to use Chinese-style rhetoric. "Mountain Princess," chapter 3, story 5 of *Tales for Comfort* (*Otogi monogatari*, 1678) introduces a maiden who lives in the mountains:

> Once when [a hunter] went deep into the mountains, there appeared a woman of twenty or so. She was clad in an exquisitely colored kimono with small sleeve openings, and her black hair was of a rare luster. It was unthinkable that there could be another like her.[4]

This story in the vernacular is not entirely without a trace of Chinese-style phrasing and rhetoric that had been fused into Chinese-Japanese mixed style writing. However, it shares with earlier narrative literature the lack of reference to the five sensory organs and body shape. The method of expressing beauty through the single point of glossy dark hair reminds us of the native Japanese idiom.

Chinese fiction of the strange often introduces a monster in the guise of a beautiful woman. Whether or not under its influence, some *kanazōshi* tales portray a lovely countenance in order to emphasize the contrast between that and her fearsome true identity.

> As [the traveling priest] went closer to see, the cottage was arranged in a refined manner with storybooks randomly spread on a low table. The faint fragrance of rare perfume was elegant. A beautiful, very graceful woman in lovely clothing sat close to the fireplace. Adding pine branches and pinecones, she tended the fire. This was a sight unfamiliar in the countryside.[5]

This passage from "The Ghost of Soga" in the *Tales for Comfort* introduces a ghost in the shape of a lovely women. The text does not refer to her facial features but portrays her mostly through her beautiful costume and graceful demeanor. In the Edo period, wordy descriptions of beautiful women more or less continued to depend upon Chinese-style expressions.

2. FROM JAPANESE COURTESANS TO SINO-JAPANESE FRAGILE WOMEN

Charms of Prostitutes

In this, Ihara Saikaku is similar. Courtesans are judged not only by looks but comprehensively by sensibility: the choice of what to wear, the knack of looking right in the clothes, training, manners of waiting upon patrons, and skill in performance. Thus, there may be no need to emphasize good looks alone.

The concept of the beautiful woman comes with different assumptions depending on the age. In ancient times, goddesses were assumed to embody beauty; next queens and princesses. There is a phrase in China, *the four beautiful women*. The combination of the four varies, but it often refers to Xi Shi (the king of Wu's consort), Diao Chan (Dong Zhuo's beloved), Wang Zhaojun (consort of Emperor Yuan of the Han and later of a nomadic ruler), and Yang Guifei (highest-ranking consort of Emperor Xuanzong of the Tang and the subject of "The Song of Lasting Regret"). With the exception of Diao Chan, the others are monarchical consorts. Considering that Dong Zhuo grasped power virtually equal to that of an emperor, Diao Chan can also be looked at as a monarchical spouse. In an age when the culture of the pleasure quarters flourished, however, the beautiful woman became a presence closer to commoners. Thus, accomplished courtesans appear onstage as representative beautiful women. In China, Li Shishi (Song courtesan), Chan Yuanyuan (of the Ming), and Sai Jinhua (of the Qing) can be mentioned. In fiction, we find endless examples like Du Shiniang (in *Stories to Caution the World*) and Li Xiangjun (in a drama called *Peach Blossom Fan*, also a real person).

In modern times, "a beautiful woman" often refers to a prostitute. From late Qing to the first half of the twentieth century there was an expression, *Yangzhou beauties*. The reason is that many courtesans were from Yangzhou and vicinity.

In Japan too, pleasure-quarter culture flourished in Edo. As long as "the beautiful woman" becomes a synonym for a courtesan, portrayal of a courtesan turns out to be a kind of portrayal of feminine beauty. How did Ihara Saikaku depict courtesans?

The first thing to notice when viewing his idiom of description of beautiful women is that he hardly uses Chinese-style rhetoric and vocabulary. The absence of flamboyant rhetoric and fixed phrases sometimes helps description of external appearances to be quite exact.

> No need for her to view herself in the mirror or neatly tie up her hair; habitually without makeup and barefooted, she carries herself in unhurried, delicate ways. Graceful and plump, her eyes are always alert. Good mannered, possessed with skin that rivals the snow in whiteness, skilled in bed, famously amorous, she enchants souls. She enjoys drinking, has a good singing voice, plays the thirteen strings, the three strings being her forte, and entertains the party. With a refined style of writing, she is a writer of long letters. She begs for nothing, gives without stint, shows compassion, and expertly uses feminine wiles.[6]

This is a description of an ideal courtesan by the name of Yūgiri (Evening Mist) in "Even If Put into the Fire" in chapter 6 of *The Life of an Amorous Man* (*Kōshoku ichidai otoko*, 1682). The passage suggests that, more important than just good looks, is whether a courtesan is cultured and pleasing to her patrons. In fact, it is written from such a point of view. The majority of the description relates to techniques of pleasing men, like artistry and personal charms. Regarding external appearance, reference is to plumpness and snow-white skin.

For Saikaku, clothing constitutes an important point for demonstrating a courtesan's sensibility. Therefore, in describing external appearance, particular emphasis goes to the description of gorgeous robes. In portraying the exceptional beauty of the courtesan Hatsune (First Song), "Sighting the

First Outfit of the Year" in the same chapter of the novel says nothing of her facial features and body shape. Instead, it introduces at length the patterns and hues of her clothes.

> A springy sky-blue inner robe next to her skin, a second layer of reddish yellow crepe with a scattered design of fallen plum blossoms, and outside scarlet damask with five-color appliqués of shuttlecocks, battledores, and bows, along with pattern-dyed sacred straw ropes, New Year leaves, lovers' leaves and many more with great splendor. Over it she wears a purple kimono jacket, tips of its red ties hanging down, with a design of a white plum tree perched by a warbler singing its first song of the year, recalling her name, First Song. As she proceeds ceremoniously and noiselessly from her quarters to the teahouse, her sight stirs longing thoughts.[7]

References to superior looks appear, rather, in "comparative evaluations" (*shinasadame*) of courtesans. The above-quoted passage about the courtesan Yūgiri is directly preceded, in the same chapter of *The Life of an Amorous Man*, by the following:

> [The] setting sun declining toward Mount Seyama, Seyama is soon to complete her term of service. Her petite figure is a flaw, but her face is lovely and refined, and her thoughts are wise. Ōhashi is tall and beautiful, with clean eyes but a vulgar mouth, and her procession not ideal. Her manners after taking her seat at a party equal those of an Ono no Komachi who composes no poetry. She is passive in terms of thoughtfulness, so her young girl-attendant by the name of Shun lends wisdom to her in all matters. Okoto is plain looking and somewhat vulgar, but some like her for that. She is too wise and greedy in every way, and a growth on her neck is source of grief. Nobody can find a flaw as far as her handling of party guests goes, and she has her own dignity in a way. Asazuma is tall with a charming way of carrying herself. With a beautiful profile and a straight nose, what is pitiable is her nostrils. They are black, as though she were a soot-sweep.[8]

In accordance with the style of Edo writings evaluating the skills of courtesans, this passage gives the names of courtesans and reports on their strengths and shortcomings. Altogether, a tall and slender woman with lovely eyes, a straight nose, and an attractive profile is regarded as beautiful. Of particular interest is that height counts toward beauty.

Tsuga Teishō's Approach

Likewise a literary adaptation, Tsuga Teishō's *A Garland of Heroes* (*Hanabusa sōshi*, 1749), published eighty-three years after Asai Ryōi's *The Protective Doll*, uses a rather different approach. First, *The Protective Doll* hardly offers a description of beautiful looks except in the passage cited above. Portrayals in *A Garland of Heroes* are further simplified. "Baba Motome Drowns His Wife in Order to Become the Adopted Husband of the Higuchi Family" in volume 1 is taken from "Jin Yunu Beats Her Compassionless Husband" contained in *Stories Old and New* (*Gujin xiaoshuo*). In the original, the appearance of Jin Yunu, the main character, is portrayed in the form of an interpolated poem:

> Old Jin, past age fifty and bereaved of his wife, had no male heir. All he had was a daughter by the name of Yunu. She was quite beautiful. In verse, her beauty might be described:
>
> Flawless skin comparable to jewels
> Manners that abash flowers
> If only in courtly apparel
> She would be a Zhang Lihua.[9]

Zhang Lihua (died 589), a favored consort of Chen Shubao, the last emperor of the Southern Chen dynasty, was reputed to be an exceptional beauty. The above poem about Yunu does not portray her countenance; rather, it merely likens her to "jewels" and "flowers" with the use of conventional metaphors. While this was a frequently used pattern in Ming fiction, such idiomatic understanding does not seem to have been established in Edo literature of the same period. In fact, the same passage is simplified in *A Garland of Heroes*.

> Jōō, past age fifty and bereaved of his wife over seven years ago, had no boy. He had one daughter. Her childhood name was Sai. She was incomparably beautiful beyond her family standing.[10]

Portrayal of facial appearance by way of interpolated verse seems to have long troubled Japanese translators. As is well known, many of the stories in Tsuga Teishō's *A Garland of Heroes* were adapted from Chinese vernacular fiction: *Stories to Caution the World*, *Stories to Awaken the World*, *Stories Old and New*, and *Remarkable Stories New and Old*. In these collections, descriptions of facial appearances are frequently interwoven into the narrative portions in the form of interpolated verse. Moreover, unlike the narrative portions, the poems are in archaic Chinese. Thus, they are difficult to translate into Japanese kana literature. Naturally, one way would be to translate them into traditional Japanese verse (*waka*). However, its short form lacks epic quality. Even if one attempts to transpose a Chinese poem found in the original narrative into *waka* form, one would experience difficulty in conveying the original intention. The reason that Tsuga Teishō, in translation, chose to excise descriptions of beautiful appearances from the original is probably that methods of rendering them into Japanese *waka* poetry had not yet been found.

Standards for Excision

When contrasted with the seventeen-years-later *Tales of Overgrown Fields* by the same author, that is even clearer. "An Eguchi Courtesan Sinks Her Jewels Indignant at Heartlessness" in chapter 5, tale 2, takes off from "Du Shiniang Sinks Her Jewel Box in Anger," *Stories to Caution the World*, 32. Du Shiniang's lovely looks are described in the form of an interpolated poem, a form also used in stories in the "Three Words and Two Slaps." It goes, in Shuhui Yang and Yunqin Yang's translation:

Her body full of grace and charm,
Her skin soft and fragrant,
Her brows the color and shape of distant hills,
Her eyes as limpid as autumn water,
Her cheeks as lovely as lotus petals,
She was the very image of Zhuo Wenjun.
Her lips the shape of a cherry,
She was a veritable Fan Su.
How sad that such a piece of flawless jade
Has fallen by misfortune into the world of lust![11]

Zhuo Wenjun is the wife of Sima Xiangru of the Han period, and Fan Su is a concubine of Bo Juyi of the Tang period. They are named here as synonyms for a beautiful woman. The facial description in this poem reflects an often-seen pattern in Ming vernacular fiction. In contrast, in the Edo Japanese adaptation, the beautiful countenance of Shirotae, the main character, is rendered as follows:

With her face fresh like a lotus blossom and her eyes moistened like autumn water, she evoked the images of Chang'e leaving the Moon Palace and Feiyan newly attired.[12]

While the majority of the original verse was excised, details not in the original were added. For example, "she evoked the images of Chang'e leaving the Moon Palace" is quoted from *Outlaws of the Marsh*, and "Feiyan newly attired" is from a poem by Li Bo.[13] On the other hand, the tale also uses the rhetoric of comparing the woman to historical characters reputed for their beauty. In chapter 3, tale 5, titled "Lady White Chrysanthemum Shoots a Strange Bone on the Monkey Seat Shore," of the same collection contains the following passage:

> The way her black hair falls over her white ears and the makeup on her weeping face washed by tears recalls Xi Shi in torment, Consort Yu in tears, Wang Zhaojun with a melancholy countenance as she leaves the capital, and Yang Guifei with her moaning eyebrows at Mawei Station.[14]

In these two passages, *Tales of Overgrown Fields* offers relatively detailed descriptions. Otherwise, the collection only provides simple sketches like "Little Butterfly, Yukina's wife, was young and by birth pure" (chapter 2) and "within the carriage was a young lady, graceful looking, whose flowerlike countenance resembled a jewel" (chapter 3).

Takebe Ayatari's *Tale of Nishiyama* published in 1768 is more concise in portrayal. The author only mentions that the woman has "clean features" and "radiant looks" (chapter 1). By the time of Ueda Akinari's *Tales of Rain and Moon* (1768), we find relatively detailed descriptions. "A Serpent's Lust" in chapter 4, for example, introduces the main character as "not yet twenty years of age, with elegance about her face and the way her hair streamed down, clad in a fine robe with designs of distant mountains, looking distressed in the drenching rain, accompanied by a clean-looking fourteen- or fifteen-year-old maid who carried a bundle of her mistress's belongings." Still, there is not much difference. It is fine to consider this to follow the rhetoric of Asai Ryōi's *The Protective Doll*.

3. PORTRAYAL FROM *OUTLAWS OF THE MARSH*

The Format of *Outlaws of the Marsh*

It was in the genre of "reading books" (*yomihon*) that descriptions of human appearances achieved a dramatic change. In fiction by Santō Kyōden and Takizawa Bakin, we find brilliant, or at least loquacious, descriptions that go on endlessly. When we consider such rhetoric, we must naturally include in our vista vernacular Chinese fiction. For beautiful women more often appear in romances like "Three Words and Two Slaps" than in historical fiction. Needless to say, those stories exerted great influence on character portrayals in Japanese "reading books."

However, descriptions of beautiful women seen in Chinese vernacular fiction were not instantly embraced. At first, they were rather avoided. *A Popular*

Account of Loyal Outlaws of the Marsh (*Tsūzoku Suiko chūgi-den*) translated by Okajima Kanzan was published in 1757, eight years after *A Garland of Heroes*. In it, some descriptions of beauty are consciously eliminated. For example, installment 29 of the original introduces the concubine of Jiang the Gate Guard Giant:

> Her eyebrows resemble green mountain ridges, her eyes are bedewed with autumn waves. Her cherry lips are lightly rouged in a gradated fashion, her hands of spring bamboo shoots lightly unfurl tender fingers. Her crown is small, clearly spreads an amber hue and covers the clouds of raven-black hair. Her colorful sleeves are narrow, ingeniously dyeing pomegranate flowers and lightly holding lovely snow. Her golden hairpin pierces a phoenix, her jeweled bracelet surrounds a dragon. Never mind what may happen. Let Cui Hu go and get drinks. One wonders if Zhuo Wenjun were selling wine again.[15]

Okajima Kanzan simply omits this passage. Probably he judged such description to be still unfamiliar to Japanese readers. The same applies to the portrayal of Jade Orchid, General Zhang's bondmaid, in installment 30 of *Outlaws of the Marsh*:

> Her face is like a lotus calyx, her lips resemble a cherry. Her two eyebrows are blue portraying distant mountains, her two eyes are clear, moistened like autumn water. Her slender waist is graceful, the green skirt covers golden lotus; her natural body is fragrant, her silken sleeves lightly hold bamboo shoot arms. A hairpin going diagonally stays in the cloud of chignon, holding her ivory castanet high as she stands on a mat.[16]

The first four phrases are nearly identical to those of a poem in "Du Shiniang Sinks Her Jewel Box in Anger," *Stories to Caution the World*, chapter 32, except for the phrase order.

In Okajima Kanzan's translation, this section too was cleanly excised. In Ming and Qing vernacular fiction, narrative passages were indeed written in spoken Chinese, but descriptions of characters and landscapes were written in rhymed literary Chinese. Such passages heavily used flowery rhetoric, and, to complicate the matter, mixed spoken language here and there. This made it more challenging to apply the *kundoku* approach that had been developed for reading literary Chinese in literary Japanese. Even so, they are not impossible to translate into Japanese. In fact, as stated earlier, Tsuga Teishō's *Stories of Overgrown Fields* translates such passages, if partially.

In *A Popular Account of Loyal Outlaws of the Marsh*, Okajima Kanzan himself retains some descriptions of beautiful looks. For example, he directly translates a passage about Golden Orchid:

Her eyebrows resembled willow leaves of early spring, always containing the rain's resentment and the cloud's melancholy, while her countenance was like peach blossoms of March, secretly holding the wind's feelings and the moon's thoughts. Above all, her jewel-like appearance was enchanting, and her fragrant looks were charmingly graceful.

The language here is quite close to the Chinese style of expression that had been accepted into Japanese tales of war. The reader must have at least been thoroughly familiar with this kind of rhetoric, and it could not have been difficult to follow, so Okajima Kanzan must have judged. Perhaps his judgment as linguist and translator was correct.

Elimination for Absorption's Sake

Of the dozen or so major descriptions of beauty in *Outlaws of the Marsh*, including the above three, excepting the example of Golden Orchid, the majority are untranslated, or in some cases translated in quite a simplified manner. For example, the courtesan Li Ruilan, meaning Fresh Orchid, is described as follows in the Chinese original:

> Li Ruilan was really of an outstanding class by birth. To put it into verse:
>
> Adequate in all ten thousand kinds of art,
> Pear blossoms moistened in the rain, a jewel giving off fragrance,
> A jade-colored bird calling to wake a dreamer in Mount Luofu,
> One almost doubts if one saw a plum blossom's dawn coiffure.[17]

Okajima Kanzan quotes just the first half of the verse, without adopting the form of an interpolated poem:

> In the first place, this Li Ruilan was a famous courtesan, skilled in all ten thousand kinds of art and equipped with performing arts of one hundred kinds. Her appearance was extremely beautiful, suggestive of pear blossoms moistened in the rain or a jewel giving off fragrance. There was none in those days who did not think fondly of her.

Here, Okajima Kanzan does not simply write out the first two lines of the Chinese verse in *kundoku* Japanese. While retaining the Sino-Japanese (*kanbun*) tonality, he changes difficult Chinese expressions into a form somewhat close to the mixed Japanese and Chinese style (*wakan konkōbun*). Where he says, "Her appearance was extremely beautiful, suggestive of pear blossoms moistened in the rain or a jewel giving off fragrance," he expands the original line into two lines. He also adds a phrase not in the original—a conventional expression recurring in Japanese tales: "There was none in those days who did not think fondly of her."

Cultural Context and Selection

In installment 42 of the *Outlaws of the Marsh* is a scene in which the outlaw leader Song Jiang encounters a goddess in his dream. Clad in "a gold-threaded, deep red silk robe" with a sash of jewels from a famous mountain, she wears "nine-dragon, flying-phoenix loops on her head," and "a scepter of white jade is held in a colorful sleeve." Her face is "like a lotus calyx," her eyebrows "shine under her chignon of clouds," her lips "resemble a cherry." Her immortal visage is "beyond portrayal" and her dignified form "refuses depiction."[18]

Many expressions used here were still rather unfamiliar in Japan. Despite that, *A Popular Account of Loyal Outlaws of the Marsh* rendered the majority of the lines directly into *kundoku* Japanese. The portrayal of Jade Orchid quoted above also included a couplet: "Her face is like a lotus calyx, her lips resemble a cherry." But this was omitted in the Japanese translation. In contrast, the original here was put into Japanese nearly in its entirety except for the last two lines, which are condensed into a conventional Japanese phrase: "Indeed she did not look like an ordinary woman."

The same can be also observed in the description of two fairy maids who appear in installment 88: "Their garments were of red silk and gold thread, their faces were like the full moon, their hands like tender bamboo shoots."[19] Okajima Kanzan, in *A Popular Account of Loyal Outlaws of the Marsh*, chapter 41 (volume 3), provided a *kundoku* rendition, although skipping the fourth phrase. Why he skipped the portrayal of Jade Orchid but left this description is unclear.

Excision was probably done with an eye to the flow of the passage. Descriptions of appearances that take the form of interpolated poetry are wordy and tend to interfere with the story. While poetic interpolations were a point of appreciation in vernacular Chinese fiction, this was not an implicit understanding in Japan. Excising them caused hardly any hindrance to enjoying the development of the story. Consideration for the reader's taste or lack of familiarity may have contributed to his standard of selection.

However, we cannot ignore the meaning of including some portions by way of *kundoku* instead of skipping all such interpolations. Okajima Kanzan's attempts were passed down into the styles of Takebe Ayatari in his *Japanese Outlaws of the Marsh* (*Honchō Suikoden*, 1773) and Santō Kyōden in his *Loyal Retainers: Outlaws of the Marsh* (*Chūshin Suikoden*, 1801), thereby exerting great influence on the idiom of "reading books."

Double Eyelids Enter the Stage

By the time *Japanese Outlaws of the Marsh* was published, the situation had changed greatly. Revolving around an eighth-century battle against Dōkyō, a charlatan and pretender to the throne, this fiction echoes the style of Chinese *Outlaws* but is rendered into smooth, native Japanese. Compared with the *Tale of Nishiyama*, the difference is so great that one almost wonders if it belongs to the same author. For example, we find the following description of a fair-looking woman, who appears before a man called Yumiya no Toshio, who is selecting an ugly woman for a servant:

> She seemed about seventeen or eighteen years of age, with eyebrows very slim, eyelids charmingly overlapping, nose neat looking, lips deep red, hair jet black and long, and a face white and shiny. Her limbs were slender and graceful, the front and back of her body were flawless in a garment dyed the color of wisteria over white and red inner robes, and a brocade sash nicely tied with its ends richly hanging down. As she walked in, the other women present seemed darker than mountain crows on the snow and more terrible than spines on the shoots of trifoliate orange side by side with the first cherry blossoms of the year.[20]

In comparison with Heian period narrative tales and Kamakura period tales of war, description of beauty has become extremely concrete. While titled after *Outlaws of the Marsh*, its content is unrelated to the Chinese source. Nor is anything equivalent to the above quotation found in the original. We can call this approach to the realistic details of the facial features epoch-making. Although Chinese fiction in the vernacular may refer to such details as eyes and nose in describing women's good looks, it depended much on the rhetoric of comparison to flowers and leaves. The above example is largely free of such convention.

This description finally begins to make visible the standards for female beauty. While retaining the traditional aesthetic view that favors white skin, red lips, and long, black hair, it also reveals significant changes. Regarding slim eyebrows as beautiful is the same as in *The Story of Yoshitsune* (*Gikeiki*, Muromachi period), but slender limbs clearly represent a new sense of beauty. "Three Words and Two Slaps" and *Outlaws of the Marsh* frequently use such expressions as *delicate fingers, jewel-like bamboo shoots,* and *spring scallion*, and white, slender fingers served as a metaphor for a beautiful woman. The small size of bound feet, as represented by Golden Lotus (a name alluding to her delicate lotus-petal footprints), was also viewed as symbolic of feminine beauty. The phrase *her limbs were slender* in the above passage probably reflects such foreign aesthetic.

What is most surprising is "eyelids charmingly overlapping." No mention whatever of double eyelids is seen in Chinese literature before the late Qing. It is unclear whether double eyelids were ever thought beautiful in China before the introduction of Western culture. Takebe Ayatari's *Japanese Outlaws of the Marsh* indicates that in Japan the aesthetic sense favoring double eyelids already existed prior to that.

Finding double eyelids attractive was probably not a matter of fiction removed from reality, but of everyday life. *Customs, Manners, and Fashions of the Capital* records an eye makeup method in "Part I, Face." It does not at all say that double eyelids are attractive, but cosmetic illustrations include such eyes. There may not have been today's adoration of double eyelids then. But it was probably known that double eyelids gave brighter looks to the eyes than single eyelids.

Reception of "Slender Fingers"

Another noteworthy phenomenon is the introduction of the description of slender fingers. If the aforementioned translation by Okajima Kanzan had provided a start, we may say that Takebe Ayatari's *Japanese Outlaws of the Marsh* played a greater role in establishing related expressions. In fact, besides the above quotation, the same fiction contains a more detailed reference:

> Thus seen face-to-face, she looked particularly clean and graceful. As she intentionally rumpled her hair just slightly, slender nails show through the jet-black, glossy strands, and between the front lapels of her robe her skin just like snow.[21]

Although the reference is to slender nails, the passage in fact seems to celebrate slender fingers. While, in China, the aesthetic sense that holds slender fingers to be an attribute of a beautiful woman goes back to the rhyme-prose of the Six Dynasties period, it does not seem to have been accepted until the Muromachi period in native Japanese literature. Similar expressions began to recur in Edo period "reading books," but this was not because of the influence of Chinese classics. Rather, it was because they began to adopt the idiom for the portrayal of beautiful women from fiction in literary Chinese like *New Lamp-Wick Trimming Tales* and *Supplementary Lamp-Wick Trimming Tales*, and vernacular fiction like the "Three Words and Two Slaps." A poem called "Delicate Fingers" in "An Account of Lanlan" in *Supplementary Lamp-Wick Trimming Tales* praises slim, white fingers in the following manner:

Delicate tender jewel carved into spring scallions
Long remained within fragrant thin robes and green sleeves.
Yesterday they were on the strings of a zither.
Visibly dyeing the entire back of her hand crimson red.

Here delicate fingers are likened to thin scallions of the spring. "An Account of Lanlan" raises, as representative features of beauty, six parts of the body: "chignon of clouds" (topknot), "willow brows" (slender eyebrows), "*dan* mouth" (red lips like *dan* leaves in the fall), "yoghurt" (milky smooth, white chest), "slender fingers" (thin, delicate fingers), "fragrant hooks" (bound feet). The list places slender fingers fifth. This suggests that, in comparison with the preceding period, slim fingers were even better liked in the Ming and Qing periods. Okajima Kanzan, Takebe Ayatari, and others contributed toward forming the idiom for beautifully depicting slender fingers in Japanese literature as well.

Not just in literature, there may already have been the awareness of slender fingers as beautiful in real life. Section 1 in chapter 3 of Saikaku's *The Life of an Amorous Man* (*Kōshoku ichidai otoko*, 1682) refers to "having [girls] sleep with rings around their fingers and *tabi* socks on their feet." In the Kyoto area, the sentence conveys, young girls were encouraged to sleep with rings on their fingers so that they would remain slim when they grow older. If this was indeed a fact, depiction in "reading books" was no mere rhetorical imitation but had a real-life background.

Such being the case, Takizawa Bakin's fiction often rhetorically equates slim fingers and feminine beauty. As I will discuss later, "books of human feeling" (*ninjōbon*) by Tamenaga Shunsui (1790–1843) also portray slender fingers as part of feminine beauty.

Because the aesthetic sense favoring small, white hands exists in the West as well, perhaps we can say there is a certain amount of universality about it. Possibly, a similar aesthetic had existed in Japan before it was transmitted from the continent. At least, there must have been readiness for reception thereof.

A trace of similar aesthetics can be found in real life. "Section 2, Hands and Feet" in part 2 of *Customs, Manners, and Fashions of the Capital* not only states that "when hands and feet are delicately slender and gracefully supple, that is called an indication of beauty," but introduces cosmetic methods for making hands and feet slender. Massage methods are detailed in sections such as "How to Make Fat Fingers of Hands and Feet Slender, Knuckled and Hard Fingers Tender, and Short Fingers Longer" and "How to Make Hands and Feet White and Glossy, Fat Hands Slender and Supple."

4. ALLEGORY OF FLOWERS

Beautiful Women in Santō Kyōden

In Chinese literature, indescribable female beauty is often compared to flowers. Fiction in the vernacular, especially, frequently uses that sort of metaphor.

Japan first encountered this idiom through Chinese verse and prose as in "The Song of Lasting Regret." In native Japanese literature, comparisons of beautiful women to flowers are seen in *The Tale of Genji* as well as in poetic anthologies predating it.

In "companion tales," shorter prose narratives known as *otogizōshi* that flourished from the Muromachi to early Edo period, comparisons to flowers likewise occur, but in later times flowers increased in variety. "Little Atsumori" ("Ko-Atsumori") introduces the child's mother and Atsumori's bereaved wife as follows: "With dark blue eyebrows, radiant red-fruit lips, an iris form, the red of the lotus blossoms of the Taikei Lake, the green of the willows by the Miō Palace with eyebrow ink charmingly lustrous, the skin of white ovata blossoms, the fragrance of orchid—her countenance was entrancing."[22] Here are not only "lotus" and "willow" but "iris," "white ovata," and even orchid. Particularly interesting is a passage in "The Bowl Wearer" ("Hachikazuki"), which describes a maiden who wore a pot over her head because of a divine oracle that commanded it: "If one were to liken the Bowl Wearer's appearance to things, it would be the fragrance of bayberry, peach, and plum blossoms, over which the moon shines through the clouds; the way weeping willow branches sway in the wind in the middle of the second month; or pinks within the fence looking fragile under heavy dew and shyly facing sideways—her charming face was so beautiful."[23] Besides quickly listing bayberry, peach, and plum blossoms, it also compares the maiden to "pinks," a traditionally favored metaphor in Japan but absent in Chinese literature. Among such Japanese versions of rhetorical speech are also "early spring weeping cherry" in the same story and "maiden flowers abloom in profusion" in "The Story of the Melon Princess" ("Urihime monogatari").

Authors of "reading books" inherited such idioms and further adopted expressions from Chinese fiction in the vernacular. As mentioned earlier, Okajima Kanzan's translation, *A Popular Account of Loyal Outlaws of the Marsh*, skips some descriptions of women. In "reading books," however, voluble portrayals with ornate rhetorical speech came to be favored. For example, Santō Kyōden creatively arranges in *Loyal Retainers: Outlaws of the Marsh* a portrait of Lady Kaoyo on the basis of the depiction in *Outlaws of the Marsh*:

A group of women dressed in courtly style advanced. Each wore a veil over her. From afar, they suggested colorful clouds flying in the wind. Looked at nearby, they were mistaken for fragrant flowers smiling in the rain. As Moronao fixed his eyes to gaze, there was a lady at the center with many maids and child servants on her left and right holding a hinoki fan in one hand up close to her forehead to shade the sun. Lightly treading in lotus steps, she was coming this way like a flowering branch lured by the wind. Indeed, she appeared ready to move a man of fully sophisticated taste. He simply saw:

A shiny, gold hairpin diagonally pierces the raven clouds,
Skillfully tailored jade sleeves cover the snow-white skin.
Her cherry-like mouth lightly assumes a soft red shade,
Her hands of spring bamboo extend tender fingers halfway.
Her face resembles charming flowers of the third month,
Secretly holds the wind's sentiment and the moon's thought.
Her eyebrows are like tender willow of early spring,
Always containing the rain's resentment and the clouds' sorrow.
Her jewel-like countenance is enchanting, her fragrant shape graceful.
Unless this were Chang'e of the Moon Palace descending to earth,
Certainly it must be the Dragon Princess of the Seashell-Built Palace visiting
    the human world.

This woman was none other than Lady Kaoyo, wife of Lord En'ya.

The descriptive method here perfectly follows the idiom in Chinese fiction in the vernacular, adopting the form of an interpolated poem following the phrase, "He simply saw" (Chinese *dan jian*; Japanese *tada miru*). The verse blends depictions of two young women in *Outlaws of the Marsh*, Jade Orchid and Golden Lotus. Lines 5–9, in particular, are virtually identical to the metric portrayal of Golden Lotus.

Attempts at Japanization

Santō Kyōden was probably the first to freely use the technique of character portrayal in Chinese vernacular fiction. He did not merely accept the idiom of describing beautiful women in *Outlaws of the Marsh*. What is significant is that, after digesting the original, he assimilated it into the Japanese language. His addition of *kana* for Japanese pronunciation at the side of Chinese words particularly contributed to Japanization of the foreign style. Efforts to incorporate Chinese verse and prose into a native Japanese context had repeatedly been made since *The Taiheiki*. Nevertheless, Santō Kyōden's bold application is striking. His imitation of the form of expression and the use of rhetoric and cliché—like "he simply saw"—of Chinese vernacular fiction exerted great influence on later "reading books." Takizawa Bakin's fiction, in particular, richly inherits such technique.

Expectedly, Kyōden brought into his vision earlier Chinese literature as well as vernacular fiction. The depiction of the heroine in a section of *The Full Account of Sakurahime* (*Sakurahime zenden akebono sōshi*) is based on "The Song of Lasting Regret" rather than on vernacular fiction.

> The lovely side locks resembled the wings of an autumn cicada, while the gently curved moth eyebrows were easy to mistake for the color of distant mountains. It was like waiting for the moon of an autumn night and seeing the clear light that barely shines forth from behind the mountains. It was more refreshing than thinking of lotus flowers of a summer's day and seeing the red splendor when they first break out of the water. Indeed she was not a person of the human world; one simply wondered if Chang'e of the Moon Palace descended to the soiled world below or the Dragon Daughter of the seashell walled palace emerged on the common earth. Because she was raised within inner chambers, she resembled fragrant plum blossoms under the eaves or a warbler flying out of the valley with an enchanting voice. (Story 7, "Monk Seigen of the Kiyomizu Temple Longs for Sakurahime")

Regardless of whether the source is classical verse and prose or vernacular fiction, by Kyōden's time it was possible to assimilate descriptions of beauty from Chinese literature. But he did not simply render original passages into *kundoku* Japanese. In the above example, the first two phrases echo "The Song of Lasting Regret." But the next lines, about the moon and lotuses, are his own addition in a style not found in works like *Outlaws of the Marsh*. The passage represents an arrangement of Chinese expressions with the use of an original device.

It is also noteworthy that Kyōden rewrote Chinese clichés into Japanese-style equivalents. *The Tale of Udumbara Flowers* describes a beautiful woman whom Kyōjirō, the central male character, encounters:

> She seemed sixteen or so years of age. Her eyes of lotus petals and form of willow were elegant, and eyebrows of katsura and dark-green hair were striking. The way the scent was fragrant on a robe as thin as cicada wings, of what weave he did not know, was also unparalleled. Seeing this, Kyōjirō wondered if a Heavenly Maiden descended to visit the human world, or the Maiden of the Dragon Palace emerged from the bottom of the sea to enjoy herself. Thinking that she could not be a child of a human, his soul and heart wandered out of him, and he was bewildered that he was unable to control himself. (Part 2, section 3)

Both "lotus" and "willows" are metaphors for beauty in Chinese literature. At first glance, the words here seem to be clichés in the manner of "The Song of Lasting Regret," but in fact combinations of words like *eyes of lotus flowers*, *form of willow*, and *eyebrows of katsura* (where the name of the tree in the moon stands for the crescent moon itself) do not appear in Chinese literature. Such rhetoric is based on earlier Japanese literary works. Kyōden resorts here to *eyes of lotus flowers* and *appearance of willows* found in Asai Ryōi's "The Peony Lantern." As suggested by such expressions as "a Heavenly Maiden descended to visit the human world, or the Maiden of the Dragon Palace emerged from the bottom of the sea to enjoy herself," methods had already been prepared to replace the Chinese "divine woman" and "immortal woman" by more Japanese expressions and legendary figures, including the beautiful maiden in the Urashima legend, in which Urashima Tarō visits the underwater Dragon Palace and lives with her for three immortal years. With the use of such devices, difficult Chinese expressions came to be offered in a more accessible form either in a mixture of Chinese and Japanese literary styles (*wakan konkōbun*) or in an eclectic style combining the literary and the vernacular (*gazoku setchūtai*).

However, in describing beautiful women, Kyōden seems to have hardly considered whether his portrayal matched Japanese reality. For example, "Mount Shinobu," part 1 of *An Account of the Loyal Vassal Utō Yasukata* (*Utō Yasukata chūgi den*, 1806), contains the following description:

> To begin with, this daughter was a beauty so beyond compare that she could be called the country's finest or a lady of an immortal's appearance. She looked as if the moon appeared over green mountains, and her makeup resembled plum blossoms blooming within the fence. Lovely side locks pretend to be the wings of a fall cicada, and a pair of gently curved moth eyebrows appears to be the color of distant mountains.

The last line consists of set phrases Kyōden fondly used, but in "lovely side locks pretend to be the wings of a fall cicada, and a pair of gently curved moth eyebrows appears to be the color of distant mountains," he renders Chinese-style descriptions into native Japanese. As with "almost mistaken for plum blossoms putting on dawn makeup" in installment 69 of *Outlaws of the Marsh*, "plum blossom makeup" is a makeup method (figure 7.1). However, there probably was no similar makeup in Japan then. In fact, *Customs, Manners, and Fashions of the Capital* contains no such cosmetic approach. Kyōden simply uses plum blossoms as a metaphor for a beautiful woman rather than describing an actual makeup.

When Kyōden introduced such Chinese diction, at the same time he adopted expressions from Japanese literature basically written in *kana*. Such an approach later spread as a convention for the portrayal of beautiful women. Similar expressions are still frequently found in Meiji era translations. I would like to discuss this further in chapter 8.

Figure 7.1. *Woman with Plum Blossom Makeup*. The Museum of Xinjiang Uyghur Autonomous Region. *Source:* Gao Chunming and Zhou Xun, *Zhongguo lidai funü zhaungshi (Generations of Chinese Women's Makeup)*. Xuelin Publishing House, 1988, figure 172.

Associations between Flowers and Beautiful Women

Kyōden's description of appearances still strongly retains Chinese fragrance. Takizawa Bakin, while inheriting Kyōden's method, approached one step closer to vernacular Japanese. Bakin is bolder in adopting the vocabulary and rhetoric of Chinese vernacular fiction. Part 1 of Bakin's *The Crescent Moon (Chinsetsu yumiharizuki*, 1811) contains the following passage:

> A beautiful woman of about twice eight years of age, she wore an outfit neither of the capital nor of the country. Even the faint fragrance on her two-layered robe, light blue outside and deep red inside, was exquisite. Her eyebrows of the moon were elegant, her waist of willow supple, no different from making crab apple blossoms bloom on a cherry branch and assume color and scent of lotus flower.... The sight of her plucking a thirteen stringed zither made him wonder if a Heavenly Maiden came to visit the temple or the Princess of the Dragon's Palace was enjoying herself in the human world, so that he felt as if his heart was melting and his soul vanishing.[24]

This imitates the above-quoted passage from Kyōden's *The Tale of Udumbara Flowers*, but the first half hardly resembles the source. The imitation seems to start with "wonder if a Heavenly Maiden came." Considering that portrayals of feminine beauty in Chinese fiction in the vernacular often show little difference from story to story, it may be the case that Bakin also simply repeated conventional phrases.

When comparing the first half of the quotation with the source, we notice, in Bakin's rhetoric of likening the eyebrows to the moon and the waist to willow, his intention is to emphasize a difference from Kyōden. Reading it closely, it may be that Bakin not only did not take note of Kyōden's rhetorical adventure but even tried to suggest that his predecessor had "misused" the rhetoric. Bakin may have been confident of having greater descriptive skills than Kyōden.

Rhetoric comparing beautiful looks to flowers was common in Chinese literature. In Japan too, as discussed earlier, a beautiful woman is sometimes likened to a flower in *The Tale of Genji*. However, as a whole, there are relatively few such cases in Heian narrative literature.

Starting with *The Tale of the Heike*, through quotations from Chinese sources, the same rhetoric began to be brought into Japanese writings of the mixed Japanese and Sino-Japanese style. "Countenance of peach and plum" and "form of lotus flower" ("The Empress Takes the Tonsure") are examples. By association, a method of likening women to other familiar flowers like cherry blossoms eventually came to be used. That is the reason that chapter 21 of *The Taiheiki* compares feminine beauty to cherry blossoms of Arashiyama and Yoshino, two places famous for cherry trees. The passage quoted above from *The Crescent Moon* also includes "cherry branch."

Flowers as metaphors change over time in China, too. "Lotus" and "willow" came to be widely known through "The Song of Lasting Regret," but later, in addition to "lotus" and "peach blossoms" ("her face was like peach blossoms of the third month"), "crab apple," "pear blossoms" (also in "The Song of Lasting Regret"), "lotus flowers," "peony flower," and "orchid flowers" too gained their places as metaphors.

There are examples in fiction in literary Chinese as well, but the following can be listed from *Outlaws of the Marsh*: "her face like a lotus calyx" (installment 44), "a naturally beautiful face, crab apple blossoms" (48), "a mouth of cherry, face of apricot, chin of peach, waist of willow, heart of orchid, temperament of *hui* (a kind of orchid)" (51), "capable of every art, pear flowers wet in the rain giving off a lovely fragrance" (69), "her countenance was like crab apple holding morning dew" (81), "her face resembled peony embracing spring mist" (88, the Rung'yu Studio edition).

Rhetoric of Wordplay

In Chinese literature, comparing beautiful looks to flowers goes back to olden days. But from the Ming period it began to be used in the form of fixed phrases. This is probably related to the genre of writings devoted to evaluating courtesans, which often compared famous women of the arts to flowers in ranking them. This approach contributed to establishing correspondence or associative relations between beauty and flowers. Later, such rhetoric was also used in fiction in describing beautiful women.

Under the influence of Chinese fiction in the vernacular, flower metaphors were adopted in Edo period "reading books." In the description quoted above, Bakin uses "crab apple blossoms" precisely in that context. In the first place, "making crab apple blossoms bloom on a cherry branch" is hyperbole. If we were to examine the passage literally, it is nearly impossible to interpret what "making crab apple blossoms bloom on a cherry branch and assume color and scent of lotus flower" means. It must be because the rhetorical context already existed that such an expression was acceptable.

However, likening a beautiful woman to a flower is already seen in "companion tales." "The Tale of the Rat" (mid-Muromachi period) describes Yanagiya Saburozaemon's daughter: "Her form was a willow swaying in the wind, a crab apple in the garden that smiles in the spring rain with its sleeping blossoms, from whose shade, as if there were more to the spring than flowers and birds, rises a hazy moon through the mist bringing a dimly lit night that a poet once sang of as having no peer."[25] This is quite close to Bakin's style. Both passages may share common sources, but the process of reception may have been more complicated in this tale. Even today a beautiful woman may be described as "She stands a peony, she sits a tree peony, and when she walks, walks a lily flower." It is unknown who introduced this, but it may be somehow related to the rhetoric in "reading books."[26]

On the other hand, as in *The Crescent Moon*, in some cases "wildflowers" may serve as a metaphor instead of any specific flower:

> Her skin was so very white that it could rival the snow on Mount Su, her long and lovely black hair could be mistaken for the willows by the Night-Is-Young Palace, a faint scent remaining on her old clothes—her appearance was not lowly. She resembled Xi Shi before entering the Wu court, a wildflower simply beautiful to the eyes; or Komachi when reciting a poem about the jeweled curtain at court, as evening clouds released the moon.[27]

"A wildflower simply beautiful to the eyes" is a phrase found in "Over Fifteen Strings of Cash, a Jest Leads to Dire Disasters" in *Stories to Awaken the World*.[28] "Wildflower" was originally a metaphor for a beautiful woman of lowly status, but Bakin's fiction carries no such nuance. It uses "wildflower" in the same way as "lotus." Chapter 4 of the "Opening Series" of his *Eight Dog Chronicles* used the "first flower" of the season in the same way: "As Fusehime turned sixteen, she was all the more beautiful—like the first flower giving off fragrance under the hesitant moon of the sixteenth night."

The metaphor of "rivaling the snow" is often seen in "reading books." It originated in Chinese vernacular fiction, especially in "The Three Words and Two Slaps." One example is a line in a verse in "Secretary Qian Leaves Poems on the Swallow Tower," story 10 of *Stories to Caution the World*: "Her body defeats the brilliance of the felicitous snow." Story 19, "With a White Falcon, Young Master Cui Brings an Evil Spirit upon Himself," also likens the whiteness of the moon to that of the snow: "Its white sheen rivals the felicitous snow."[29]

Tamenaga Shunsui's Beautiful Women

Did Bakin's descriptions of beauty match reality? In fact it is difficult to verify that. In the first place, his text arranges ornate phrases without necessarily indicating clearly how a face or body is shaped. References to physical features are quite limited, not going beyond white skin, narrow waist, black hair, slim fingers, and so forth. In some descriptions rhetorical excess even makes the reader think they say nothing after all.

Literary styles in the Edo period differed depending upon the audience. The portrayal of beautiful women in "books of human feeling" assumes a somewhat different character than that in "reading books":

> The top courtesan in the room is eighteen or nineteen years of age. She looks exactly like Kikunojō, the late kabuki actor who impersonated women. She wears a divided chignon with fine hairpins. Her neck showing above lowered kimono collar is whiter than snow. Her light makeup, with white powder called Immortal Woman's Scent applied to the skin polished with rubbing bran, is particularly elegant. She wears a kimono with the solid-color sleeves and hem framing the torso part made of foreign print, and over it a light brown unpadded sash braided with lace. Having put away the bedding and neatly cleaned the room, she sits with one knee raised.[30]

This passage is found in Tamenaga Shunsui's *The Love-Tinted Plum Calendar*. The woman's hairstyle is portrayed "realistically," and greater emphasis goes to clothing and posture than to countenance. The author's aesthetic sense that values white skin is no different from that of Bakin, but Chinese-style rhetoric is avoided here. Because Tamenaga Shunsui adopted vernacular Japanese, he may have captured his object with greater visual accuracy than authors of "reading books."

His gaze also differs from Bakin's. Worthy of particular note is his detailed observation of hairstyle and hairdo methods:

There emerges a woman of twenty-one or two with a Shimada-style chignon, tied up after a hair wash, coming loose and tilting somewhat to one side. Her face not yet made up after her bath is unaffectedly beautiful, with a hint of flush showing at the corners of eyes faintly tinted of cherry blossoms. She lets out a sigh, smiles, then a curt word or two as she slides a paper door shut.[31]

On reading this passage, I almost doubt whether there was any need, in early Meiji, to imitate character descriptions from Western literature. In this vivid portrayal of the woman after bathing, sketches of the chignon, facial color, expression, and gesture can even be said to be a model of realism. With the absence of such Chinese-style clichés as "green hair" and "willow waist," the text captured the character's looks and gestures all the more precisely.

Naturally, Tamenaga Shunsui did not totally abandon Chinese-style expressions. Such phrases as *flowery smile and melancholy eyes* (series 1, part 3, section 6) and *fifteen years of age with a face of the moon of the fifteenth day, a lovely form with a mouth of a blossom* (series 1, part 3, section 6) are probably derived from Chinese wordings.

In "books of human feeling" like *The Love-Tinted Plum Calendar*, white skin, red lips, black hair, and slim fingers remain symbols of feminine beauty. As far as this goes, this genre does not differ from "reading books." But the texts not only compare white skin to the snow but sometimes describe it directly, as in "lucky that her facial features are perfect and her skin is white" (*The Love-Tinted Plum Calendar*, series 2, chapter 6, section 12). Fingers also sometimes receive naturalistic treatment, as in "slim fingers lightly holding the large coral bead attached to the tip of her silver hairpin, and, eyebrows knit, she scratches herself under one earlobe" (*The Love-Tinted Plum Calendar*, series 3, chapter 9, section 18).

However, emphasis on slender torso does not appear in works like *The Love-Tinted Plum Calendar*. Nor are white teeth held as beautiful. Neither Bakin nor Shunsui refers to white teeth in depicting beautiful women. Shunsui does once refer to "an innocent girl with appealing white teeth" (*Love-Tinted Garden of Fukagawa*, series 1, part 3, installment 5), but this in fact is designed to introduce a double meaning: "a girl with white teeth innocent of romantic interest," punning on the word "innocent" (*shirazu*) with "white teeth" (*shiraha*).

How far the descriptions in fiction match real life is difficult to determine. This applies not only to Shunsui, but to Bakin as well. Reading Bakin's fiction, I notice that he avoids referring concretely to eyebrows and teeth. Naturally, he praises thin eyebrows when following a Chinese-style portrayal. For example, "the moon eyebrows so elegant" (*The Crescent Moon*, part 1, chapter 5) emphasizes the beauty of thin eyebrows curved like the moon of the third day. However, on the whole he introduces few descriptions of this type; rather, in most cases he avoids describing eyebrows. Nor does he refer to a woman's white teeth.

Bakin was not uninterested in eyebrows. In describing men, he refers to thin eyebrows and white teeth. Moreover, he sometimes applies to men expressions originally for women. *Eight Dog Chronicles* says, "The skin of his face is white and his beard is green. His fine eyebrows are like distant mountains, his clear eyes resemble the twin stars. With a tall nose and red lips, he is one likable man" (series 5, part 2, installment 44). But "fine eyebrows are like distant mountains" originated as an expression used for women.

This of course is not Bakin's rhetorical innovation. Such an approach is already seen in Chinese fiction in the vernacular. For example, *Outlaws of the Marsh*, chapter 9, introduces an idling aristocrat nicknamed "Little Whirlwind" as possessing "lustrous teeth, vermilion lips," and in *Outlaws of the Marsh, a Sequel* (1664), chapter 1 contains an expression, "his face is white and lips are red, eyebrows are dark and eyes excellent." Influence of such expressions is certainly conceivable.

In Edo, it was customary for married women to shave their eyebrows. The reason that Bakin did not describe women's eyebrows in detail probably has something to do with this. Likewise, the reason he did not praise white teeth also seems connected to the custom of teeth blackening.

Concerning what sort of aesthetic sense there was in real life, another late-Edo author Shikitei Sanba writes something interesting in series 2, chapter 1, of *The Barbershop of the Floating World* (*Ukiyodoko*, 1813):

> She must already be thirty-seven or eight, but she's still with her eyebrows. Talk about lovely, this is a woman who doesn't shave off her eyebrows when she should, so she's handicapped. True. Kin with monsters, so to speak. Not in the same group as human beings.[32]

According to this description, a married woman is better looking without eyebrows, and she is akin to a monster if she keeps them. Tamenaga Shunsui also refers to the shaving of eyebrows. In *Love-Tinted Garden of Fukagawa*, a comment runs: "Then, she'll shave her eyebrows and tie her hair up with a round chignon, and she'll turn into such a good-looking mature woman" (part 3, chapter 7). This too suggests that in Edo married women were more appealing with eyebrows shaven. Utamaro's *A Beautiful Reader* (figure 7.2) can serve as supporting evidence.

However, we must be careful about the fact that, from portrayal in fiction, we can see only a portion of the actual sense of beauty. By bringing together literary representations with visual representations, we have the best possibility of grasping standards of beauty.

Figure 7.2. *Ten Types of Women's Physiognomies: A Beautiful Reader.* Tokyo National Museum. Source: Yamaguchi Keizaburō, ed., *Utamaro I, Meihin soroimono ukiyo-e (Illustrated Sets of Ukiyo-e)*, 12 vols. Gyōsei, 1991, figure 1.

NOTES

1. Matsuda Osamu, Watanabe Morikuni, and Hanada Fujio (annotators), *Otogi bōko* (SNKBT 75, 2001), 78.
2. Qu You, *Jiandeng xinhua*. Translated from "Botan dōro" in Iizuka Akira (tr.), *Sentō shinwa* (*Tōyō Bunko* 48) (Heibonsha, 1965).
3. Hiroshi Kitagawa and Bruce T. Tsuchida (trs.), *The Tale of The Heike*, vol. 1 (University of Tokyo Press, 1977), 34.
4. Noma Kōshin (ed.), *Otogi monotagari* (*Koten Bunko* 65, 1952), 99–100.
5. Ibid., 200–01.
6. Asō Isoji, Itasaka Gen, and Tsutsumi Seiji (annotators), *Saikaku shū*, vol. 1 (NKBT 47, [1957] 1977), 154–55.
7. Ibid., 164.
8. Ibid., 154–55.
9. Cf. Tatsuma Shōsuke's translation in Komada Shinji and Tatsuma Shōsuke (trs.), *Kokin kikan*, vol. 2 (*Chūgoku Koten Bungaku Taikei* [hereafter CKBT] 38, Heibonsha, 1973). The verse, not appearing in Tatsuma's translation, was provided by the author.
10. Nakamura Yukihiko et al. (annotators and translators), *Hanabusa sōshi* (in *Nihon Koten Bungaku Zenshū* 48, 1973), 91.

11. Shuhui Yang and Yunqin Yang (trs.), *Stories to Caution the World: A Ming Dynasty Collection*, vol. 2 (University of Washington Press, 2005), 548.

12. Tokuda Takeshi and Yokoyama Kuniharu (annotators), *Shigeshige yawa, Kyokutei denki hanakanzashi, Saibara kidan, Toribeyama shirabe no itomichi* (SNKBT 80, 1992).

13. Li Linian et al. (editors), *Shuihu zhuan* (Jiangsu Guji Publishing House, 1989), 352. Cf. Komada Shinji (tr.), *Suikoden*, vol. 1 (CKBT 28). The phrase "Feiyan newly attired" comes from the second of the three "Poems in the Pure and Plain Mode" ("Qingping-diao ci") by Li Bo.

14. *Shigeshige yawa* (SNKBT 80), 52.

15. Chapter 14 (installment 29) of the original. *Suihu zhuan* (Jiangsu Guji edition), 316. Cf. *Suikoden*, vol. 1 (CKBT 28), 363.

16. *Shuihu zhuan* (Jiangsu Guji edition), 322.

17. *Shuihu zhuan* (Jiangsu Guji edition), 753. Cf. *Suikoden*, vol. 2 (CKBT 29), 397.

18. *Shuihu zhuan* (Jiangsu Guji edition), 464.

19. Sidney Shapiro (tr.), *Outlaws of the Marsh*, vol. 5, 2677, based on the Rong'yu Studio edition of *Shuihu zhuan* (951 in the Jiangsu Guji edition), which Okajima Kanzan seems to have used. This passage does not appear in the Japanese translation of Komada Shinji, whose work is not based on the Rong'yu Studio edition.

20. Takada Mamoru et al. (annotators), *Honchō Suikoden* (SNKBT 79, 1992), 118.

21. Ibid., 240.

22. Ichiko Teiji (annotator), *Otogizōshi* (NKBT 38 ([1958] 1977), 233.

23. Ibid., 70.

24. Gotō Tanji (annotator), *Chinsetsu yumiharizuki*, vol. 1 (NKBT 60, [1958] 1976).

25. A reference to a celebrated poem by Ōe no Chisato ("Shin Kokinshū," no. 55): "Neither all clear / nor totally cast over / the spring night's / hazily shining moon / has no peer indeed."

26. The Japanese original is in the 7/7/7/5 rhythm known as *dodoitsu*, a form of popular origin that was perfected by Dodoitsu Bōsenka in 1838.

27. *Chinsetsu yumiharizuki*, vol. 2 (NKBT 61), 192, in chapter 2 of the "Gleanings."

28. "Wildflowers are more eye-catching" in Shuhui Yang and Yunqin Yang's translation, *op. cit.*, vol. 2, 773.

29. See ibid., vol. 2, 150 and 301. Bakin uses the expression *rival the snow* about handsome men as well in his fiction. Installment 33, chapter 2 of the fourth series of *The Eight Virtuous Heroes*, for example, describes Kobungo's skin in that manner: "Well-fattened, the whiteness of his skin could rival the snow."

30. Nakamura Yukihiko (annotator), *Shunshoku umegoyomi* (NKBT 64, [1962] 1978), 151 (in series 3, chapter 7, section 7).

31. *Shunshoku umegoyomi*, 179 (in series 3, chapter 9, section 18).

32. Honda Yasuo (annotator), *Ukiyodoko, Shijūhachi-kuse* (*Shinchō Nihon Koten Shūsei* 52, 1982), 134.

8

Until Naomi Was Born

1. ENCOUNTER WITH WESTERN BEAUTY

Similarities and Differences between West and East

Over the last one hundred years, various aesthetic premises of Western cultures have become familiar in East Asia. There are no tremendous differences in contemporary East Asian views of feminine beauty from those of the West. Before modern times this was not the case, however. Large eyes, for example, are regarded as beautiful today and are made abnormally large in such things as visual fiction targeted at girls and young females (*shōjo manga*). The situation was totally different just one century or so ago. Li Yu of Qing era China said, in his *Occasional Contemplations*, that women with "large, wild eyes" are tough and unyielding, and that those with "thin, long eyes" are gentle-hearted. Not only did he not evaluate large eyes positively, but he considered them a shortcoming.

So, too, in Edo Japan. The author of *Customs, Manners, and Fashions of the Capital* considered that women "should, when going out or attending a formal occasion, keep their eyes at eight-tenths level, looking down rather than straight ahead." He further introduces a concrete method for achieving this eye level: "'Eyes at eight-tenths level' means you should, when standing, look about two yards away from your feet; and, when seated, just beyond one yard away from your knees. If you follow this rule, your eyes will be downcast by themselves, looking narrow." Wide eyes were considered ugly.

As mentioned in the previous chapter, small hands and feet were regarded as traits of feminine beauty in early modern China. The desire to make feet small even went to the extent of physical alteration by foot binding. Although Japan did not go to this extreme, according to *Customs, Manners, and Fashions of the Capital*, dainty hands and feet were "indications of feminine beauty."

Still, there were certain common features between "the beautiful woman" of the East and that of the West before modern times. For example, a straight nose was evaluated highly in both West and East. A statement in *Customs, Manners, and Fashions of the Capital* is illustrative: "Because the nose is at the center of the face and catches others' eyes, it is desirable that its ridge is straight" (chapter 1, "Face"). The view that white skin is beautiful had also existed before receiving the influence of the West.

Naturally, things vary from region to region within the East. In late Qing China, for example, narrow eyebrows and white teeth were important elements of feminine beauty. No similar aesthetic awareness existed in Edo Japan, where the custom of blackening the teeth and shaving the eyebrows prevailed.

Such differences aside, the ideal images of beauty in Qing China and Edo Japan share a number of common features. Their shared views can be roughly summarized as follows: The ideal skin is white and smooth; the nose straight and the hair luxurious; double eyelids are pretty, but single eyelids are acceptable if they are clear. The phrase *cool-looking eyes* lacks concreteness, but it can be interpreted to refer to eyes that give a likable impression. The shape of the face was not so important, but relatively speaking, oval faces were favored over round faces.

In terms of physique, slenderness was generally favored. Breasts and hips were not objects of evaluation of beauty. Erotic literature sometimes praised wide hips; but publicly at least, they were not aesthetic objects. Large breasts were hardly regarded as beautiful, not only in principle but also in reality. We find some examples portraying ample breasts in *ukiyo-e* art (figure 8.1), but the number is limited, and no fantasy about well-developed breasts seems to have existed. In China, no example representing large breasts is found even in erotica.

In daily life as well, it was not good either to emphasize breasts and hips or to bring out the body line. Not only that, it was thought to be women's indispensible etiquette to cover breasts and hips by appropriate clothing. *Customs, Manners, and Fashions of the Capital* takes the trouble to include a section on "How to Conceal Protruding Hips to Look Good," and introduces appropriate postures and dress so as to de-emphasize the hips. The reason

Figure 8.1. *Five-Color Ink of the Northern Region: A Low-Class Prostitute* (*Kitaguni goshiki-zumi: teppō*). Source: Kitagawa Utamaro, Musée Guimet. *Utamaro I*, figure 54.

is that "even if a person is by and large good-looking, protruding hips make her deportment greatly inferior and unattractive."

Long legs are thought beautiful today, but such a standard did not exist before modern times.

Single and Double Eyelids

When examining earlier views of feminine beauty, we often turn to literary works. But premodern poetry and fiction, often restricted by stylistic and rhetorical conventions, do not necessarily copy facts as they are. Some fictitious descriptions are at odds with real life.

Paintings tend to be somewhat closer to reality, but varying degrees of stylization exist. More solid evidence than artworks can be found in photographs from Japan's late Tokugawa and China's late Qing. The photograph of Zhenfei, the favorite consort of Emperor Guangxu (1871–1908), is a good example. Concubines were often chosen by looks, and those who received imperial favor were beautiful almost without exception. Zhenfei's photograph (figure 8.2) shows her as straight-nosed and clear-eyed. With a lovely mouth, she is certainly beautiful by today's standard as well.

Figure 8.2. Zhenfei, Emperor Guangxu's Consort. *Source:* Liu Changle et al., *Zhonghua guwenming datuji* II, Shifong. *People's Daily* et al., 1992, 145.

The same is also the case in Japan. A photograph of Niimura Nobu, consort of Tokugawa Yoshinobu, the last shōgun, shows her to be oval-faced and straight-nosed. She is said to have been fair-skinned and slender (figure 8.3).

Looking at these photographs, we realize that traditional aesthetic sense does not clash with Western concepts of beauty but even shares certain common elements. Such overlapping served as a foundation later when accepting mainstream Western conceptions of beautiful women.

Among a number of changes that occurred under the influence of Western sense of beauty, double eyelids and deep-sculpted face should first be mentioned.

Figure 8.3. Niimura Nobu, Consort of Tokugawa Yoshinobu, the Last Shōgun. In the Possession of Ibaraki Prefectural Museum of History. *Source:* POLA Research Institute of Beauty and Culture, ed., *Bakumatsu-Meiji bijinchō*. Shin Jinbutsu Ōraisha, 2002, 18.

Photographs reveal the process of that change. Early Meiji photographs of women include those with single eyelids. However, winners of Japan's first beauty contest, held in 1907 to 1908, overwhelmingly possessed double eyelids. In particular, Suehiro Hiroko, who placed first nationally, is deep-sculpted and double-eyed (figure 8.4). Hinatsu Mineko, who won first place in the Kyoto regional, is one of the few winners who had single eyelids (figure 8.5). How close a woman was to Western beauty probably became a new standard.

Figure 8.4. Suehiro Hiroko, Top National Winner of Japan's First Beauty Contest. In the Possession of POLA Research Institute of Beauty and Culture. *Source:* POLA Research Institute of Beauty and Culture, ed., *Bakumatsu-Meiji bijinchō*. Shin Jinbutsu Ōraisha, 2002, 105.

Figure 8.5. Hinatsu Mineko, Top Kyoto Regional Winner of the Same Contest. In the Possession of POLA Research Institute of Beauty and Culture. *Source:* POLA Research Institute of Beauty and Culture, ed., *Bakumatsu-Meiji bijinchō*. Shin Jinbutsu Ōraisha, 2002, 144.

Beauty in Sino-Japanese Style Literature

In the process of accepting Western sense of beauty, images of attractive women in literature exerted great influence. Naturally, changes in images of beauty in literature are affected by such elements as conventions of expression, so that they do not always follow the same path as in reality. However, literary descriptions certainly play an important role in shaping aesthetic values.

Fiction in translation poses numerous problems of style. If "golden hair" and "blue eyes" abruptly occurred in the text, the intended sense of beauty would not be conveyed to Chinese and Japanese readers. Worse, the reader might think of a monster. Translators were sensitive to such problems.

In fact, there are few examples of faithful rendering of descriptions of beautiful women in early Meiji translations. In those days, there were two distinctive approaches to translation: using the style of Sino-Japanese (*kanbun*) and writing in the style of popular Japanese-language fiction that developed in the Edo period known as "books of human feeling" (*ninjōbon*, narratives of love) or "reading books" (*yomihon*, full-length didactic books). Niwa Jun'ichirō's *Love Story of Flower and Willow* (*Karyū shun'wa*), published in 1878, belongs to the former category. This abridged translation from Edward George Earle Bulwer-Lytton's *Ernest Maltravers* and its sequel *Alice*, departs from the original almost shockingly. A passage runs as follows (rendered in English):

> Not yet twice eight years of age, the woman is so charming that she rivals a precious jewel, with her clouds of hair at the temples slightly in disarray and falling onto her eyelids. She has clear eyes, a tall nose, kingfisher-green eyebrows that arc like crescent moons, and red lips with a peach blossom on them. Once she beamingly smiles, she assumes an appearance of one who might bring the country to ruin with her natural beauty.[1]

This describes Alice, daughter of a wretched factory worker living in a lonely abode, as she first appears in chapter 1 of *Love Story of Flower and Willow*. The style is thoroughly Sino-Japanese (*kanbun*) in nature, studded with conventional Chinese expressions. The language is harder to follow than Japanese-language fiction by such popular late Edo authors as Santō Kyōden and Takizawa Bakin. Rather, it is closer to Okajima Kanzan's *A Popular Account of Loyal Outlaws of the Marsh*, a mid-Edo partial translation of *Outlaws of the March*. The passage in fact resembles portrayals of countenances interpolated in *Outlaws of the Marsh* and other vernacular Chinese fiction. The style of *Love Story of Flower and Willow* must have been felt fairly difficult even in those days when knowledge of premodern Chinese was rather widespread in Japan. The translator must have assumed an audience of a certain cultural level, not of common citizens.

Chapter 19 of *Love Story of Flower and Willow* similarly describes the appealing looks of a society woman called Madame de Ventadour (as retranslated to English):

> Her flowery face reflected stars' light and shone above the railing, clouds of her side locks swayed in the wind and fell onto her lovely eyelids: her graceful form was charming beyond description.... Her hands were delicate and transparent like jeweled branches—beautiful flowers would give way to her in elegance.[2]

Comparison between this and the portrayal of Alice highlights nearly identical patterns of expression. The vocabulary does not differ much between the two, either. The translator achieves some variety merely by combining words differently and replacing some figures of speech with others. As Alice acts timidly elsewhere, "Shyness reveals itself on her face, crab apple suddenly grows red as she turns her head to see the wall" (chapter 1); and on another occasion "lips half smiling, language warm and docile, she demonstrates her naturally beautiful hue like a wildflower blooming in the remote countryside" (chapter 3). There is nothing new about these descriptions.

This style, heavy with Chinese literary diction, is not used throughout the work, however. In chapter 6, Alice is presented "with lips half smiling, speech soft sounding, eyes radiating charm without losing their focused gaze—indeed she should be called a beauty representing an era." Here the tone is close to Edo popular fiction of the "reading books" and "books of human feeling" types.

In the first place, the translation of *Ernest Maltravers* is far from faithful. Depending upon the translator's convenience or fancy, words are arbitrarily added or the original is changed. It is precisely "a crazy translation in which it is hard to know where each passage is translated and how."[3] In short, it is impossible to infer from comparison of the original text and translation the reasons for the translator's choice of style and rhetoric. However, such early translations provide interesting material for learning what images of beauty their translators spontaneously visualized when reading portrayals of characters in foreign literature.

Bakin-Style Western Beauties

Now the second approach: translation of Western literature in the style of "reading books" and "books of human feeling." *Lingering Fragrance of Plum Buds* (*Bairai yokun*) by Ushiyama Ryōsuke (Ushiyama Kakudō) is a typical example. It purports to be a translation of Sir Walter Scott's *Ivanhoe*, but, as with *Love Story of Flower and Willow*, the content is changed to the extent that it is nearly impossible to call it a translation. Of the translation in two parts, the first was published in December of 1886, and the second the following February. The heroine Rowena is given the following description:

> Delicate yet in a nobly gentle attire, and followed by her female servant Elgitha, Rowena slowly carried her lotus steps her skirt fluttering lightly, smiles on her face, she came to this place. Her eyes were cool and compassionate, her eyebrows were neither too dark nor too thin, her mouth was small with lips like a red flower, her teeth thoroughly delicate and white and moreover lustrous, and her freshly knit hair reflected the bright light of the candles on silver stands, her fragrance gave off its scent along with the flowers on the floor. They simply saw: like a doll that came to birth as a result of the artistry and infinite energy of the world's top class sculptor, one smile meant a thousand pieces of gold, and one coquettish look ten thousand *yi*. A monarch of one thousand carriages would lose his state. . . . She was now twice eight years of age, the time when plum buds send their fragrance secretly awaiting a yellow bird. Gentle, gracefully pliant and yet dignified, she carried herself in ways that nobody thought her a maiden of twice eight years of age. She was so well mannered and gentle spoken that at times she would bewitch talented men.[4]

Contrasting this against the original, we find that, except for proper nouns, the content is almost entirely the translator's creation. The style of writing imitates that of "reading books," and terms like *attire*, *lotus steps*, *twice eight* as well as fixed phrases like *eyes cool* and *lips like a red flower* take after Bakin's work.[5] Some Chinese-style expressions are simply read in Sino-Japanese pronunciation, while others are intended for native Japanese reading. This mixed style basically follows the notation method of "reading books." Probably, while conscious of *Love Story of Flower and Willow*, Ushiyama tried to create a different effect. In his approach to description, hardly any originality is recognizable. In those days, when the vernacular writing style known as "unity of written and spoken languages" (*genbun itchi*) had not yet been discovered, it may be that the description itself was impossible without adopting the literary style from the past. Among late-Edo and early Meiji pictorial representations, we also find examples of Western women depicted in a Japanese-looking manner.

Imaginary Western Beauties

Creative works around the same time also used both Sino-Japanese style and the style that mixes literary and vernacular elements. Both cases were at an experimental stage, and the Edo period method of portrayal was basically followed unchanged. Tōkai Sanshi's *Strange Encounters with Beautiful Women* (*Kajin no kigū*, 1885-1897) belongs to the former category. Authors of political novels attempted to use literature as a tool for enlightenment. For this reason, they do not seem to have taken much interest in descriptive techniques.

> As Sanshi lifts his head and looks into the distance, a lady has already come out and waits at the entrance. The sight is as vague as wispy clouds hazily covering the crescent moon, but as he approaches she appears to be like a shining white crane standing on the steps of the immortals' palace. About twenty years of age, although without full makeup or rich ornaments, her cool beauty perfectly rivals the snow; her eyebrows trace the jade of distant mountains and her phoenix side locks are greener than the clouds; although the autumn waves of her eyes carry emotion, their piercing gaze shoots out with hidden dignity and her red cheeks contain a smile, slightly exposing her lustrous teeth; a long skirt of light silk trails down from her slender waist, and as she moves with polished lotus steps in colorfully embroidered light shoes with lingering fragrance reaching out, slow steps come down the steps to meet him. Indeed, one suspects that a beautiful heavenly creature has descended to the human world.[6]

This is a description of a beautiful woman in chapter 1 of *Strange Encounters with Beautiful Women*. The style of portrayal is repeatedly used in other chapters, with different vocabulary and different combinations of words. Words and rhetoric in use offer absolutely nothing new. "Lotus steps," an expression that refers to bound feet, is such a misuse that one might break out laughing. However, the text does not totally ignore facts. The same chapter includes this passage: "Already one lady approaches Sanshi with slow steps, holding her light skirt. Aged twenty-three or four, with green eyes, lustrous teeth, and golden hair flowing down her back." Right after this, the author parenthetically explains: "Westerners regard the green-eyed with shiny, golden hair as beautiful." He seems to pay unexpected attention to the differences in aesthetic sense and context between East and West.

Fiction written in the eclectic style that combines the literary and the vernacular (*gazoku setchūtai*) more often uses a descriptive idiom of "reading books" and "stories of human feeling." Suehiro Tetchō's *Plum Blossoms in the Snow* (*Setchūbai*, 1886) contains such a description in part 1, installment 1:

> She seems to be sixteen or seventeen, with a white face and a straight nose, superior eyebrows and cool-looking eyes. With no makeup, she has natural beauty. Her Shimada-style chignon, which seems to have been done a few days ago, is

slightly in disarray, wisps of black hair falling onto her face; the way she pays attention to her mother's sleeping face as she sheds beads of tears and wipes them with a hand cloth indeed recalls "A branch of pear blossoms wet in the rain in spring."[7]

Here, phrases like *a white face and a straight nose, superior eyebrows and cool-looking eyes* and *a branch of pear blossoms wet in the rain in spring* (the latter being a line from Bo Juyi's "The Song of Lasting Regret") are clichés in the manner of "reading books." They were probably familiar to everyone.

Whether in Sino-Japanese style or "reading book" style, such expressions reiterate stereotypical responses to given situations rather than reflecting actual scenes. We can catch a glimpse of the great influence Edo period literature had in the reception of Meiji political novels.

2. CREATION OF THE IMAGE OF THE MODERN BEAUTIFUL WOMAN

The Beautiful Woman of the Modern Type

The year 1885, which marks the publication of *Strange Encounters with Beautiful Women*, is also the year when Tsubouchi Shōyō published *Temperaments of Contemporary Students* (*Tōsei shosei katagi*). Shōyō advanced a concept of new literature in *The Essence of the Novel* (*Shōsetsu shinzui*, 1885) and attempted to implement his approach in creative work. Did his portraits of characters really differ from those of the past? If they did, what was new?

> Shaped slender and petite, she appears far younger than her age. When she walks golden lotuses emerge beneath her feet, and her grace of bearing moves the hearts of people who watch her. How can hers be inferior to the slender waist of Feiyan, who was famous in China long ago? White-skinned and straight-nosed, her eyes are cool and her mouth is small. The only thing to regret is that she lacks personal charm and rarely laughs even softly. Although she occasionally beams with a smile, dimples are nowhere to be seen. In particular, her eyebrows form straight lines, instead of being curved in the so-called distant mountain shape.[8]

This portrayal of a normal school graduate appears in installment 3 of *Mirrors for Wife and Husband* (*Imo-to-se kagami*, 1886).

The passage merely depicts an Edo-period-style beauty as nothing like an educated Meiji girl who would symbolize Westernization. Describing the walking of this student with her modern education as "golden lotuses emerge under her feet, and her grace of bearing moves the hearts of people who watch her"—this beats me. This is no teachers' school graduate but a courtesan of the Yoshiwara licensed quarters!

Despite the fact that Tsubouchi Shōyō criticizes Bakin thoroughly in his *Essence of the Novel* (*Shōsesu shinzui*, 1885), his own style here remains in Bakin's shadow. It is difficult to spot any revolutionary innovativeness in the above passage. Rather, it conveys the impression that his intellectual energy produces no forward motion.

What strikes me as surprising is that few readers found this odd. Shōyō himself seems to have thought his work "new literature." The content of his fiction certainly was new. Yet the art of expressing details failed to move along with it.

Even so, Shōyō himself probably assumed he had introduced some innovations. In fact, "shaped slender and built petite" is an expression close to spoken language. The sentence, "In particular, her eyebrows form straight lines, instead of being curved in the so-called distant mountain shape," is perhaps intended to emphasize deviation from Bakin's approach. Some effort goes, in its own way, into the characterization of the student's smile: "rarely laughs even softly. Although she occasionally beams with a smile." It may be that Shōyō puts into practice in these sketches what he calls "reproduction" (*mosha*), or "depicting nothing else than scenes that can be found in society and making them seem real."

The Limitation of the Spoken Style

Tsubouchi Shōyō's portrayal of beautiful women in this novel is, so to speak, a rendering of *ukiyo-e* pictures of beautiful women into written prose, and thus conveys no feeling of contemporary real life. To begin with, beauty of human features first forms itself as an aesthetic image when depicted in connection with concrete scenes of social life such as movements and conversations. Beauty is conveyed vividly when filtered through bodily movements with which a speaker gestures, and expressions on the face with which words are uttered. However, regardless of whether the writing is in Sino-Japanese style or Japanese eclectic style combining the literary and the vernacular, many works from that era offer no portrayal appropriate to the situation in the story.

Drifting Clouds (*Ukigumo*, 1887) by Futabatei Shimei can be called a turning point. With a style that differed both from Tōkai Sanshi's Sino-Japanese style and Tsubouchi Shōyō's eclectic style, Futabatei's images of beautiful women were quite different from those of his predecessors.

"How lovely," Osei said with no sincerity. She looked up with a smile for no reason, pretending to be attracted by the moon. As Bunzō stole a glance at her profile, although the beauty of her facial features was just as usual, her slightly pale oval face in the moonlight with two or three strands of stray hair hovering around her cheeks in the breeze made by her fan was frightful enough to make him tremble. As he gazed steadily at her for a while, that frightful profile gradually turned toward him—wide-open, cool eyes starting to move with a sharp stare—those eyes directly met his. Concealing the beaming smile on her small, tightly pursed mouth behind the fan in her hand, like five ice fish lined up next to a thin white radish, she made a bashful gesture.[9]

The comparison of the character's hands to "five ice fish next to a thin white radish" makes the contemporary reader smile, but this bold, almost reckless, expression can be said to demonstrate the author's determination to break with traditional rhetoric. His attempts at thoroughly colloquial style are glimpsed through the use of Japanese mimeses: *shigeshige* (steadily), *patchiri* (wide-open), *jirori* (with a sharp stare), and *pittari* (directly).

From today's perspective, the style of Futabatei's *Drifting Clouds* feels more familiar than that of Shōyō's *Temperaments of Contemporary Students*. In those days, however, the latter may have looked more "literary." As the author himself testified, volume 1 of *Drifting Clouds* "jumbles" spoken language with the styles of "Shikitei Sanba, Fūrai Sanjin, Zenkō, Aeba Kōson, and others."[10] In other words, he follows the styles of the kind of popular literature known as *gesaku* (playful writing) from Edo to early Meiji. The resulting style is close to daily language, but it may give an impression of a popular novel. One can write in this kind of colloquial style without much classical training. Shōyō's style, on the other hand, is difficult to reproduce without knowledge of premodern Japanese and Chinese literatures.

Futabatei Shimei claims: "I choose to adopt no established or conventional phrases. What I just barely used as reference is the so-called Fukagawa idiom found in Shikitei Sanba's work."[11] He did not allow himself to be fettered by the rhythm and conventions of classical Chinese and the eclectic style. It may be that he was thus able to write more "freely." This is particularly apparent in chapter 2 and thereafter:

> Osei stopped under a large elm, closed the umbrella she held above her, gave a quick look around. With a charming smile, she looked at Norobu and abruptly said,
> "That person was quite good-looking!"
> "Yes? That person?"
> "You know, that person introduced as the section head's younger sister or something."

"Oh, I wondered who you might be talking about—yeah, she's quite good-looking."

"And I understand you said she looked prettier than at home. So, you know, you too must . . ." Looking Noboru straight in the face with smiles brimming around her eyes and mouth, she let out a gentle laugh.[12]

Jealous of the section head's sister-in-law, Osei exchanges words with Noboru in a scornful tone that vividly conveys her intricate feeling. The passage does not directly portray her appearance, but a kind of beauty is expressed through the description of her gaze, movement, and way of speech.

The Impact of "The Tryst"

The most epoch-making character portrayal may have occurred in translation rather than in fiction. In comparison with the novels Futabatei Shimei laboriously produced while imitating Dostoyevsky and Goncharov, his translation work conveys greater freshness. In 1888, the year after *Drifting Clouds* was published, "The Tryst" ("Aibiki"), a translation of a story from Ivan Turgenev's *Sketches from a Hunter's Album*, was published in the *Kokumin no tomo* magazine. Readers must have been surprised by the unprecedented portrayal of personal features.

> As I focused my eyes to look, it was a girl—perhaps a peasant's daughter. She sat straight, twenty or so paces away, head pensively hung and hands languid on her lap. One hand, half bare, gently rolled over her striped petticoat each time the bundle of wildflowers on her lap breathed. She decorously wore a clean white gown buttoned at the neck and wrists, two strands of large, yellow beads streaming down from the collar to the chest. She was quite pretty, wearing a narrow, scarlet ribbon around her ivory-white hairline. Beautiful and well-kempt thick hair, light yellow yet shining white in the sun, spilled out from under the ribbon left and right in two semicircles. The rest of her face was sunburned, but looked charming because her skin was thin. I couldn't see her eyes—she kept them downcast. But thin, attractive eyebrows and long eyelashes were clearly visible. The lashes were moist. The trace of falling tears was clearly visible in the evening sun on her cheeks down to her pale lips. She had a lovely neck. Her nose was somewhat large and round, but not so much as to offend the eyes. Particularly likable was her facial expression. It was gentle and graceful without pretention, worried and innocently lost.[13]

The passage captures unintentional physical motions and easy-to-overlook details. For readers of that time, this must have been a rather shocking representation conveying the charm of new descriptive art. There had been a variety of vivid descriptions of women's hair in *kana* literature, but the translation offered strikingly more graphic depiction: "The beautiful and well-kempt thick hair, light yellow yet shining white in the sun, spilled out from under the ribbon left and right in two semicircles." In particular, it must have been surprising to see a description of how color changed reflecting the light. The translation of these details was possible because they were rendered in colloquial Japanese free of traditional restrictions related to diction and rhetoric.

In his "How I Came to Use *Genbun Itchi*" ("Yo ga genbun itchi no yurai"), Futabatei characterizes his style as one of rejection of the use of classical Chinese (*kanbun*) or literary Japanese (*gabun*): "I do not use Chinese expressions that have not obtained citizenship within our language . . . nor do I use obsolete Japanese expressions in the style of *haberu* [a sentence ending indicating humbleness], because they have already completed their lifetime service. I intend to adhere to today's language." This principle is carried through in his translations.

Futabatei's translation of "The Tryst" provides a good manual for describing a beautiful countenance. However, the presence of a manual did not immediately change the literary approach as a whole. Literary style is always accepted one step behind reception of foreign aesthetics, and in many cases it requires a long passage of time. From the start, whether a given manner of depiction is good or bad is a relative issue. "The Tryst" certainly demonstrated an approach to expression that had not existed earlier. This does not mean that portrayal in Asian literature is inferior to that of modern Western literature. Thus, it is no wonder that some authors continued to favor old Edo period ways of writing. In fact, the styles of "reading books" and "stories of human feeling" long continued to cast their shadows. That was the case not only with fiction but also with translation.

Mixture of New and Old Images

The Lady of the Camellias (*Tsubakihime*), Osada Shūtō's translation of *La Dame aux Camélias* by Alexandre Dumas, fils, started being serialized in the newspaper *Yorozu chōhō* on August 30, 1902. A translation had been carried in *White Lily* (*Shirayuri*) in May to June 1896. The year 1902 is when Nagai Kafū published *Flowers of Hell* (*Jigoku no hana*), and Kunikida Doppo had published "Musashino" the year before. But translation does not necessarily trace the same route as fiction. The portrayal of Tsuyuko (Marguerite) offers something quite interesting.

> In this wide world, I have not yet heard of one equipped both with graceful beauty and an outpouring of charm like her. . . . Her slender height is already attractive beyond words, but look at the skillful way of dressing herself—other women can hardly rival her.

The phrase "one equipped both with graceful beauty and an outpouring of charm" cannot be found in the original. Probably it freely translates "it was impossible to see more charm in beauty than in that of Marguerite. Excessively tall and thin, she had in the fullest degree the art of repairing this oversight of Nature by the mere arrangement of the things she wore."[14] Obviously, priority went to the context of appreciation rather than to faithfulness to the original expression. In such cases, the style of late Edo long fiction is invariably adopted.

Premodern portrayals of beautiful women may thoroughly exaggerate their fine-looking physical features, but they never refer to flaws. As I mentioned in the prologue, in ancient times beautiful appearance was a metaphor for virtue, and a beautiful women meant a virtuous, chaste woman.

That kind of understanding infused Meiji era translation as well. The original *La Dame aux Camélias* contains an expression that suggests that Marguerite was too thin ("Tall and thin to the extent of exaggeration, she possessed to the supreme degree the art of repairing the oblivion of nature by the simple arrangement of things she wore.")

The Japanese translation omits this and instead says, "her slender height is already attractive beyond words," with sole emphasis on beauty.

On the other hand, new ways of portrayal were also adopted. In particular, detailed depiction of specific portions of the face and body was directly carried into translations.

> The distant-mountain eyebrows drawn above long, clear, lively black eyes; polished pale pink cheeks over which long eyelashes cast a faint shade each time she looks down; the naturally straight ridge of the nose that strictly forms neither a straight nor curved line; the well-shaped mouth; snow-white, well-aligned pearly teeth that show when the flowery lips barely open; the hue of the face suggestive of shining, smooth velvety nap on a pink portion of a peach on the branch—there was no other word but "beauty," none but "charm."

An expression like *polished pale pink cheeks over which long eyelashes cast a faint shade each time she looks down* had existed either in Chinese or Japanese context. The *hue of the face* in the above translation was correctly *the hue of the skin*. Aside from a few such alterations, the realistic portrayal in the original is on the whole reflected in the translation.

In the original novel, after the description of the nose, is a sentence: "The nostrils are somewhat swollen because of a strong yearning for a lustful life." This is omitted in the translation. The idea of not including flaws in the depiction of a beautiful woman was probably also at work here.

It is certain that both translations, "The Tryst" and *The Lady of the Camellias*, offered character descriptions that had not existed earlier in Japanese literature. On the other hand, there is the issue of context in understanding early translations. When Western literature had not yet been widely known to readers at large, the context of literary expression could hinder understanding and appreciation of the work. In nineteenth-century English literature, mention of blue eyes and blonde hair suffices for the reader to reflexively know that the character is "a beautiful woman." This is the same as a look at the four Chinese characters indicating "bright iris, lucent teeth," making the reader's imagination soar. In the East, however, the sight of the four characters referring to "golden hair, jasper eyes" (Chinese *jinfa piyan*, Japanese *kinpatsu hekigan*) did not traditionally evoke beauty. At worst, it may have conveyed an unpleasant impression.

Cultural context too was a large problem. Nineteenth-century Western fiction portrays cheerful disposition, social response and manners, witty conversation, and so forth as part of a woman's beauty and charm. If directly translated, such elements would not have been understood. It was somewhat later that such "translation of culture" came to be attempted.

3. PHYSICAL APPEARANCE AS INFORMATION ON CUSTOMS AND MANNERS OF THE DAY

The Influence of Newspapers

As translations from Western literature increased, creative writing also gradually changed. Narrative structure is simplest to imitate. Descriptive methods cannot readily be copied because they are related to grammar and syntax. Thus, a method was devised to use style, vocabulary, and rhetoric familiar to the reader in prose expressions while making use of plot development in Western fiction. The first attempts were by authors of the Ken'yūsha (1885–1903), the first serious Japanese literary clique. Such attempts, it would be safe to say, were a result of the natural course of events rather than conscious endeavor.

The Golden Demon (1897–1902) by Ozaki Kōyō, the Ken'yūsha's founder and leader, was vastly popular and influential. It was recently pointed out that this novel used as its source *Weaker than a Woman* by the American author Bertha M. Clay, making it less than a completely creative work. However, Kōyō "simply picked up 'materials,' and the majority of *The Golden Demon* is his original contribution. Its direction as a whole does not necessarily *follow* that of the source."[15] The novel does not detail the antagonist Shigisawa Miya's appearance before her marriage. Her beauty begins to be portrayed after she becomes wealthy following her union with Tomiyama Tadatsugu.

> This clear autumn sky was cheerful and wide to the heart's content, as she stood with a dreamy expression on her face. The sunlight shining in through every window illuminated her form diagonally, the pearl on a pin holding the lapels of her kimono gleaming as if ready to flare up. Her form, purer and fresher than seen before, standing against a spotlessly, totally clear background, suggested a white flower put in a jeweled vase. . . .
>
> Her eyes were refreshing and brimful of compassion, her eyebrows were as if an artist drew them to his satisfaction, her mouth seemed like a bud already fragrant, her nose was so well shaped that there could be nothing like it, her skin, smooth and even shiny, was transparently white. If one sought to find flaws, one could say that, although her dark and lustrous hair was tied up in a way that made her head seem heavy, the hairline was somewhat in disarray, that although her posture appeared so delicate that it seemed not to withstand a breeze, her face was now so thin that it evoked grief and loneliness, and her neck, so thin that it seemed susceptible to breaking, was painful to see.[16]

This passage corresponds to chapter 25 of *Weaker than a Woman*, but the portrayal itself is not in the source; it is Kōyō's amplification.

The Golden Demon began newspaper serialization starting on the New Year of 1897, approximately one year after the publication of *The Lady of the Camellias* in Japanese translation. Compared with Tsubouchi Shōyō's work, the description of carriage and expression is considerably more skilled. But Kōyō focuses so much on writing style that he does not necessarily explain in clear terms in which way the character is beautiful. Aside from white, shiny skin, a slender neck, and a thin face, nothing is mentioned.

Even while he consults Sino-Japanese writings and "reading books," Kōyō's style and metaphor uses unique rhetoric. Phrases like "her eyebrows were as if an artist drew them to his satisfaction" and "so delicate that it seemed not to withstand a breeze" still follow traditional clichés. Excluding such few examples, however, most are his original expressions. He also uses a realistic approach to the description of clothing.

That aside, we do encounter some abstract descriptions, as in "her eyes were refreshing and brimful of compassion" and "her mouth seemed like a bud already fragrant, her nose was so well shaped that there could be nothing like it." As such figurative speech exemplifies, depiction of facial features gives an impression that the text repeats embellished phrases derived from "reading books" and "stories of human feeling." While describing the face and hair if figuratively, the text hardly refers to the body shape and limbs. Here too, *The Golden Demon* resembles Chinese-style literature and "reading books."

Considering the number of newspaper subscribers, Ozaki Kōyō's portrayal of beauty must have had a great influence. On this point, *Drifting Cloud* and *Temperaments of Contemporary Students* probably do not compare. Reality is sometimes reflected in fiction; at other times physical appearances and fashion described in fiction influence real society. Although the description in *The Golden Demon* gives an impression of being somewhat stereotyped, it is sufficiently plausible that its image of beauty does not remain within the literary work but is absorbed into daily language life.

Stylistic Restrictions

Of widely read novels, we must not forget Tokutomi Roka's *Namiko* (*Hototogisu*), which was serialized on the *Kokumin shinbun* beginning on November 29, 1898. The novel handles problems of modern society, and its interest in family and marriage is connected to today. It begins with a description of the heroine Namiko:

> A screen door on the third floor of the Chigira Inn in Ikaho in Jōshū opened, revealing a lady viewing the evening landscape. She was eighteen or nineteen years of age. Her hair was tied into a graceful *marumage* chignon, and she wore a kimono jacket of fine-patterned silk crepe with grass-color braided ties.
> She had a white-complexioned narrow face. Her eyebrows somewhat close together and the flesh around her cheeks somewhat devoid of fullness could be called flaws, but her slender figure conveyed a graceful personality. This was a lady who could be compared neither to a plum blossom proud of its strength in the north wind nor a cherry blossom flying in the guise of a butterfly in spring mist, but an evening primrose faintly fragrant on a summer evening.

It would be fine to consider the description of the hairdo and outfit as realistic. While the passage contains a concrete description like "eyebrows somewhat close together," it also uses such rhetoric reminiscent of Edo literature as "an evening primrose faintly fragrant on a summer evening." Based upon this depiction, the artist Kuroda Seiki contributed a frontispiece portraying Namiko. It provides interesting material for considering how literary imagination resonates with artistic imagination.

Tokutomi Roka was not as obsessed with colloquial Japanese as was Futabatei Shimei. It may be that Roka felt some reservation about which should be regarded as "spoken Japanese" (*kōgo*) among the variety of dialects. However, the eclectic mixing of literary and vernacular Japanese solved the difficult problem. It was inevitable that Roka chose the style he chose. As long as the mixture of literary and vernacular Japanese is used, rhetoric that corresponds to that style naturally accompanies. Rather than a matter of the author's consciousness, portrayal of beauty is above all directly connected to language.

Whatever style is used, as long as modern life is the material, aesthetic sense of the era is naturally reflected in fiction. Further, as a literary work reaches its readers through the newspaper, it contributes to common sense. Within this kind of interconnection, a kind of implicit understanding is formed between author and reader.

Attempts at a Literary Style

Japan in 1887 continued its slow attempts at finding a writing style without reaching an answer. Amidst a variety of attempts, some authors continued to experiment using literary Japanese (*gabun*) besides the vernacular and mixed literary-vernacular styles. Mori Ōgai was one of them. His *Dancing Girl* (1890) describes the German girl Elise in that style:

> As I was passing this place, I saw a maiden in silent tears leaning on the closed door of a church. She seemed sixteen or seventeen years of age. Her hair spilling out of a scarf on her head was light gold, and her clothes gave no hint of grime or stain. Her face as she turned around surprised by my footsteps was impossible to describe because I lack the pen of a poet. Why did those clear, blue eyes, inquisitive and grief-filled, covered by half-moistened long eyelashes, penetrate into my wary heart with but one gaze?[17]

This passage provides precise details like the blue eyes that seem to question something and the narrator's psychological change. In comparison with Chinese-style clichés, the description here conveys a kind of freshness.

However, if one questions whether the use of literary Japanese allowed description beyond what is possible for either the eclectic or the vernacular style, the answer will probably be in the negative. While literary Japanese is suited for expressions laden with implied meanings, it is not suited for expressing double or triple qualifying relationships in complex sentences.

Women Writers' Gaze

While also using literary Japanese, the works of Higuchi Ichiyō are quite different. In comparison with male authors, women authors do not seem to be particularly interested in portraying beautiful women. Unless they are showing their own projections or ideal images of feminine beauty, they do not describe beautiful appearances. This also applies to art. The majority of portraits of beautiful women (*bijinga*) were painted by men.

Heian period narrative literature was created by women writers. Works of this genre tended not to contain extensive portrayals of feminine beauty. In this context, it is interesting to consider how modern women authors who used literary Japanese described beautiful looks. There were not yet many women authors in the second decade of the Meiji era. In that situation, Higuchi Ichiyō's depiction is all the more striking.

> Undone, her hair would reach her feet. She wore it swept up and pulled into a heavy-looking roll in the "red bear" style—a frightening name for a maiden's hairdo, but the latest fashion even among girls of good family. Her skin was fair and her nose was nicely shaped. Her mouth, a little large perhaps, was firm and not at all unattractive. If you took her features one by one it is true, they were not the classic components of ideal beauty. And yet she was a winsome girl, exuberant, soft-spoken. Her eyes radiated warmth whenever she looked at you.[18]

This is the physical appearance of Midori, the heroine of *Child's Play* (*Takekurabe*, 1895–1896, also known as *Growing Up*). Ichiyō mentions that Midori is far from beautiful when individual features are looked at, but a male author would have lined up flowery phrases to forcefully turn her into one. This novel was published in mid-nineteenth century, when portrayal in the manner of "stories of human feeling" and "reading books" was still in fashion. However, Ichiyō never used those conventions of portraying beautiful characters. Flowery words that male authors would favor do not necessarily suit women's aesthetic sense. That she paid no attention to such a stereotypical portrayal may be because she intuitively disliked it.

4. WESTERNIZATION OF HEROINES

Description in Perspective

The style in which "reading books" and "stories of human feeling" were written developed by absorbing the essence of prose expression from both Chinese-type and *kana*-type literatures. Given its development over a long period of time, creation of a new style that surpasses it is no easy matter.

The moment when modern literature came to be fully liberated from the shadows of both types was probably around the time when Natsume Sōseki began writing fiction. In the forties of the Meiji period, techniques of fiction writing made great strides. It no longer was necessary to use such a clumsy method as portraying the heroine's features with focus on the scene of her first appearance.

Mineko in Sōseki's *Sanshirō* (*Sanshirō*, 1908) is presented as a beautiful woman, but the description of her features is not concentrated in one place; rather, it is scattered here and there as the narrative develops. The technique of portraying a character from plural points of view was also discovered. The novel describes Mineko not only from the narrator's viewpoint but also through the protagonist Sanshirō's eyes. Indeed, there are more cases of the latter.

When first happening to see Mineko by the side of the pond on campus, Sanshirō instantly feels curious about this young woman holding a round fan. Because her face is hidden behind the fan, he cannot quite tell what she looks like. The impression he receives is simply one of "pretty colors."

Soon, inhaling the fragrance of a white flower she holds in her left hand, and accompanied by another woman, she approaches where Sanshirō is. He hears their voices. Her eyes meet his. At that point, "Sanshirō was fully conscious of the instant her deep, black eyes were upon him," and the impression of color was replaced by "something inexplicable."[19] Here his curiosity begins to gradually change to a favorable feeling.

Only after such a change within him does Mineko's external appearance become visible. It does not suddenly begin with her facial features or physical shape. All he sees is this: "He could see her obi now, dyed in bright colors except for a frond of autumn grass in the white of the cloth. In her hair she wore a pure white rose. It shone brilliantly against the black hair, in the shadow of the tree."[20] After they pass by, Sanshirō picks up the flower the woman had dropped, marking a point where the distance between the two begins to be slowly reduced. However, he does not yet even know her name. She remains "the woman from the pond," and is so referred to in the novel. Thus, first entering the stage as "a woman of mystery," she gradually approaches from a distance.

From the External Appearance to the Heart

Sanshirō does not see Mineko for a while. The image of "the woman" grows in his imagination, and good feelings for her gradually *build up* in his young heart. On his way out of the hospital after delivering at Nonomiya's request a lined kimono for his younger sister, he finds "the woman by the pond standing at the bright entrance that reflected the green foliage outside."

"The woman from the pond" is not yet identified, but the description of her looks finally begins here. Still, it is not a direct portrayal.

> She soon turned toward him again. Eyes downcast, she moved two steps in Sanshirō's direction, then suddenly raised her head and looked directly at him. Her eyes were well shaped, the outer corners chiseled deep and long into the face, the flesh of the lids softly creased. The eyes were alive, beneath brows of remarkable blackness. He could see her beautiful teeth now as well. The contrast between her teeth and the color of her skin was, for Sanshirō, something unforgettable.
> Today she wore a trace of white powder. It was not in such poor taste, however, as to hide the skin beneath. With its glow of color, the smooth flesh looked as though it would be unaffected by strong sunlight, and she had given it but the slightest touch of powder. The face did not shine. The flesh—the cheek, the jaw—was firm, with no more than necessary on the bone. And yet the face overall was soft. The very bone, it seemed, and not the flesh, was soft. It was a face that gave a sense of great depth.[21]

Although this passage describes the eyes and teeth, it does not refer to the nose and mouth. It mentions that the eyebrows are "strikingly black," but it deliberately avoids directly calling them beautiful. Instead, it emphasizes the harmony between eyebrows and eyes.

Sōseki had his own theory about the portrayal of beauty. He did not at all think that Western literature was unconditionally superior. In particular, he criticized in his *Literary Theory* (*Bungakuron*, 1907) the approach often seen in nineteenth-century Western novels of describing a character completely in one place. The reason is that "depicting everything from head to toe leaving nothing out," he thought, made "the overall impression of the beautiful woman, which is the purpose of depiction, extremely unfocused," and failed in true-to-life portrayals of beauty.

> It is an indisputable fact that an overly detailed passage is often not as effective as a concise, strong phrase . . ., and, with something like a woman's countenance, when one minutely describes everything starting with the nose and eyes, the result is often that only a vague impression remains in the brain. I consider this a flaw of aiming at being successful with parts and leaving the overall impression behind.

This aesthetics probably explains why he describes Mineko not collectively in one place in *Sanshirō* but in response to scenes and occasions.

Beauty That Speaks to the Inside

Including Sōseki's works, Western women who appear in Japanese modern literature are either extraordinarily beautiful or terribly plain.[22] Behind this there may have been an idea that ideal beauty is found in a Westerner's face. In *Sanshirō*, however, despite praising a Western woman to the skies, Sōseki did not give Mineko a Westerner-like face.

For Sōseki, feminine beauty does not mean beauty for display. It has to be charm that stirs a man's soul. Like the portrait of a woman painted by Jean-Baptiste Greuze, Mineko's eyes "appeal with something enchanting. And beyond all doubt they appeal to the senses." Thus, facial expressions are more important than the looks of the face.

> She bowed to him. Sanshirō was less startled by this courtesy from a stranger than by the grace with which it was performed. She dropped forward from the waist, as softly as a piece of paper floating on the wind, and very quickly. Then, arriving at a certain angle, she stopped, easily, precisely. This was not something she had been taught.
> "Pardon me..."
> The voice emerged from between the white rows of teeth. It was crisp but had a near-aristocratic ease.[23]

By presenting good looks through alertness and loveliness of motions in this manner, the passage strengthens the impression and makes her more alluring. The reader can tell that she is slender despite the absence of direct reference. The white teeth are also smoothly introduced in a conversation scene.

At this point, we can say that the portrayal of beauty in modern literature first became fully independent, freed from Chinese, literary Japanese, and further eclectic Japanese that mixes literary and vernacular Japanese.

Fantasy about Long Legs

Natsume Sōseki's fiction openly reveals a complex about Oriental faces. It is because of that complex that, when Sanshirō sights a beautiful Western woman, he reacts with this feeling: "He even thought that he would certainly feel small if he went to the West and entered the company of such people."

On the other hand, in his fiction he never attributes a Western face or body proportion to his female protagonists. This was the case with Futabatei Shimei, Ozaki Kōyō, and Tokutomi Roka as well. Attractive women who appear in their novels are mostly kimono-clad. The beauty of the kimono receives emphasis as an important element of the portrayal of feminine charm.

However, with Tanizaki Jun'ichirō, the situation changes drastically. *Naomi* (*Chijin no ai*, also known as *Fool's Love* in English, 1924–1925), in particular, contains unconcealed praise of Western women. This may be the first case in Japanese literature of assigning a perfectly Western-looking face to a Japanese woman.

In fact, Naomi is even said to resemble Mary Pickford (figure 8.6). When working as a waitress at a café, Naomi still wears a traditional Japanese hairdo on off days. After moving in with the narrator-protagonist Jōji (homonymic to George in Japanese) as his protégé, however, she changes that to pigtails. Although she wears a kimono sometimes at first, she almost always wears Western clothes after moving in.

About Naomi's face, the narrator mentions little beyond "very shiny, pretty lines of uniformly sized teeth." Instead, he details her physique:

> Her trunk was short and her legs long, so that from a distance she looked much taller than she was. Her short trunk tapered to a wonderfully slim waist, then swelled into richly feminine hips.[24]

Figure 8.6. Mary Pickford. *Source:* Provided by Everett Collection, Inc.

This obviously suggests the physique of a Western woman. Tanizaki Jun'ichirō tries to express physical beauty not through a clear-cut face but through a healthy, sensual proportion of the body. He frankly depicts such physical characteristics as the slim waist and richly feminine hips. This passage further manifests an almost religious aesthetic sense that finds beauty in long legs.

"Sensual beauty" is also found in Sōseki's works, but he does not go so far as to directly refer to the hips. Tanizaki, on the other hand, has no hesitation in describing the shapeliness of the hips. In chapter 10 of the same novel, he again openly admires Naomi for her "thick shoulders, large hips, and protruding chest."

The emphasis on the long legs merits particular notice. The longer the legs, the more beautiful. Rather than a sense of beauty, this can be called obsession. What supported it was the aesthetics built upon *Fernweh* (longing for a distant land) and a complex in relation to Western culture.

Naturally, "long legs fantasy" did not begin with *Naomi*. If we look back, there were some signs of that in the Meiji era. In the Taishō era, it is fair to say that it was already presuppositional. Thus, when Tanizaki Jun'ichirō praised a woman's long legs, his readers experienced no sense of incongruity. Rather, the "long legs fantasy" in *Naomi* demonstrates an aspect of such commonly shared admiration.

The same point is evident in art as well. Women portrayed in paintings from the same age have awfully long legs. The proportion of the head to the body of the woman in Takehisa Yumeji's *Nostalgia for Hirado* (*Hirado kaikyū*, figure 8.7) is

Figure 8.7. *Nostalgia for Hirado.* Source: Takehisa Yumeji, *Sansai, Special Issues*, no. 242. Sansaisha, 1969, 9.

closer to one-tenth than to one-eighth. The position of her sash indicates that her upper body is extremely short, occupying only one-fourth of her height, while her legs appear to be one-and-a-half times the length of her upper body. If such a woman actually appeared before one's eyes, one would flee in shock. However, people did not at all think or find this exaggerated portrayal strange.

The beautiful women who appear in the illustration used for Shiseidō's *Ladies' Pocket Notebook* (*Gofujin techō*, figure 8.8) are also long-legged. It indicates that the idea that long legs are attractive had been perfectly established in citizens' popular culture.

Interestingly, the same phenomenon is also seen in modern China. Moreover, representation is even more extreme than in Japan. Beautiful women appearing in art are all extraordinarily long-legged (figure 8.9). In China too, then, admiration of the West took the form of adoration of Westerners.

The phenomenon of being infected with the West often appears in the guise of warped nationalism, or "return to the East." In China, women in

Figure 8.8. An Illustration in Shiseidō's *Ladies' Pocket Notebook* (A Ginza Scene). In the Possession of Shiseido Corporate Museum, 1927. *Source:* Haga Tōru, ed., *E no naka no Tōkyō*. Iwanami, 1993, 49.

Figure 8.9. A Chinese Advertisement for Cigarettes from the 1940s. *Source:* Liang Jingzhu (chief editor), *Lao guanhao (Old Advertisement, Series of the Old Days in 20th Century)*. Longmen Shuju, 1999, 77.

Ming period clothing often appear in advertisements of the 1930s. Interestingly, they are also terribly long-legged (figure 8.10). Ming clothing was originally presented as an allegory for "non-West" or "anti-West." Thus, long legs that would overwhelm Western women here symbolize rivalry with Europe and the States. At a glance, it may seem to flaunt Eastern values, but in that imagined scenery it is recognized as a trajectory of excessive adoration of the West. In the first place, the mentality itself of "surpassing the West" is completely dominated by the way of thinking of the modern West.

On that point, China shares much with Japan. Modern Japanese art frequently portrays beautiful women in kimono. But almost without exception, they are shaped like Western women. And they are extremely long-legged. Painters may not necessarily have been clearly aware of this. But such portrayal itself was drawn from Western art. In this sense, those paintings should be understood in relation with Western aesthetic views rather than being seen as expressing "Eastern" and "traditional" beauty.

Sensuous Is Beautiful

Handling sensuality as feminine beauty is the most striking characteristic of Tanizaki's portrayal. In fact, Naomi's shoulders, chest, and arms are judged by whether they are sexually attractive rather than on their beauty.

> She had surprisingly full shoulders and a thick chest that suggested strong lungs. When I tried to fasten the buttons [of her bathing suit] for her, she'd take deep breaths and move her arms so that the muscles of her back rippled and swelled. The bathing suit, which already seemed at the bursting point, would stretch even more tightly across her bulging shoulders and threaten to split.[25]

The serialization of *Naomi* on the Osaka Asahi newspaper started in March 1924. Around then, magazines were flooded with Western-style beautiful women on color covers and in illustrations, and commuter train posters featured people in Western clothes with Western faces and body shapes. It was not just literature that idealized Western facial features. In comparison with the Meiji period, aesthetics of looks leaned much further toward Europe and the States.

Naomi can be said to demonstrate in the most extreme way the "Westerner-ization" (rather than Westernization) of the portrayal of beautiful women. In fact, Tanizaki Jun'ichirō has a character by the name of Mā-chan thoroughly disparage a Japanese-looking face:

Figure 8.10. A Chinese Advertisement for Cigarettes from the 1930s. *Source:* Liang Jingzhu (chief editor), *Lao guanhao (Old Advertisement, Series of the Old Days in 20th Century)*. Longmen Shuju, 1999, 49.

Her thick, raven black hair—not simply abundant, but heavy and oppressive—was chopped shoulder length, frizzled in a negligent sort of way, and adorned with a ribbon wrapped around her head and over her forehead. Her cheeks were red, her eyes large, and her lips thick, but the oval outline of her face, with its long, thin nose, was in the pure Japanese style of the *ukiyo-e* prints.[26]

Rich, black hair had been a symbol of feminine beauty since the Heian period, but here it is "oppressive." From an excess of dislike of the "purely Japanese" face, even the "oval face" has become the object of disgust.

Such a perception is of course a matter of Tanizaki's personal taste. However, like a magic mirror his portrayal reflects in exaggerated form the adoration of the West that spread widely in Japanese society of the Taishō era.

Not only the portrayal in literature, iconographic representations like paintings and posters also demonstrate that trend. "Emulating Westerners" (*Seiyōjinka*) proceeded all along from the Meiji to the Shōwa era, but it was perhaps most striking in the Taishō era.

This is not a phenomenon limited to Japan, but a trend widely observed in East Asia. Westerner-like deep-sculpted faces were unconditionally thought beautiful. From the last half of the nineteenth century, this aesthetic view

Figure 8.11. A Prewar Chinese Poster for Cigarettes. *Source:* Liang Jingzhu (chief editor), *Lao guanhao (Old Advertisement, Series of the Old Days in 20th Century)*. Longmen Shuju, 1999, 36.

dominated people's gaze almost obsessively. For example, it is quite common in Chinese paintings to make women look like Westerners. The trend is particularly strong with advertisements that speak directly to the sensibility of the masses. Figure 8.11, an advertisement for cigarettes, portrays a woman resembling a Westerner. In China, Westerners were already depicted on ceramic ware and so forth in the Qing period. But it was in the twentieth century that Westerner-like figures came to be considered to represent ideal beauty.

NOTES

1. The original runs: "She seemed about fifteen years of age, and her complexion was remarkably pure and delicate, even despite the sunburnt tinge which her habits of toil had brought. Her auburn hair hung in loose and natural curls over her forehead, and its luxuriance was remarkable even in one so young. Her countenance was beautiful, nay, even faultless, in its small and child-like features, but the expression pained you—it was so vacant. In repose it was almost the expression of an idiot—but when she spoke or smiled, or even moved a muscle, the eyes, colour, lips, kindled into a life, which proved that the intellect was still there, though but imperfectly awakened." (Project Gutenberg, EBook 7649, book 1, chapter 1)

2. The original: "There lay before them the still street, with its feeble and infrequent lights; beyond, a few stars, struggling through an atmosphere unusually clouded, brought the murmuring ocean partially into sight ... and by that uncertain light Valerie's brilliant cheek looked pale, and soft, and thoughtful.... As she spoke she began plucking (it is a common woman's trick) the flowers from the vase between her and Ernest. That small, delicate, almost transparent hand!" (Ibid., book 2, chapter 3)

3. Yoshitake Yoshitaka, *Meiji Taishō no hon'yakushi* (Kenkyūsha, 1955).

4. Kindai Digital Library, *Bairai yokun*, vol. 1, 26–27.

5. Cf. the present author's "*Ivanhoe no henyō*" in *Hikaku bungaku kenkyū*, no. 55 (Tokyo University Hikaku Bungaku-kai, 1989). This study discusses the influence of Bakin's *Eight Dog Heroes* on *Lingering Fragrance of Plum Buds* (*Bairai yokō*, an 1889 Japanese translation of *Ivanhoe* by Ushiyama Kakudō) and also addresses the Chinese translation of *Ivanhoe*.

6. Ōnuma Toshio and Nakamaru Nobuaki (annotators), *Seiji shōsetsu shū*, vol. 1 (SNKBT Meiji-hen 17), 25.

7. Yamada Toshiharu and Hayashibara Sumio (annotators), *Seiji shōsetsu shū*, vol. 1 (SNKBT Meiji-hen 16), 343.

8. *Tsubouchi Shōyō zenshū*, vol. 13 (Daiichi Shobō, 1977) (Bessatsu, vol. 1), 311.

9. Aoki Toshihiro and Togawa Shinsuke (annotators), *Tsubouchi Shōyō Futabatei Shimei shū* (SNKBT Meiji-hen 18), 229–30.

10. Futabatei Shimei, "Yo ga hansei no zange," *Bungaku sekai*, 1908.

11. Futabatei Shimei, "Yo ga genbun itchi no yurai," *Bunshō sekai*, 1906.

12. *Tsubouchi Shōyō Futabatei Shimei shū*, 303–4.

13. In Constance Garnett's English translation from the Russian, the passage goes: "I looked attentively; it was a young peasant girl. She was sitting twenty paces off, her head bent in thought, and her hands lying in her lap; one of them, half-open, held a big nosegay of wild flowers, which softly stirred on her checked petticoat with every breath. Her clean white smock, buttoned up at the throat and wrists, lay in short soft folds about her figure; two rows of big yellow beads fell from her neck to her bosom. She was very pretty. Her thick fair hair of a lovely, almost ashen hue was parted into two carefully combed semicircles, under the narrow crimson fillet, which was brought down almost on to her forehead, white as ivory; the rest of her face was faintly tanned that golden hue which is only taken by a delicate skin. I could not see her eyes—she did not raise them; but I saw her delicate high eye-brows, her long lashes; they were wet, and on one of the checks there shone in the sun the traces of quickly drying tears, reaching right down to her rather pale lips. Her little head was very charming altogether; even her rather thick and snub nose did not spoil her. I was especially taken with the expression of her face; it was so simple and gentle, so sad and so full of childish wonder at its own sadness." *Sketches from a Hunter's Album* (Seven Treasures Publications, 2008), 195–160.

14. *Camille* (*La Dame aux Camélias*) by Alexandre Dumas, fils. The Project Gutenberg EBook [EBook #1608, produced by Dianne Bean and David Widger], chapter 2. The original states: "Or, il était impossible de voir une plus charmante beauté que celle de Marguerite. Grande et mince jusqu'à l'exagération, elle possédait au suprême degré l'art de faire disparaître cet oubli de la nature par le simple arrangement des choses qu'elle revêtait" (#2419). Notes omitted for other quotation from the same.

15. Bertha M. Clay, *Weaker than a Woman* (Kessinger Publishing Co., 2008). Translated by Hori Keiko as *Onna yori yowaki mono: Beikokuban Konjiki Yasha* (Nan'undō Phoenix, 2002).

16. Chapter 4, section 2.

17. Mori Ōgai, *Maihime, Utakata no ki* (Kadokawa Bunko, [1954] 1990), 80.

18. Robert Lyons Danly, *In the Shade of Spring Leaves: The Life and Writings of Higuchi Ichiyō, a Woman of Letters in Meiji Japan* (W. W. Norton & Company, 1981), 259. "Red bear" refers to a yak, or more specifically its tail hair. Danly's original footnote on the term runs: "The 'red bear' (*shaguma*) was a popular hair style that had originated in the demimonde and spread in the 1890s to young women of the upper classes. It was a somewhat flamboyant hairdo, with a grand chignon and flowered hairpins, but it became quite the thing for fashionable schoolgirls."

19. Jay Rubin (tr.), *Sanshirō: A Novel* (Penguin Classics, 2009), 23–24.

20. Ibid., 24.

21. Ibid., 50–51.

22. Tsuruta Kin'ya, *Ekkyōsha ga yonda Nihon bungaku* (Shin'yōsha, 1999).

23. Jay Rubin, *op. cit.*, 51.

24. Anthony H. Chambers (tr.), *Naomi* (Originally published by Alfred A. Knopf, 1985; Vintage Books, 2001), 29.

25. Ibid., 29–30.

26. Ibid., 83.

Epilogue
Where Beauty Will Go

FROM THE FACE TO PROPORTION

Postwar Japanese views of beauty have been greatly influenced by Hollywood standards. Resemblance to the Western face became an important measure. Depending on the times and the fashion, Japanese-style beauty was also favored, but that went only side by side with a consciousness of Hollywood standards. In that sense, evaluation of Oriental good looks itself can be called a manifestation of a Hollywood complex. Naturally, it is not that no aesthetic views of the Hollywood type existed before the war. Before they could penetrate every corner of daily life through magazines and TV, however, they had to wait for the establishment of mass consumer culture.

During that time, a number of changes were seen in the idea of beauty. A deep-sculpted face, wide-open eyes—preference for these remained more or less the same from the Meiji era on. On the other hand, certain criteria changed. In particular, heightened interest in body proportion deserves the greatest attention. The physique became a yardstick to distinguish between beautiful and plain women just as, or, depending upon the case, more than, facial looks.

In the East, height was traditionally not so important in judging feminine beauty. While "medium height and build" was deemed ideal, there was leniency toward the petite and so forth. Extremely long body or strikingly short legs aside, reference to height as an indicator of beauty was rather rare.

Since the Meiji era, Western-type body shape was viewed as beautiful, and, in particular, long legs, large breasts, and round hips came to be openly discussed as a measure of feminine beauty. Such aesthetic views were further emphasized by beauty contests, advertisement photos, TV commercials, and so forth. It should be added, however, that the Western body shape had no substance; most probably it was no more than a fantasy.

Beauty contests go back to the Meiji era. Before the war, they consisted of screenings of photos, and entrants never directly presented their bodies. I discovered that it was only after the war that contestants began to appear onstage to expose themselves to the gaze of judges.[1] The history is unexpectedly short.

However, the significance of screening entrants in swimsuits is quite large. Because of the requisite exposure of legs before the judges, the balance between the upper and lower bodies came to be questioned, and the beauty of facial features alone no longer led to being selected. In addition, height, especially the length of legs, came to freshly catch attention. From the start, Asians' height complex toward Westerners was quite deep-rooted. The tendency itself goes back to prewar times, but swimsuit screening encouraged it further. The inferiority complex, which men originally experienced, was carried over to the gaze directed toward women. In fact, depending upon the contest, qualifications for applicants came to include a specification concerning height. This seems to reflect the aesthetic that, with women too, tall is beautiful. The length of legs not only relates to their balance with the body, but to height. "Long legs are beautiful." This view is correlated with emphasis on proportion.

The Birth of Shared Standards

The meaning of a beauty contest lies in demonstrating "common standards." As discussed earlier, whether a certain woman is viewed as beautiful depends to a fair degree on individual taste. How a countenance looks is often affected by complex elements like the viewer's psychology, feelings toward the person in question, and mutual relationships. A woman who appears as a matchless beauty to some may seem ordinary in others' views. It is not rare that one who finds a person beautiful in her twenties may not find her beautiful at all when encountering her five years later. This is the reason that "objective" standards, such as how many centimeters long eyes, mouth, or nose should be cannot be demonstrated.

However, by shifting the focus of selection to proportion, beauty contests were able to demonstrate "common standards." Frequently, the bust, waist, and hip sizes of entrants are publicized. In postwar Japan, Itō Kinuko, who won third place in the 1953 "Miss Universe" contest, can be said to be an early example of that. Her three sizes, reported in the media, drew wide attention.

That proportion receives greater emphasis than the face has something to do with the idea that health is beautiful. Since sports came to be seen as refined taste, women began to positively participate in sports that require an awareness of the fashions and draw the gaze of onlookers such as tennis, swimming, and gymnastics. Such social change partly contributes to the emphasis on proportion. Healthy, active women are beautiful. This idea would later connect to the vogue of wheat-colored skin.

Through the sexual liberation of the sixties, sex appeal came to be added to the indispensable conditions for a beautiful woman. This awareness was dramatically reinforced in male magazines and the like. Partly helped by the advancement in photographic technology, the bust and hips began to be emphasized and exaggerated as elements of beauty in representations.

If *beautiful woman* was a euphemism for *prostitute* in premodern times, in modern and contemporary days it is often associated with *actresses*. In fact, actresses commonly appear in TV commercials and photographic advertisements. For noncommercial purposes too, sometimes an actress's photo is used to stage an image of the beautiful woman. It is also a matter of course that a photo of an actress decorates the front cover of a weekly magazine, or an actress appears on TV as a guest on a variety show. Nor is it rare that an actress is put to use for a public advertisement. If we look around, we see that our surroundings are full of images of beautiful woman symbolized by actressess. The woman of matchless beauty is a shared object. This awareness is common to old days and today.

The image of "proportional beauty" rapidly spread through the media. Almost without exception, beauty contest winners become models or actresses. Appearing in gravure photos of magazines, they have played a large role in settling the image of "proportional beauty."

On looking at the transformation of the postwar image of beautiful women, one observes another interesting phenomenon: the size of the mouth receded from the standards for beauty. Before modern times, in most cases a beautiful woman had a small mouth. As one can tell from a look at Hollywood actresses, in the West women with mouths that are large by the Asian standard are often regarded as beautiful. At present, there is no aesthetic sense that finds beauty in a large mouth, but it is rarely considered a flaw.

Democratization of Beauty

Today, the development of cosmetic goods and the progress of cosmetic surgery have made it easy to create beauty. The percentage of success in surgeries for double eyelids, heightened nose bridges, or enhanced breasts has increased, so that, among young people, resistance to such operations is said to be gradually declining.

What is far simpler than surgery is makeup. Today, when choices can be made from countless cosmetic goods, it is possible to create not only a white skin and red lips but a straight nose bridge and double eyelids. Except for extreme cases, everyone can become a beautiful person. To become a Cinderella in terms of good looks is no longer impossible.

In the first place, deviation from the average determines the scarcity value of beauty. The situation in which everyone can look beautiful, even if of artificial creation, has reduced the impact of beautiful looks. This is the reason that today "ruining the castle, ruining the state" is no longer possible: neither the state nor a company is ruined because of a beautiful woman.

On the other hand, the fact that beautiful looks can be obtained with money is bringing an important change. Namely, there is no longer absolute beauty. If everyone becomes a more or less similarly "beautiful woman," good looks, no matter how beautiful, would be boring. Thus, beauty with individuality comes to be favored over beauty that represents the average value. In other words, as an inevitable trend, distance from the mean value comes to be viewed as beautiful.

This probably explains the fact that, while there is an upper limit to the demand for facelift surgery, the cosmetic goods market has immeasurable potential. As long as beauty is a value added to humanity, demand for beauty never ceases. On the other hand, the diversification of aesthetic sense rejects a uniform view. Thus, the cosmetics industry not only responds to the sense of beauty in fashion but can constantly design new "beautiful looks," thereby luring consumers.

Beauty for Consumption

Today, production and circulation of images of beauty are closely tied in all aspects to economic activities. From Hollywood actresses, popular singers, TV talents, and supermodels to women who appear in sources of information on fashions and cosmetic products, ideal looks are always shown as part of commercial strategies. In all cases, production of beautiful images is accompanied by economic activities. Beautiful appearances supplied to the market of gazes are thoroughly digitalized in terms of movie-house drawing power, TV audience ratings, the fashion industry, and male magazines' sales performances. Within that context, beauty is produced and consumed as merchandise.

Naturally, beautiful looks themselves do not carry the smell of a commodity economy. Because the purpose is ingeniously concealed, at least consumers are totally unaware. Supply of images of beauty is persistently carried out on the basis of the principle of pleasure. While paying attention to the average sense of beauty, the fashion industry and cosmetics makers have skillfully led popular sensibility. Through the intervention of brilliant color, pleasant smell, and a peaceful atmosphere, images repeatedly shown on the media come to be widely accepted and take root. Despite the fact that gazes are thoroughly educated, consumers firmly believe in their own sensibility.

Unlike long ago, a beautiful face is, today, no longer a distant ideal image beyond everyday life. Before, "the beautiful person" was created and circulated in the demand and supply relationship of emotions. With the birth of mass consumption culture, the ideal beautiful person ceased to be the target of adoration and became a goal that everyone can try to aim at. "The beautiful person" is no longer an unrealizable dream. The message, "you, too, can be beautiful," has immeasurable power. Not only fashion and cosmetics industries but also many business circles related to beautification, fitness, and diet, makers of daily necessities like soaps, shampoos, and conditioners as well as makers of health food, enjoy the benefits brought by this fantasy. By making consumers believe that everyone can be beautiful, they can involve them in the process of "becoming a beautiful person."

Deep Tan Represents Unconscious Cynicism

Of Japanese fashions in recent years, what I personally took greatest interest in is the young women's makeup called "intensely dark" (*ganguro*, artificial deep tan with bleached or dyed hair), along with its variant called "mountain woman" (*yamanba*, deep tan and contrasting white makeup with half-disheveled pastel-colored or blonde long hair). Not just because it was a 100 percent Japanese original makeup. I found it interesting because it was philosophically thought-provoking. By now the fashion has totally disappeared; but, in the future, when looking back at feminine beauty and makeup methods of the late twentieth century, it will undoubtedly be discussed.

From the beginning of modern times, East Asian countries single-mindedly raced toward Westernization. By the time they realized it, their aesthetic sense had been completely dyed in the hue of Western culture. I do not intend to go into detail about whether this was right or wrong. Limiting the discussion to makeup methods, it can be said that, in the past, they were never even once able to break away from Western influence. Japanese-style makeup and a revival of "tradition" are no more than a link in Westernization in the sense that they are an expression of resistance against Western culture.

What is interesting about *ganguro* is its freedom from the Western context. Not only that, thoroughly liberated from the existing grammar of makeup, it withdrew from the first time from the game called the fight against "higher" culture. The phenomenon came with neither the background of adoration of the West, nor any tinge of anti-Western sentiment. Rather, it flaunted the fact that it had become possible to free oneself from that repeated game. It can be called a makeup method that most philosophically questions what "beauty" is. I am not talking about the sense of purpose of those who apply such makeup. Unlike the response from adults, *ganguro* was probably thought rather beautiful among young females. Again, its popularity among men is a precondition for lasting as a fashionable makeup method. In that sense, it has not been liberated from the posture of fawning upon men. In other words, within young women's community, *ganguro* has no particularly philosophical implication. What deserves attention is the meaning in adults' culture. It is endlessly interesting because, when the phenomenon called *ganguro* confronts adults' culture, it signifies a kind of cynicism. In pondering the question "what constitutes the beautiful woman," *ganguro* may provide a meaningful hint.

The Beautiful Woman Only Exists in Discourse

The concept of the beautiful woman resembles that of "morality." Like the image of the beautiful woman, there are rough measures of morality but no ultimate standards. The sense of morals differs from individual to individual; it also differs by culture, area, and age. Some think holding an aged stranger's luggage an ethical act, but others consider it discrimination against the elderly.

In the Edo period, loyalty to the domain lord was a yardstick for measuring a moral sense. Today, however, loyalty for an individual is far from virtue; rather, it can be associated with the world of gangsters.

As there is no absolute morality, there is no ultimate beauty. Only in imagination can supreme morality or unsurpassed beauty exist. Despite that, people still long for unsurpassed beauty, just as they yearn for the fantasy of absolute morality.

As the beautiful woman is the mean of faces, morality too may be the mean of conscience. On the other hand, humans always seek higher morality than the mean. Likewise, they long for the beautiful woman beyond the mean.

As morality exists on the premise of immorality, so is the concept of the beautiful woman possible precisely because there is the plain woman.

Nothing is so uninteresting as everyone being a moralist. The world in which every woman is beautiful is also frightful.

Morality exists because it is talked about as an ideal, rather than exists in reality. The beautiful woman is also created by discourse and exists only in discourse.

In this sense, how the beautiful woman has been portrayed is more important than how she looks.

In contemporary fiction, anything like the portrayal of beautiful women is rarely seen. With the development of technology in image manipulation and computer graphics, the space in which literary expression displays its power has become markedly reduced. In its place, theories of feminine beauty and manuals for becoming beautiful flood the streets. However, fantasy about the beautiful woman is never a useless illusion. In contemporary society too, it is a psychological medicine that heals the souls of people.

"What constitutes the beautiful woman?"—more important than finding an answer to this question is continuing to think about it.

NOTE

1. Inoue Shōichi, *A Hundred-Year History of Beauty Contests* (*Bijin kontesuto hyakunenshi*) (Asahi Sinbunsha, 1997).

Afterword

How have beautiful women been portrayed in Japanese and Chinese cultures? I explored this question in this book with a focus on verse and prose. Before modern times, there was a close relationship between poetry and art. Poetic comments were often added on paintings, or paintings were produced on the basis of poems. In the first place, literati art can be called pictorial representation of their poesy. In terms of aesthetic awareness and representational methods too, the forms share much in common. Like Wang Wei and Deng Banqiao of China and Yosa Buson and Ike no Taiga of Japan, many poets were also painters. When considering images of beauty in literature, naturally we need to bring paintings within our vision. However, whether in poetry or art, in this book everything is no more than material for examining images of the past. References to verse, prose, or painting here are not intended as literary or art criticism. In the case of art, in particular, I generally handle it in relation to literature, or simply quote examples as sources that record customs and manners.

That I made both Japan and China the objects of my study is not merely to compare them. It is because at least two viewpoints are necessary in order to clarify the spread and acceptance of the images of beauty in the cultural sphere of Chinese characters. Ideally, the Korean peninsula and Vietnam should also be added, but regrettably that is quite beyond my ability. My claim is that this book offers a basis for discussion.

Regarding the images and views of beauty appearing in Chinese culture, I went by the theme in examining description of countenances, views equating beauty to vice, customs and manners, and so forth. Clarification of the influence on images of beauty exerted by the intersection of ethnic cultures was among the aims.

In contrast, I followed a chronological line in developing my inquiry into the images of beauty appearing in Japanese culture. I tried to trace the processes through which Japanese images of beauty were formulated, while examining how images of beauty were accepted or rejected through literature, art, customs, and manners. This was a nearly reckless challenge, but now that it is completed, I feel it was quite worth attempting.

How images of beauty were expressed is not merely a question of literature and art. It is also related to such fields as philosophy, aesthetics, history, psychology, anthropology, and sociology. Naturally it is beyond the scope if this book is to refer to all of them. If I have been able to show what the use of the images of beauty in verse and prose as materials makes visible from the angle of comparative cultural history, nothing makes me happier. To interpret various phases of cultural intersection from the viewpoint of the history of representation of beautiful women was a project since my master's degree days. Time passed while it remained incomplete. Now that my wish of many years has finally been fulfilled, I will be able to part with this theme, at least for the time being.

Chapters 2, 3, and 5 were partially published earlier, but substantially revised for inclusion in this book. They hardly retain the original form, so I skip citation. Chapter 4 was freshly rewritten on the basis of an oral presentation. The rest was newly written for this book.

Depending upon the content, each chapter is written somewhat differently. The book is designed so that any chapter can be read separately, depending upon the reader's purpose, without the need to read all in order.

Finally, I would like to thank Yamauchi Naoki, who has given me the chance for writing, and Kawasaki Mari of Shōbunsha. Without their encouragement, I would not even have resolved to challenge this vast theme.

I have just looked at my notebook to find that we first met to make arrangements on May 21, 1998. I thought then that I would be able to complete the manuscript in one year, but my curiosity continued to expand as I wrote. In particular, the Japanese portions took considerably longer than was planned. That I am able to put my work together into one volume is entirely thanks to the two, who continued to patiently wait and give constant encouragement.

Cho Kyo
August 2001

Glossary of Selected Chinese and Japanese Names, Titles, and Terms

Account of Seaside Excursions, An (*Haizou yeyou lu* 海陬冶遊録). A Qing literary work on courtesans.

Account of the Loyal Vassal Utō Yasukata (*Utō Yasukata chūgiden* 善知鳥安方忠義傳, 1806). A *yomihon* conspiracy story by Santō Kyōden, illustrated by Utagawa Toyokuni (歌川豊國).

"Account of the Wo People, An" ("Woren zhuan" 倭人傳). A section on Japan contained in the *Book of Wei* portion of the *Records of the Three Kingdoms* (*Sanguo zhi*, compiled around 280–290), popularly called "Records of Wei: An Account of the Wo People" (Chinese: "Weizhi Woren zhuan"; Japanese: "Gishi Wajinden" 魏志倭人傳).

Accounts of the Dressing Chamber (*Zhuanglou ji* 妝樓記). Fragmentary anecdotes about women and their things by Zhang Mi (張泌) of the late Tang period.

Accounts of the Dressing Table (*Zhuangtai ji* 粧臺記). Written by Yuwen Shiji (宇文士及, ?–642).

All about the North (*Beibian peidui* 北邊備對). A geohistorical work by Cheng Dachang (程大昌, 1123–1195) of the Song period.

Analects of Confucius (*Lun yu* 論語). A record of the words and acts of the philosopher Confucius (Kongzi 孔子, 551–479 BCE) and his disciples.

Anthology of Myriad Leaves (*Man'yōshū* 萬葉集). Also known as *A Collection of Ten Thousand Leaves*, or *A Collection for Ten Thousand Generations*. It is the oldest extant collection of Japanese poetry, in which the last datable poem is from 759. The final compiler is said to be Ōtomo no Yakamochi (大伴家持).

Asai Ryōi (淺井了意, 1612–1691). A *kanazōshi* writer and priest in the early Edo period; author of *The Protective Doll* (*Otogi bōko* 御伽婢子, 1666).

Awake at Night (*Yoru no nezame* 夜の寝覺; also *Yowa no nezame* 夜半の寝覺). A late Heian narrative, probably from the end of the twelfth century.

baihua (白話). Vernacular, as opposed to literary, Chinese. In literature, the term is used in connection with *baihua xiaoshuo* (白話小説), referring to Chinese fiction written mostly in colloquial language as opposed to traditional fiction written in literary Chinese. Major vernacular fiction includes *Outlaws of the Marsh*, *The Plum in the Golden Vase*, and *A Dream of Red Mansions*.

Baopuzi (抱朴子). An alias of Ge Hong (葛洪 283–343) and the title of a philosophical book by him. Ge Hong was a minor southern official during the Jin dynasty (263–420) and known for his interest in Daoism, alchemy, and techniques of longevity.

Bao Si (褒似). First consort, then queen, of King You of Zhou (795–771 BCE). Legends say that the king repeatedly lighted the warning beacons as a way of making Bao Si smile at the lords who gathered. No one reported when a real emergency occurred.

Beginner's Guide (*Meng Qui* 蒙求). A children's primer in four-character verse written by Li Han (李瀚) of the Tang period.

bijinga (美人画), also **bijin-e** (美人絵). Pictures of beautiful women in Japanese art, especially in woodblock printing of the *ukiyo-e* genre.

Bin Chun (斌椿, b. 1804). Author of *Occasional Jottings aboard a Raft* (*Chengcha biji* 乘槎筆記) and the chief envoy of the first Qing period mission sent to European countries in 1866.

"Biographies of Assassins" ("Ceke liezhuan" 刺客列傳). A chapter in "Biographies" in the *Records of the Grand Historian*.

Biographies of Exemplary Women (*Lienü zhuan* 列女傳). A book compiled by the Han dynasty scholar Liu Xiang (劉向) around 18 BCE. It includes 125 biographical accounts of women exemplars in early China, taken from Chinese histories.

Bo Collection, The (*Bozhi wenji* 白氏文集). A collection of writings by the Tang poet Bo Juyi.

Bo Juyi (白居易, also spelled Bai Juyi, 772–846). A Tang period poet.

Book of Han (*Han shu* 漢書, completed in 111 CE). One of the official dynastic Chinese histories. The main portion was compiled by Ban Gu (班固, 39–92). Also called *The History of Former Han*.

Book of Later Han (*Hou Han shu* 後漢書). One of the official Chinese histories, compiled by Fan Ye (范曄, 398–445) in the fifth century.

Book of Songs (*Shi jing* 詩經). The earliest extant collection of Chinese poems and songs, some possibly from as early as 1000 BCE, also known as the *Classic of Poetry*, the *Book of Odes*, or simply *The Odes*.

Book of Wei (*Wei shu* 魏書). A component of the *Records of the Three Kingdoms* (*Sanguo zhi* 三國志), compiled around 280–290 by Chen Shou (陳壽).

"Bowl Wearer, The" ("Hachikazuki" 鉢かづき). An *otogizōshi* tale.

Cao Cao (曹操, 155–220). One of the central figures of the Three Kingdoms period, also skilled in poetry. He was posthumously titled Emperor Wu of Wei.

Cao Zhi (曹植, 199–232). Cao Cao's son and a poet who lived during the late Han dynasty and Three Kingdoms period of Chinese history.

Categorized Compendium of Ancient Matters (*Koji ruien* 古事類苑). A Japanese encyclopedia published in 1896–1914, compiling materials from ancient times to 1867.

Child's Play (*Takekurabe* たけくらべ, 1895–1896). A novel by Higuchi Ichiyō (樋口一葉). Also known in English as *Growing Up*.

Chōbunsai Eishi (鳥文齋榮之, 1756–1829). An Edo-period *ukiyo-e* artist.

Chronicle of the Great Peace, The (*Taiheiki* 太平記). A fourteenth-century story of battles and political turmoil, covering the period between 1318 and 1367. The first twelve of the forty volumes were translated by Helen Craig McCullough in 1979 as *The Taiheiki: A Chronicle of Medieval Japan*.

Chu ci (楚辭／楚辞). Also called *Songs of the South* or *Songs of Chu*. An anthology of Chinese poems by Qu Yuan (屈原) and Song Yu (宋玉) from the Warring States period and later imitators of their poetic style. It is the second-oldest extant collection of Chinese poems.

Collection of Chinese and Japanese Poems for Singing (*Wakan rōeishū* 和漢朗詠集). A Chinese and Japanese poetic anthology compiled in 1018 by the Heian period *waka* poet and critic Fujiwara no Kintō (藤原公任, 966–1041).

Collection of National Polity (*Keikokushū* 經國集, 827). Early Heian *kanshi* collection. Ordered by Junna (ruled 923–935) and compiled by Yoshimine no Yasuyo (良岑安世) and others.

Commentaries on Things Now and Old (*Gujin zhu* 古今注). A dictionary by Cui Bao (崔豹) of the Jin period. Also translated as *Commentaries on Antiquity and Today*.

Commentaries on Things Now and Old in Central China (*Zhonghua gujin zhu* 中華古今注). A dictionary by Ma Gao (馬縞) of the Five Dynasties period.

Commentary of Zuo (*Chunqiu Zuozhi zhuan* 春秋左氏傳／春秋左氏传). The earliest Chinese work of narrative history, said to be a commentary on the *Spring and Autumn Annals* and attributed to Zuo Qiuming (左丘明). Also called the *Chronicle of Zuo*, or simply *Zuo zhuan*. It covers the period from 722 BCE to 468 BCE.

Compendium of Materia Medica (*Bencao gangmu* 本草綱目). A book by Li Shizhen (李時珍), late Ming.

Confessions of Lady Nijō, The (*Towazugatari* とはずがたり). An early fourteenth-century memoir and travelogue written by Go-Fukakusa-In Nijō (後深草院二條, b. 1258), a late Kamakura poet and diarist who served Go-Fukakusa (ruled 1246–1259). The original title literally means "Telling a Tale Unrequested."

"Contemporary Makeup" ("Shishi zhuang" 時世粧). A poem by Bo Juyi (白居易).

Court Library's Treasury Cases (*Shiqu baoji* 石渠宝笈). Catalogue of the painting and calligraphy collection of the Qing court. The three parts were completed in 1745, 1793, and 1816.

Crescent Moon, The (*Chinsetsu yumiharizuki* 椿説弓張月, 1811). A fictitious *yomihon* account of the warrior Minamoto no Tametomo by Takizawa Bakin, illustrated by Katsushika Hokusai.

Cui Bao (崔豹). Author of *Commentaries on Things Now and Old* (*Gujin zhu* 古今注, the Jin period).

Customs, Manners, and Fashions of the Capital (*Miyako fūzoku kewai den* 都風俗化粧傳, 1813). Written by the late Edo cosmetics researcher Sayama Hanshichimaru (佐山半七丸).

Daji (妲己, eleventh century BCE). A favorite consort of King Zhou of Shang, the last king of the Shang dynasty in ancient China. She is a classic example of how a beauty causes the downfall of a kingdom in Chinese culture.

"Dancing, a Rhyme-Prose" ("Wu fu" 舞賦). A poem by Fu Yi (傅毅) of the Han period.

Dancing Girl (*Maihime* 舞姬, 1890). A novel by Mori Ōgai.

Diary of Izumi Shikibu (*Izumi Shikibu nikki* 和泉式部日記). A memoir by the mid-Heian *waka* poet and court lady Izumi Shikibu (born 977?).

Diary of Murasaki Shikibu, The (*Murasaki Shikibu nikki* 紫式部日記). A memoir by Murasaki Shikibu covering a period from the early autumn of 1008 to the beginning of 1010. Known also as *The Diary of Lady Murasaki* in Richard Bowring's revised edition of his earlier work, *Murasaki Shikibu: Diary and Poetic Memoirs*.

"Divine Woman, The" ("Shennü fu" 神女賦). A rhyme-prose piece by Song Yu (宋玉) of the Warring States period, also known in English as "Rhapsody on the Goddess."

Dream of Red Mansions, A (*Honglou meng* 紅樓夢). A novel in vernacular Chinese written in mid-eighteenth century in the Qing period. The main portions are said to have been written by Cao Xueqin (曹雪斤). Also translated as *Dream of the Red Chamber*.

Drifting Clouds (*Ukigumo* 浮雲, 1887). A novel by Futabatei Shimei (二葉亭四迷).

"Early Spring's Faint Rain." A poem by Li Shanfu (李山甫).

Eight Dog Chronicles (*Nansō Satomi hakkenden* 南總里見八犬傳, 1814–1842). Long fiction by Takizawa Bakin (瀧澤馬琴). Also known as *Tale of Eight Dogs* and *The Story of Eight Virtuous Heroes*.

Empress Consort Wu (Zetian Wu Hou 則天武后, or Wu Zetian 武則天, 624–705). She was the only woman in the history of China to assume the title of emperor (*huangdi* 皇帝), or empress regnant.

Empress Dowager Lü (d. 180 BCE). The wife of Emperor Gaozu of the Han dynasty.

Erya (爾雅). The oldest extant Chinese dictionary or encyclopedia, probably dating from the third century BCE. It has been translated as *The Literary Expositor*, *The Ready Rectifier*, *Progress towards Correctness*, and *Approaching Elegance/Refinement*.

Essence of Japanese Prose (*Honchō monzui* 本朝文粹). A mid-eleventh-century Japanese anthology of exemplary Chinese-language prose and poetic prose, compiled by Fujiwara no Akihira (藤原明衡, 989–1066).

Essence of Medical Prescriptions, The (*Ishinbō* 醫心方, 984). The earliest extant Japanese medical text covering all areas of health. Compiled by Tanba no Yasuyori (丹波康賴, 912–995).

Essence of the Novel, The (*Shōsesu shinzui* 小説神髓, 1885). A treatise by Tsubouchi Shōyō (坪内逍遥, 1859–1935), critiquing late Edo prose and advocating conventions of Western realism.

Essential Skills for People (*Qimin yaoshu* 齊民要術, ca. 544). An ancient Chinese agricultural text written by the Northern Wei dynasty official Jia Sixie (賈思勰). Also known as *Main Techniques for the Welfare of the People*.

Etymological Dictionary of Names (*Shiming* 釋名). A dictionary compiled by Liu Xi (劉熙) of the Later Han (25–220).

"Eyebrow Ink" ("Haizumi" はいずみ). A piece in *The Tales of the Riverside Middle Counselor*.

Feng Menglong (馮夢龍, 1574–1645). Man of letters of the Ming period and the editor of *Stories Old and New*, *Stories to Awaken the World*, and *Stories to Instruct the World*.

Five Miscellanies (*Wu zazu* 五雜組; 五雜俎). Also translated as *Five Assorted Offerings*. Essays under the five categories of heaven, earth, humans, things, and affairs, written by Xie Zhaozhe (謝肇淛, 1567–1624).

Forest of Gems in the Garden of the Dharma (*Fayuan zhulin* 法苑珠林). An encyclopedia of Buddhism, completed by Dao Shi (道世) in 668.

"Fox of Kowata" ("Kowata-gitsune" 木幡狐). An *otogizōshi* tale, in which a fox maiden marries a human.

fu (賦). Rhyme-prose, also called *rhapsody* in English. A form of prose-poem popular in ancient China, especially during the Han dynasty and the Six Dynasties period. Usually consists of a combination of prose and rhymed verse.

Full Account of Sakurahime: Dawn Light Storybook, The (*Sakurahime zenden akebono sōshi* 櫻姫全傳曙草紙, 1805). Long fiction by Santō Kyōden (山東京傳) and illustrated by Utagawa Toyokuni (歌川豊國).

Fūrai Sanjin (風來山人). An alias of Hiraga Gennai (平賀源内, 1728–1780), an Edo period doctor, author, and painter.

Futabatei Shimei (二葉亭四迷, 1864–1909). A Japanese author, translator, and literary critic.

ganguro. Apparently from *gangan kuroi*, meaning "intensely dark," is an artificial deep tan makeup accentuated by contrasting white color and dyed blonde hair. This style was particularly popular in the late 1990s and early 2000.

Garland of Heroes, A (*Hanabusa sōshi* 英草紙, 1749). A *yomihon* by Tsuga Teishō (都賀庭鐘) of nine stories.

gazoku setchūtai (雅俗折衷体). An eclectic style in Japanese literature combining the literary and the vernacular.

Ge Hong (葛洪, 283–343). A Jin dynasty writer and the author of *Baopuzi*.

genbun itchi (言文一致). Usually translated into English as "unification of spoken and written language." It is also short for *genbun itchi tai*, "unified style," modern written Japanese that emerged out of the literary effort in the Meiji era to write in a style that is close to the modern vernacular.

giko-monogatari (擬古物語). "Pseudo-classic tales" or "stories modeled after old tales." Narratives of the Kamakura period (1185–1333), most of them indebted to *The Tale of Genji* and *The Tale of Sagoromo* (which is also considered a *giko-monogatari*).

Gleanings from the Kaiyuan and Tianbao Eras. See *Memorabilia of the Kaiyuan and Tianbao Eras*.

Gleanings of the Daye Era (*Daye shiyi ji* 大業拾遺記). Tang accounts of the events of the court of Emperor Yang of Sui (隋煬帝, 569–618).
Glories and Graces (*Bunka shūreishū* 文華秀麗集). Early Heian *kanshi* collection. It was ordered by Saga (ruled 809–823), and compiled by Fujiwara Fuyutsugu and others by 818. It contains 148 poems by twenty-six poets.
"Goddess of the Luo, The" ("Luoshui-shen fu" 洛水神賦). A rhyme-prose piece by Cao Zhi (曹植, 199–232).
Goddess of the Luo Illustrated, The (*Luoshui-shen fu tu* 洛水神賦圖). A scroll painting by Gu Kaizhi illustrating Cao Zhi's rhyme-prose, "The Goddess of the Luo."
Golden Demon, The (*Konjiki yasha* 金色夜叉, 1897–1902). A novel by Ozaki Kōyō (尾崎紅葉).
"Grand Beauty, The" ("Shiren" 碩人). A poem in the "Odes of Wei" in *The Book of Songs*.
Great Learning for Women (*Onna daigaku* 女大學). A general name referring to the lessons for women and their variants that came to be used for women's education in the mid-Edo period. It is so named after *The Great Learning*, one of the Four Books and Five Classics of China.
Grotto of Immortals, The (*Youxian ku* 遊仙窟). Fiction by Zhang Wencheng (張文成) (also known as Zhang Zhuo 張鷟, 660?–741).
Gu Kaizhi (顧愷之, 344–405?). A celebrated Chinese painter of the Eastern Jin period.
Han Xizai's Night Revels (*Han Xizai yeyuan tu* 韓熙載夜宴図). A painting by Gu Hongzhong (顧閎中) from the mid-tenth century.
Han Yu (韓愈, 768–824). A Tang period essayist and poet, and also a precursor of Neo-Confucianism.
Higuchi Ichiyō (樋口一葉, 1872–1896). A Meiji woman writer.
History of Southern Dynasties, The (*Nanshi* 南史). One of the official Chinese dynastic histories. It covers the period from 420 to 589 and was completed between 643 and 659.
Records of the Three Kingdoms (*Sanguo zhi* 三國志). A book complied around 280–290, also known as *History of the Three States*.
Ihara Saikaku (井原西鶴, 1642–1693). An Edo poet and author.
Imperial Readings of the Taiping Era (*Taiping yulan* 太平御覽). An encyclopedia compiled by Li Fang (李昉) and others from 977 to 983.
Japanese Outlaws of the March (*Honchō Suikoden* 本朝水滸傳, 1773). A free adaptation by Takebe Ayatari (建部綾足) of the Chinese *Outlaws of the Marsh*.
Jeweled Chamber Secrets (*Yufang mijue* 玉房秘訣). A manual ascribed to the Six Dynasties period (222–589).

Kaibara Ekiken (貝原益軒, 1630–1714). An early Edo Neo-Confucian scholar and botanist.

kanazōshi (假名草子). A general term for popular works published between 1600 and 1682, referring to a book of short tales written primarily in *kana* (Japanese phonetic characters) and in accessible Japanese rather than in Chinese or Sinicized Japanese in which learned books were written.

kanbun (漢文). A Japanese term referring to composition, by Japanese, of prose in premodern Chinese. In a broad sense it refers to any literary Chinese-language prose, by Chinese or any others, and read in literary Japanese.

kanshi (漢詩). A Japanese term referring to verse composition in literary Chinese, written by Chinese or any others and read in literary Japanese.

kanshibun (漢詩文). Verse and prose in literary Chinese.

Ken'yūsha ("Friends of the Inkstone" 硯友社). A literary coterie, 1885–1903. Under the leadership of the novelist Ozaki Kōyō, it developed into Japan's first modern literary clique.

Kitagawa Utamaro (喜多川歌麿, ca. 1755–1806). A representative Edo period *ukiyo-e* artist.

kundoku (Sino-Japanese reading 訓読). The way of reading literary Chinese as literary Japanese following Japanese grammar, usually with the help of pointers and added *kana*. The Chinese text remains intact, but word order is changed in reading to suit Japanese grammar, and Japanese verb endings and particles are added to facilitate "translation." It is also called *yomikudashi*.

Kyokutei Bakin (曲亭馬琴, 1767–1848). A late Edo period author best known for *Eight Dog Chronicles* (*Nansō Satomi hakkenden* 南總里見八犬傳, 1814–1832) and *The Crescent Moon* (*Chinsetsu yumiharizuki* 椿説弓張, 1811). Also known as Takizawa Bakin (瀧澤馬琴).

"Lady Li, a Rhyme-Prose" ("Li furen fu" 李夫人賦). A poem by Emperor Wu (武帝) of Han.

Lady of the Camellias (*Tsubakihime* 椿姫, 1902). A Japanese translation by Osada Shūtō (長田秋濤) of *La Dame aux Camélias* by Alexandre Dumas, fils.

"Lady Who Loved Caterpillars, The" ("Mushi mezuru himegimi" 蟲めづる姫君). A piece in *The Tales of the Riverside Middle Counselor*.

"Lament, The" ("Lisao" 離騷). A poem by Qu Yuan (340–278 BCE) of the State of Chu, a representative piece in the *Songs of the South* (*Chu ci*). Also translated as "Encountering Trouble."

"Legend of Dame Ren" ("Ren-shi zhuan" 任氏傳). Written by Shen Jiji (沈既済, ca. 740–799). A Tang period story about a certain Zheng who falls in love with a woman and marries her. In fact a bewitching fox, she remains loyal to her husband. In the end, she is killed by a dog.

Leng Mei (冷枚). A Qing period artist.

Lessons with Illustrations for Admonishing Women (*Jokai e-iri onna jitsugo-kyō* 女誡繪入女實語教, 1695). Moral lessons for women written and illustrated by the woman author Isome Tsuna (居初津奈).

Life-Nourishing Principles (*Yōjō-kun* 養生訓). A medical-philosophical instruction book by the Edo period Neo-Confucianist Kaibara Ekiken (貝原益軒, 1713).

Life of an Amorous Man, The (*Kōshoku ichidai otoko* 好色一代男, 1682). A novel by Ihara Saikaku.

Li He (李賀, 790–816). A Tang period poet.

Li Ji (驪姬 ?–651 BCE). A concubine and later wife of Duke Xian of Jin, ruler of the State of Jin between 676 and 651 BCE during the Spring and Autumn period. She is known for starting the Liji Incident that led to the suicide of Prince Shensheng.

Lin Biao (林彪, 1907–1971). A Chinese Communist military leader who rose to prominence during the Cultural Revolution, climbing as high as Mao Zedong's designated successor. He died in a plane crash in Mongolia after what appears to have been a failed coup to oust Mao.

Lin Daiyu (林黛玉). A character in *A Dream of Red Mansions*. The given name means Blue-Black Jade.

Lingering Fragrance of Plum Buds (*Bairai yokun* 梅蕾餘薫, 1886–1887). A loose Meiji translation by Ushiyama Ryōsuke (牛山良介) of Sir Walter Scott's *Ivanhoe* (1819).

Li Shanfu (李山甫). A Tang period poet.

Literary Selections (文選). One of the earliest existing collections of Chinese poetry. It contains verse and prose from the Qin dynasty, Han dynasty, and later. It was compiled around 520 CE during the Southern dynasty by Prince Zhaoming (昭明太子), the eldest son of Emperor Wu of Liang, and a group of scholars he had assembled.

Literary Theory (*Bungakuron* 文學論, 1907). A treatise by Natsume Sōseki (夏目漱石).

"Little Atsumori" ("Ko-Atsumori" 小敦盛). An *otogizōshi* story about the legendary child left by Taira no Atsumori, who died during the so-called Genpei (Taira-Minamoto) War of 1180–1185.

Liu Xiang (劉向, about 77–76 BCE). Biographer and scholar. Author of *Biographies of Exemplary Women*.

Liu Yiqing (劉義慶, 403–444). A man of letters in the North and South period, known as the author of *A New Account of Tales of the World*.

Li Yu (李漁, 1610–1680). Dramatist of the Qing period, pen name Li Liweng (李笠翁). Author of *Complete Collection of Li Yu* and *Occasional Contemplations*.

Love Story of Flower and Willow (*Karyū shun'wa* 花柳春話, 1878). A free translation by Niwa Jun'ichirō (丹羽純一郎) of Edward George Earle Bulwer-Lytton's *Ernest Maltravers* and its sequel *Alice*.

Love-Tinted Garden of Fukagawa (*Shunshoku Tatsumi no sono* 春色辰巳園, 1833–1835). A sequel to *The Love-Tinted Plum Calendar*.

Love-Tinted Plum Calendar, The (*Shunshoku umegoyomi* 春色梅児誉美, 1832–1833). A *ninjōbon* story by Tamenaga Shunsui.

Loyal Retainers: Outlaws of the Marsh (*Chūshin Suikoden* 忠臣水滸傳, 1799–1801). A *yomihon* adaptation of the Chinese *Outlaws of the Marsh* by Santō Kyōden (山東京傳).

Ma Gao (馬縞). Author of *Commentaries on Things Now and Old in Central China* (*Zhonghua gujin zhu* 中華古今注).

Mandarin-Duck Coverlets (*Yuanyang bei* 鴛鴦被). A Yuan dynasty drama.

Memorabilia of the Kaiyuan and Tianbao Eras (*Kaiyuan Tianbao yishi* 開元天寶遺事). A collection of episodes from the two eras of Emperor Xuanzong of the Tang, written by Wang Renyu (王仁裕 880–956) of the Five Dynasties period.

Mirrors for Wife and Husband (*Imo-to-se kagami* 妹と背鏡, 1886). A novel by Tsubouchi Shōyō (坪内逍遥).

Miscellaneous Morsels from Youyang (*Youyang zazu* 酉陽雜俎). A collection of legends, reports, and so forth by Duan Chengshi (段成式, d. 863). The title is also more literally translated as *Miscellaneous Delicacies from the South Slope of Mount You*.

Miscellaneous Notes on a Journey to the East (*Tōyū zakki* 東遊雜記, 1788). A travelogue by the mid-Edo geographer Furukawa Koshōken (古川古松軒, 1726–1807).

Mori Ōgai (森鷗外, 1862–1922). A novelist, playwright, translator, and army doctor of the Meiji to Taishō eras.

Morisada's Rambling Writings (*Morisada mankō* 守貞謾稿, sometimes written 守貞漫稿). An encyclopedic work by Kitagawa Morisada (喜田川守貞) primarily based on firsthand observations. The writing began in 1837 and continued to 1867. There is a publication date of 1853. The work is sometimes referred to now as *Customs and Manners of the Recent Times* (*Kinsei fūzoku-shi* 近世風俗志).

Moxi (妹喜). A consort of the notorious King Jie (桀, 1728–1675 BCE) of the Xia dynasty of China.

Mr. Lü's Spring and Autumn Annals (*Lüshi Chunqiu* 呂氏春秋). An encyclopedic Chinese classic text in twenty-six volumes compiled around 239 BCE under the patronage of the Qin dynasty chancellor Lü Buwei (呂不韋).

Murasaki Shikibu Diary (*Murasaki Shikibu nikki* 紫式部日記). A memoir written by the author of *The Tale of Genji*. It covers a brief period from the early autumn of 1008 to the beginning of 1010.

Namiko (*Hototogisu* 不如歸, 1898–1899). A novel by Tokutomi Roka (徳富蘆花). Namiko is the name of the female protagonist. The original title refers to "lesser cuckoo," a bird with many Chinese and Japanese legends.

Natsume Sōseki (夏目漱石, 1867–1916). Novelist and scholar of English literature.

New Account of Tales of the World, A (*Shishuo xin'yu* 世説新語). An early fifth-century collection of tales by Liu Yiqing (劉義慶, 403–444).

New Lamp-Wick Trimming Stories (*Jiandeng xinhua* 剪燈新話). A Ming collection of supernatural stories compiled by Qu You (瞿佑) around 1378.

New Songs from a Jade Terrace (*Yutai xinyong* 玉臺新咏). An anthology of love poems compiled c. 545 by the court poet Xu Ling (徐陵).

New Year pictures (*nianhua* 年画). A form of Chinese colored woodblock print for decoration during the Chinese New Year holiday.

Niimura Nobu (新村信, d. 1905). Consort of Tokugawa Yoshinobu, the last shōgun (1837–1913).

ninjōbon (人情本). "Books of human feeling," or narratives of love that developed in the Edo period.

nishiki-e (錦絵). Color *ukiyo-e* prints that developed during the Edo period.

Niwa Jun'ichirō (丹羽純一郎, 1851–1919). A Meiji translator and critic; also known as Oda Jun'ichirō (織田純一郎), a name he adopted from 1879 on.

Occasional Contemplations (*Jianqing ouji* 閒情偶寄). A Qing period book by Li Yu (李漁, 1611–1680), also called *Casual Writings of Leisurely Mood*.

Occasional Jottings aboard a Raft (*Chengcha biji* 乘槎筆記, 1866). A record of personal experiences by Bin Chun (斌椿, b. 1804).

Ōe no Asatsuna (大江朝綱, 886–957). Heian period writer of Chinese poetry and prose.

"Oil Peddler Wins the Queen of Flowers, The" ("Maiyoulang duzhan huakui" 賣油郎獨占花魁). A piece in *Stories to Awaken the World* (*Xingshi hengyan* 醒世恒言, 1627).

Okajima Kanzan (岡島冠山, 1674–1728). A mid-Edo Confucian scholar and translator.

Old Book of Tang (*Jiu Tangshu* 舊唐書). Also simply *Book of Tang* (*Tangshu*). It is the first classic work about the Tang dynasty. The book was begun at the order of Gaozu (高祖) of Later Jin in 941 and was presented to the Emperor Chudi in 945 by its chief editor, Liu Xu (劉昫).

Onna daigaku. Confucian moral lessons for women in Edo period Japan. The first 1716 publication was followed by a number of variations.

Origins of Things, The (*Shiwu jiyuan* 事物紀原). A dictionary of origins compiled by Gao Cheng (高承) of the Song period.

otogizōshi. Shorter prose narratives flourishing from Muromachi to early Edo, often called "companion tales" in English.

Outlaws of the Marsh (*Shuihu zhuan* 水滸傳). A Ming period novel, also known as *Water Margin*, *All Men Are Brothers*, *Men of the Marshes*, or *The Marshes of Mount Liang*, attributed to Shi Naian (施耐庵) or Shi Naian and Luo Gaunzhong (羅貫中). One of the four great classical novels of Chinese literature.

Ozaki Kōyō (尾崎紅葉, 1868–1903). A Meiji novelist and founding member of the Ken'yūsha (1885–1903), the first serious Japanese literary coterie.

Pan Jinlian (潘金蓮). A female character in *Outlaws of the Marsh* and *The Plum in the Golden Vase*, known as Golden Lotus in English. She conspires with her lover Ximen Qing to kill her husband Wu the Elder.

"Peony Lantern, The" ("Botan no tōro" or "Botan dōro" 牡丹燈籠). A story in Asai Ryōi's *The Protective Doll* and adaptation from the Chinese ghost story called "The Account of the Peony Lantern" in *New Lamp-Wick Trimming Stories*.

Peony Pavilion, The (*Mutan ting* 牡丹亭). A play written by Tang Xianzu (湯顯祖) in the Ming period and first performed in 1598 at the Pavilion of Prince Teng. Also called *The Peony Pavilion: A Record of a Return to Life* (*Mutan ting huanhun ji* 牡丹亭還魂記) or simply *A Record of a Return to Life* (*Huanhun ji* 還魂記).

Pillow Book, The (*Makura no sōshi*). A collection of essays by the mid-Heian woman author Sei Shōnagon (清少納言).

"Pledge of Mandarin Ducks unto Death, The." A piece in *Qingpingshan Studio Promptbooks* (*Qingpingshantang huaben*) of the Ming period.

Plum Blossoms in the Snow (*Setchūbai* 雪中梅, 1886). A Meiji political novel by Suehiro Tetchō (末廣鐵腸).

Plum in the Golden Vase, The (*Jinping mei* 金瓶梅). Also known in English as *Gold Vase Plum*, or *The Golden Lotus*. A spin-off from *Outlaws of the*

Marsh. A Chinese vernacular novel composed between 1573 and 1620 during the late Ming period by Lanling Xiaoxiao Sheng (蘭陵笑笑生), "The Lanling Laughing Scholar."

"Poem on a Hapless Beauty" ("Boming jiaren shi" 薄命佳人詩). A poem by the Northern Song poet Su Shi (蘇軾, 1036–1101). The phrase "fair women, hapless fate" ("jiaren boming" 佳人薄命) is said to come from this poem.

Popular Account of Loyal Outlaws of the Marsh, A (*Tsūzoku chūgi Suikoden* 通俗忠義水滸傳, 1757–1784). A Japanese translation by Okajima Kanzan (Edo scholar of Chinese studies, ?–1728) of the *Outlaws of the Marsh*.

Portrait of Ladies-in-Waiting at the Go Board (*Yiqi Shinyü tu* 奕棋仕女圖). A painting from a tomb in Turpan prefecture in Xinjiang.

"Powder Girl." A story in *Records of Light and Dark*.

Priest Kyata (僧伽多). An Indian priest in *Stories Gleaned at Uji*, volume 6, story 9 (or story 91 consecutively numbered). Priest Jialuo (僧伽羅) in the source story in *The Great Tang Records on the Western Regions* (*Da Tang Xiyu Ji* 大唐西域記).

Protective Doll, The (*Otogibōko* 御伽婢子, 1666). A collection of sixty-eight ghost stories by Asai Ryōi, including adaptions of Chinese stories from *Stories for Trimming the Lamp Wick* and its sequels as well as other collections. An *otogibōko* is a stuffed doll believed to protect children.

"Qiao Yanjie's Concubine Ruins the Family." A chapter in *Stories to Caution the World*.

Qingpingshan Studio Promptbooks (*Qingpingshantang huaben* 清平山堂話本). A Ming period collection of vernacular short stories compiled around 1541 by Hong Pian (洪楩) of the "Clear and Peaceful Mountain Studio."

Qu You (瞿佑, 1341–1427). Writer and poet of the Ming period, author of *New Lamp-Wick Trimming Stories*.

Qu Yuan (屈原, about 339–278 BCE). A poet, scholar, and minister to the king of the Southern Chu during the Warring States period.

Record of Ancient Matters (*Kojiki* 古事記). A Japanese chronicle compiled in 712.

Records of Light and Dark (*Youming lu* 幽明錄). A collection of tales of the strange by Liu Yiqing (劉義慶, 404–444) of the Six Dynasties period.

Records of the Grand Historian (*Shi ji* 史記). A Chinese history written from 109 BCE to 91 BCE by Sima Qian (司馬遷).

Records of the Three Kingdoms (*Sanguo zhi* 三國志). The history of the Three Kingdoms period covering the years 189–280. Written by Chen Shou (珍壽) in the third century.

Red Poppy, The (*Gubijinsō* 虞美人草, 1907). A novel by Natsume Sōseki (夏目漱石).

Remarkable Stories New and Old (*Jingu qiguan* 今古奇觀). A late Ming collection of vernacular stories by Baoweng Laoren (抱甕老人).

Restored to Life (*Huanhun ji* 還魂記). Drama in fifty-five scenes by Tang Xianzu of the Ming period. See *The Peony Pavilion* (*Mudan ting* 牡丹亭).

Rise and Fall of the Minamoto and the Taira (*Genpei jōsuiki* 源平盛衰記). Also known as *An Account of the Genpei Wars*. Late Kamakura or early Nanboku tale of war.

Romance of the Western Bower (*Xixiang ji* 西廂記). A Chinese drama by the Yuan period playwright Wang Shifu (王實甫, ca. 1260–1336). and set in the Tang dynasty. Also known in English as *West Chamber Romance*.

"Saiki" ("Saiki" さいき). An *otogizōshi* tale.

Sanshirō (*Sanshirō* 三四郎, 1908). A novel by Natsume Sōseki.

Santō Kyōden (山東京傳, 1761–1816). Mid-Edo poet, writer, and *ukiyo-e* artist with another pseudonym of Kitao Masanobu. He is particularly known for his "reading books" as well as novels depicting visitors to licensed quarters.

"San'yan Erpai" (三言二拍). See "Three Words and Two Slaps."

"San'yue Performances, a Relief." Unearthed from the tomb of Wang Chuzhi in Quyang County, Hebei province.

Sarashina Diary, The (*Sarashina nikki* 更級日記). A memoir by Sugawara no Takasue's daughter (b. 1008).

Sayama Hanshichimaru (佐山半七丸). Edo researcher of cosmetics and the author of *Customs, Manners, and Fashions of the Capital* (*Miyako fūzoku kewai den*, 1813).

Sequel to a Treatise on Curiosities (*Xu Bowu-zhi* 續博物誌). A dictionary by Li Shi (李石) of the Song period.

"Seven Explications" ("Qishi" 七釋). A writing by the Later Han scholar Wang Can (王粲, 177–217).

Shikitei Sanba (式亭三馬, 1776–1822). An Edo period author and *ukiyo-e* artist, particularly known for *The Bathhouse of the Floating World* (*Ukiyoburo*, 1809–1813) and *The Barbershop of the Floating World* (*Ukiyodoko*, 1813–1814).

shinü-hua (仕女画). Chinese paintings of court ladies.

shōjo manga (少女マンガ). Contemporary Japanese visual fiction targeted at girls and young females.

Shōtoku Tennō (稱德天皇, 718–770). A Japanese female emperor who ruled first as Kōken (孝謙, 749–758), then as Shōtoku (764–770).

Sikong Shu (司空曙, ca. 720–ca. 760). A poet of the Tang period.

Sima Xiangru (司馬相如, 179–117 BCE). A minor official of the Western Han dynasty, well known for his poetic skills and controversial marriage to the widow Zhuo Wenjun (卓文君).

Somedono no Kisai (also Kisaki) (染殿后, 829–900). "Empress at the Somedono," real name Fujiwara no Akirakeiko, and empress of Montoku.

"Song of a Sleepless Night" ("Yezuo yin" 夜坐吟). A poem by Li He (李賀, 790–816).

"Song of Lasting Regret, The" ("Changhen ge" 長恨歌). A celebrated poem by Bo Juyi (白居易). Also known as "The Song of Everlasting Sorrow."

Songs of Chu (*Chu ci* 楚辭). Also called *Songs of the South*. An anthology of Chinese poems by Qu Yuan (屈原) and Song Yu (宋玉) from the Warring States period and subsequent imitators of their poetic style. It is the second-oldest collection of Chinese poems on record.

Song Yu (宋玉, 303?–221? BCE). A well-known Chinese poet in the State of Chu; the author of "The Divine Woman" (also known as "Rhapsody on the Goddess"). Several poems in the *Songs of the South* are attributed to him.

"South of the River Tune" ("Jiangnan qu" 江南曲). A poem by Wen Tingyin (温庭筠).

Spring Outing of the Lady of the State of Guo (*Guo-guo Furen youchun tu* 虢国夫人遊春図). A painting by Zhang Xuan, also known in English as *Spring Outing of the Tang Court*.

Stories Gleaned at Uji (*Uji shūi monogatari* 宇治拾遺物語). Early Kamakura collection of tales (ca. 1190–1242). The title is also understood to mean *Stories Gleaned by the Uji Great Counselor*, but the identity of the compiler(s) is unknown.

Stories Old and New (*Gujin xiaoshuo* 古今小説). A collection of stories (1620 or 1621) edited by Feng Menlong, also known as *Stories to Instruct the World* or *Illustrious Words to Instruct the World* (*Yushi mingyan* 喻世明言).

Stories to Awaken the World (*Xingshi hengyan* 醒世恒言, 1627). A collection of stories edited by Feng Menlong, also known as *Constant Words to Awaken the World*.

Stories to Caution the World (*Jingshi tongyan* 警世通言). A collection of stories (1624) edited by Feng Menlong, also known as *Comprehensive Words to Caution the World*.

"Story of Yingying" ("Yingying zhuan" 鶯鶯傳). A Tang period supernatural story attributed to Yuan Zhen (779–831).

Story of Yoshitsune, The (*Gikeiki* 義經記). A Muromachi period tale of war in eight parts. Yoshitsune, the title character, is also one of the main characters in *The Tale of the Heike*.

Strange Encounters with Beautiful Women (*Kajin no kigū* 佳人之奇遇, 1885–1897). A Meiji political novel by Tōkai Sanshi (東海散士).

Strange Tales from Make-Do Studio (*Liaozhai zhiyi* 聊齋志異). A late seventeenth-century collection of stories by Pu Songling (蒲松齡, 1640–1715), also known in English as *Strange Tales of Liaozhai*.

Strategies of the Warring States (*Zhanguo ce* 戰國策). An ancient Chinese historical work and compilation of materials on the Warring States period compiled between the third and first centuries BCE, and put together by Liu Xiang (77–6 BCE) of the Han period.

Suehiro Tetchō (末廣鐵腸, 1849–1896). A Meiji activist and writer.

Sugawara no Michizane (菅原道眞, 845–903). A scholar, *kanshi* poet, and courtier of Heian Japan. The author of *Sugawara Poems* (*Kanke bunsō*, probably 900).

Supplementary Lamp-Wick Trimming Stories (*Jiandeng yuhua* 剪燈餘話). A collection of stories by Li Zhen (李禎).

Su Shi or **Su Dongpo** (蘇軾, 蘇東坡, 1036–1101). The Northern Song poet and the author of "Poem on a Hapless Beauty" ("Boming jiaren shi").

Suzuki Harunobu (鈴木春信, 1725–1770). A mid-Edo *ukiyo-e* artist.

Taiheiki (*Taiheiki* 太平記). See *The Chronicle of Great Peace*.

Takebe Ayatari (建部綾足, 1719–1774). Mid-Edo haiku poet and author of *yomihon* and travelogues.

Takehisa Yumeji (竹久夢二, 1884–1934). A Japanese painter and poet who represents Taishō-era romanticism.

Takizawa Bakin (瀧澤馬琴, 1767–1848). Late Edo writer of *yomihon* ("reading book") and *kusazōshi* (illustrated fiction for popular audiences). Author of *Eight Dog Chronicles*.

"Tale of Bunshō" ("Bunshō sōshi" 文正草子). An *otogizōshi* tale.

Tale of Flowering Splendor, The (*Eiga monogatari* 榮花物語; 榮華物語). Late Heian historical tale in forty parts, believed to have been written by a number of mostly female authors over the course of roughly a century, from 1028 to 1107. It relates the events in the life of the courtier Fujiwara no Michinaga. In William and Helen McCullough's translation it is called

A Tale of Flowering Fortunes: Annals of Japanese Aristocratic Life in the Heian Period.
Tale of Genji, The (*Genji monogatari* 源氏物語). Early eleventh-century long fiction by Murasaki Shikibu (紫式部).
Tale of Middle Counselor Hamamatsu, The (*Hamamatsu Chūnagon monogatari* 濱松中納言物語). An eleventh-century tale, traditionally ascribed to Sugawara no Takasue's daughter (b. 1008).
Tale of Nishiyama (*Nishiyama monogatari* 西山物語, 1768). A *yomihon* story by Takebe Ayatari (建部綾足).
Tale of Ochikubo, The (*Ochikubo monogatari* 落窪物語). A mid-Heian narrative dating from the later tenth century.
Tale of Sagoromo, The (*Sagoromo monogatari* 狹衣物語). A late Heian narrative attributed to Rokujō Saiin Baishi Naishinnō no Senji (?1022–1092).
Tale of the Heike, The (*Heike monogatari* 平家物語). A Kamakura period martial tale about the struggles between the Heike (Taira) and Genji (Minamoto) houses, covering the period about 1131–1191.
Tale of the Hollow Tree, The (*Utsuho monogatari* 宇津保物語). Early Heian fiction in twenty parts and a predecessor of *The Tale of Genji*.
"Tale of the Rat, The" ("Nezumi no sōshi" 鼠草子). A mid-Muromachi *otogizōshi* and picture scroll about a rat marrying, under disguise, a young human woman.
Tale of Udumbara Flowers, The (*Udonge monogatari* 優曇華物語, 1804). A *yomihon* revenge story by Santō Kyōden (山東京傳).
Tales for Comfort (*Otogi monogatari* 御伽物語, 1678). A collection of supernatural stories of the *kanazōshi* genre.
Tales of Moon and Rain (*Ugetsu monogatari* 雨月物語, 1768). A collection of nine stories by Ueda Akinari (上田秋成) inspired by Chinese ghost stories.
Tales of Overgrown Fields (*Shigeshige yawa* 繁野話, 1766). A collection of nine tales of the *yomihon* genre by Tsuga Teishō (都賀庭鐘).
Tales of the Riverside Middle Counselor, The (*Tsutsumi Chūnagon monogatari* 堤中納言物語, ca. 1055). Late Heian collection of ten short tales and a fragment.
Tales of the Strange (*Zhiguai xiaoshuo* 志怪小説). Chinese supernatural stories.
Tales of Yamato (*Yamato monogatari* 大和物語). A Heian collection of brief tales centering on *waka*.
Tamenaga Shunsui (爲永春水). A late Edo author of *ninjōbon* (1790–1843). Author of *The Love-Tinted Plum Calendar* (*Shunshoku umegoyomi*, 1832–1833).

Tanizaki Jun'ichirō (谷崎潤一郎, 1886–1965). A twentieth-century Japanese novelist.

Temperaments of Contemporary Students (*Tōsei shosei katagi* 當世書生気質, 1885–1886). A novel by Tsubouchi Shōyō (坪内逍遙).

Ten Nights of Dream (*Yume jūya* 夢十夜, 1908). A series of short dream pieces by Natsume Sōseki (夏目漱石).

"Three Words and Two Slaps" ("San'yan Erpai" 三言二拍). A collective name for the Chinese anthologies of stories in the vernacular in the Ming period: *Constant Words to Awaken the World*, *Comprehensive Words to Caution the World*, *Illustrious Words to Instruct the World*; and *Desk-Slapping Wonders, First Collection* and *Desk-Slapping Wonders, Second Collection*. The first three are better known in English as *Stories to Awaken the World*, *Stories to Caution the World*, and *Stories to Instruct the World*. The last two titles are also translated into *Slapping the Desk in Amazement, First Collection* and *Slapping the Desk in Amazement, Second Collection*.

Tōkai Sanshi (東海散士, 1853–1922). A Meiji to Taishō era politician and novelist.

Tokutomi Roka (德富蘆花, 1868–1927). A Meiji to Taishō era novelist.

Tosa Diary (*Tosa nikki* 土佐日記). Written by Ki no Tsurayuki (ca. 872–945), ca. 935, and presented as if it were a travelogue recorded by a woman. The oldest piece of Japanese prose literature extant in its original form.

Treasury of Great Learning for Women (*Onna-Daigaku takarabako* 女大學寶箱). A Japanese book of lessons published in 1716 and the first published version of a set of lessons for women derived from a piece by Kaibara Ekiken.

Treatise on Curiosities (*Bowu-zhi* 博物志). A dictionary compiled by Zhang Hua (張華, 232–300) of the Jin period.

Tsubouchi Shōyō (坪内逍遙, 1859–1935). Playwright, novelist, literary theorist, and translator.

Tsuga Teishō (都賀庭鐘, 1718–1794). A mid-Edo period *yomihon* author, Confucian scholar, and physician.

Twenty-Four Histories (*Ershisi shi* 二十四史). A collection of Chinese historical books covering a period from 3000 BCE to the Ming dynasty in the seventeenth century. The number is twenty-five with the *New Yuan History* (新元史), and twenty-six with *Draft History of Qing* (*Qingshi gao* 清史稿) compiled in 1927 under Zhao Erxun (趙爾巽).

Ueda Akinari (上田秋成, 1734–1809). An Edo period author, scholar, and *waka* poet, especially popular for *Tales of Moon and Rain* and *Tales of Spring Rain*.

ukiyo-e (浮世繪). A genre of art that developed in the Edo period in woodblock prints and paintings. The term *ukiyo* (floating world) partly means "contemporaneous," and thus the genre features motifs of the customs and manners of the day as well as of landscapes, tales from history, the theater, and pleasure quarters.

Ushiyama Ryōsuke (牛山良助). The Meiji translator of Sir Walter Scott's *Ivanhoe*. Also known as Ushiyama Kakudō (牛山鶴堂).

Utagawa Toyohiro (歌川豊廣, 1773–1830). An Edo period *ukiyo-e* artist.

Utagawa Toyokuni (歌川豊國, 1769–1825). A master of *ukiyo-e*, known for his *bijinga* and kabuki actor prints.

"Viewing a Beauty." A poem by Shi Jianwu (施肩吾).

"Viewing a Courtesan." A poem by Sikong Shu (司空曙).

waka (和歌). In the broadest sense, Japanese poetry as opposed to Chinese poetry; in the most restricted sense, synonymous with *tanka* ("short verse" in 5/7/5/7/7 rhythmic units).

wakan konkōbun (和漢混淆文). An eclectic style mingling literary Japanese and Sino-Japanese readings as opposed to *wabun*, which exclusively uses Japanese readings and diction, and *kanbun*, which uses Sino-Japanese.

Wang Can (王粲, 177–217). A man of letters and politician of late Later Han period.

Wang Shifu (王實甫, c. 1250–c. 1337). Playwright of the Yuan period, author of *Romance of the Western Bower*.

Wang Tao (王韜, 1828–1897). A Qing dynasty translator, reformer, political columnist, newspaper publisher, and fiction writer.

Wang Xifeng (王熙鳳). A female character in *A Dream of Red Mansions*, known as Sister Phoenix or Splendid Phoenix in English. She is the male protagonist's elder cousin-in-law.

Wang Zhaojun (王昭君). A Han woman who entered the rear palace of Emperor Yuan probably after 40 BCE. In 33 BCE she was presented to Huhanye, the ruler of the Xiongnu (匈奴), a confederation of nomadic tribes from Mongolia, when he visited the Han court as part of the tributary system between the two countries.

Wen Tingyun (温庭筠, c. 801–866). A Tang period poet.

"White-Haired Woman of the Shangyang Palace" ("Shangyang baifaren" 上陽白髮人). A poem by Bo Juyi (白居易).

"Woman in Mount Hua, The." A poem by Han Yu (韓愈).

Wu the Elder (武大). A character in *Outlaws of the Marsh* (*Shuihu zhuan* 水滸傳), where he is called Wu Dalang (武大郎), and *The Plum in the Golden Vase* (*Jinping mei* 金瓶梅).

Xie Zhaozhe (謝肇淛, 1567–1624). A man of letters of the Ming period; the author of *Five Miscellanies*.

Ximen Qing (西門慶). A character in *The Outlaws of the Marsh* and *The Plum in the Golden Vase*.

Xi Shi (西施). A Chinese woman said to have lived during the end of Spring and Autumn period in the capital of the ancient State of Yue. King Goujian of Yue, after being defeated and imprisoned by King Fuchai of Wu, presented Xi Shi to Fuchai in 490 BCE as part of a military strategy, which proved successful.

Yang Guifei (楊貴妃, 719–756). The beloved consort of Emperor Xuanzong of Tang during his later years. *Guifei* referred to the highest rank for imperial consorts during her time.

Yan Shigu (顔師古, 581–645). A famous Chinese author and linguist of the Tang dynasty. He wrote commentaries on several Chinese classic texts, including the *Records of the Grand Historian* and *Book of Han*.

yomihon (讀本). Reading books, or full-length didactic books popular around 1750–1867.

yomikudashi (読み下し). See *kundoku* (訓読).

yomikudashi-bun (読み下し文). A Chinese-language text written out in the *yomikudashi* style.

Zhang Hua (張華, 232–300). A man of letters of the Western Jin dynasty. Author of *A Treatise on Curiosities* (*Bowu-zhi* 博物誌).

Zhang Mi (張泌). A man of letters of the late Tang period.

Zhang Xuan (張萱, 713–755). A high Tang painter. Among his works are *Spring Outing of the Lady of the State of Guo* (*Guo-guo Furen youchun tu* 虢國夫人遊春圖) and *Preparing Newly Woven Silk* (*Daolian tu* 搗練圖).

Zhao Feiyan (趙飛燕, c. 32–1 BCE). Empress of Emperor Cheng of the Han period, known for her beauty and dancing skills as well as for the palace intrigue she and her sister, Consort Zhao Hede, engaged in. In the end, when she was demoted to a commoner and ordered to guard her husband's tomb, she committed suicide.

Zhenfei (珍妃, 1876–1900). The favorite consort of Emperor Guangsu of late Qing.

Zhou Fang (周昉, c. 730–800). A mid-Tang painter of portraits such as *Courtiers Playing Backgammon*.

Zhuge Liang (諸葛亮, also Zhuge Kongming 諸葛孔明, 181–234). A great strategist of the Three Kingdoms period.

Zhuo Wenjun (卓文君, second century BCE). A Chinese poet of the Western Han dynasty. As a young widow, Zhuo Wenjun eloped with the poet Sima Xiangru.

Selected Bibliography

Brownmiller, Susan. *Femininity*. Simon and Schuster, 1994. Translated into Japanese as *Onnarashisa* by Ikushima Sachiko and Aoshima Junko, Keiso Shobo, 1998.

Corson, Richard. *Fashions in Makeup: From Ancient to Modern Times*. Peter Owen Publishers, 1972. Translated into Japanese as *Mēku-appuno rekishi* by POLA Institute of Beauty and Culture under the supervision of Ishiyama Akira, Pōra Bunka Kenkyūjo, 1982.

Daibō, Ikuo. *Miryoku no shinrigaku (Psychology of Charm)*. POLA Institute of Beauty and Culture, 1997.

Freedman, Rita. *Beauty Bound: Why We Pursue the Myth in the Mirror*. Lexington Books, 1986. Translated into Japanese as *Utsukushisa to iu shin'wa* by Tsuneda Keiko, Shinjuku Shobō, 1994.

Fujimoto, Yukari. *Watashi no ibasho wa doko ni aru no?: shōjo manga ga utsusu kokoro no katachi (Where Is My Place to Be? The Mental Shape That Graphic Fiction for Young Girls Reflects)*. Gakuyō Shobō, 1998.

Haiken, E. *Venus Envy: A History of Cosmetic Surgery*. Johns Hopkins University, 1997. Translated into Japanese as *Purasuchikku byūtī: biyō seikei no bunkashi* by Nonaka Kuniko, Heibonsha, 1999.

Haniwara, Kazurō. *Japanese Faces: Do Small Faces and Beautiful Faces Mean Evolution? (Nihonjin no kao: kogao bijingao wa shinka nano ka)*. Kōdansha, 1999.

Harashima, Hiroshi. *Kaogaku e no shōtai (Invitation to the Study of Faces)*. Iwanami Science Library 62. Iwanami Shoten, 1998.

Harashima, Hiroshi, and Baba Yukio. *Hito no kao wo kaeta no wa nanika: genjin kara gendaijin, miraijin made no "kao" wo kagaku suru (What Changed the Human Face: Science of "Face" from Primitive Men to Modern and Future Men)*. Kawade Yume Shinsho. Kawade Shobō Shinsha, 1996.

Haruyama, Yukio. *Keshō: oshare no bunkashi 1* (*Makeup: Cultural History of Dressing Up, 1*). Haruyama Yukio no hakubutsushi 3. Heibonsha, 1988.

Ikeda, Shinobu. *Nihon kaiga no joseizō: jendā bijutsushi no shiten kara* (*Images of Women in Japanese Art: From the Viewpoint of Gender Art History*). Chikuma Purimā Books. Chikuma Shobō, 1998.

Inoue, Shōichi. *Bijin no jidai* (*The Era of Beautiful Women*). Bunshun Bunko, 1995.

Ishida, Kaori. *Keshō sezu ni wa ikirarenai ningen no rekishi* (*History of Humans Who Cannot Live without Making Up*). Kōdansha Gendai Shinsho, 2000.

Ishikawa, Tadahisa (ed.). *Chūgoku bungaku no joseizō* (*Female Images in Chinese Literature*). Kyūko Shoin, 1982.

Kamei, Hideo. *Shintai: kono fushiginaru mono no bungaku* (*Human Body: Literature of This Strange Thing*). Renga Shobō Shinsha, 1988.

Kawamura, Kunimitsu. *Otome no karada: onna no kindai to sekushuariti* (*The Virgin's Body: Women's Modernity and Sexuality*). Kinokuniya Shoten, 1994.

Kitayama, Seiichi. *Ifuku wa nikutai ni nani wo ataeta ka: gendai mōdo no shakaigaku* (*What Clothes Gave to the Body: Sociology of the Modern Mode*). Asahi Sensho, 1999.

Kodama, Miiko, and Ningen Bunka Kenkyūkai (ed.). *Bijo no imēji* (*Images of Beautiful Women*). Sekai Shisōsha, 1996.

Kōhara, Yukinari. *Kao to hyōjō no ningengaku* (*Humanics of Faces and Expressions*). Heibonsha Library, 2000.

Kondō, Haruo. *Chūgoku no kaiki to bijo: shikai, denki no sekai* (*The Strange and the Beautiful in China: The World of the Tales of the Strange and the Romantic*). Musashino Shoin, 1991.

Kura, Takuya. *Bijin wo aishita idenshitachi: ii onna wo sukinano wa bokura no sei ja nai* (*Genes That Loved Beautiful Women: It's Not Our Fault That We Like Good-Looking Women*). Wani Books, 1994.

———. *Naze, hito wa bijin wo aisuru no ka?* (*Why Do Humans Love Beautiful Women?*). Chiseiteki Ikikata Bunko. Mikasa Shobō, 1998.

———. *Utsukushisa wo meguru shinkaron: yōbō no shakaiseibutsugaku* (*The Theory of Evolution around Beauty: A Sociobiology of Looks*). Keisō Shobō, 1993.

Lakoff, Robin Tolmach, and Raquel L. Scherr. *Face Value: The Politics of Beauty*. Routledge & Kegan Paul, 1984. Translated into Japanese as *Feisu varyū: bi no seijigaku* by Minami Hiroshi, POLA Institute of Beauty and Culture, 1988.

Mainichi Shinbun Gakugeibu (ed.). *Nihon no bijo* (*Beautiful Women of Japan*). Mainichi Shinbunsha, 1966.

Matsuura, Tomohisa. "Gabi'-kō: shigo to kago 2" ("On Moth-Feeler Eyebrows: Chinese Poetic Diction and Japanese Poetic Diction"), in the enlarged edition by the same author of *Shigo no shosō: Tōshi nōto* (*Aspects of Poetic Diction: Notes on Tang Poetry*), Kenbun Shuppan, 1995.

Minami, Shinbō. *Kao* (*Face*). Chikuma Bunko. Chikuma Shobō, 1998.

Natori, Haruhiko. *Vīnasu konpurekkusu* (*Venus Complex*). Magazine House, 1999.

Takashima, Toshio. *Suikoden to Nihonjin: Edo kara Shōwa made* (*Outlaws of the Marsh and Japanese People: From the Edo Period to the Shōwa Era*). Taishūkan Shoten, 1991.

Tsuda, Noriyo, and Murata Takako. *Mayu no bunkashi: mayugeshō kenkyū hōkokusho (A Cultural History of Eyebrows: A Report on Eyebrow Makeup)*. POLA Institute of Beauty and Culture, 1985.

Washida, Kiyokazu. *Kao no genshōgaku: mirareru koto no kenri (Phenomenology of the Face: The Right to Be Seen)*. Kōdansha Gakujutsu Bunko, 1998.

———. *Mirarerukoto no kenri: "kao" ron (The Right to Be Looked at: On the Face)*. Metarōgu, 1995.

Wolf, Naomi. *The Beauty Myth: How Images of Beauty Are Used against Women*. William Morrow, 1991; Anchor Books, 1992. Translated into Japanese as *Bi no inbō: onnatachi no mienai teki* by Soda Kazuko, TBS Britannica, 1994.

Index

Account of Seaside Excursions, An, 23
Accounts of the Dressing Table, 119, 121
Asai Ryōi: "The Peony Lantern" (in *Protective Doll*), 185–89, 205; *Protective Doll*, 192, 195
Awake at Night, 162–65, 167–70

Ban Zhao, "Lessons for Women," 54
Beauty with Infants at Play, A, 71, *72*, 73, 75, 82, 87, 92
bijinga (pictures of beautiful women), 71, 73, 85, 88, 91, 234
Biographies of Exemplary Women, 44–45, 52–53
biographies of exemplary women, 45, 53–54, 67
Bo Collection, 134–35, 138, 140
body shape, 7, 22; body proportion 7, 73, 102, 240, 247–49; height, 160, 171–72, 192, 229, 247; petiteness, 82, 160, 172, 224, 247; plumpness, 29–33, 36–37, 59, 95–96, 99, 111, 149, 165, 168, 172, 191; slenderness, 7, 22, 29–30, 37–38, 58, 60, 73, 77, 111, 135–37, 144, 149–50, 160, 165, 167–68, 185–87, 192, 206, 209, 216, 218, 224, 238; sloping shoulders, 77, 95

Bo Juyi (Bai Juyi): "Contemporary Makeup," 127, 129, 140; "Pulling a Silver Jug from the Bottom of a Well," 135; "The Song of Lasting Regret," 139, 146, 152, 155, 173–78, 186, 190, 202, 204, 207, 224; "White-Haired Woman of the Shangyang Palace," 99, 119–20, 134; "Willow Branches," 151
Book of the Later Han, 25–26, 53, 129, 165
Buddhist ethics: 48, 62, 65
Bulwer-Lytton, Edward George Earle: *Alice*, 220; *Ernest Maltravers*, 220–21

"Cao Baiming Is Mistaken for a Robber" (in *Qingpingshan Studio Promptbooks*), 51
Cao Zhi: "The Goddess of the Luo," 10, 20–22, 25, 94–95, 104, 132; "Miscellaneous Poems," 173–74
Chang'e, 194, 204
Cheng Dachang, *All About the North*, 116
Chen Hongshou, *Female Immortals*, 74, 75, 102–103
Chōbunsai Eishi, *A Beauty under Cherry Blossoms*, 71, *72*, 73
Clay, Bertha M., *Weaker Than a Woman*, 230–31

clothing, 10, 77, 85, 95, 162–63, 168, 174, 191, 197, 199, 204, 209
Collection from above the Clouds, A, 143
Collection of Chinese and Japanese Poems for Singing, 135–36
Collection of National Polity, 143–44, 188
Commentary of Zuo (*Zuo zhuan*), 44, 50, 111
"companion tales" (*otogizōshi*), 178, 187, 202, 208; "The Bowl Wearer," 179, 187, 202; "The Fox of Kowata," 179; "Little Atsumori," 202; "The Story of Melon Princess," 202; "The Tale of Bunshō," 179; "The Tale of the Rat," 208
Confessions of Lady Nijō, The, 168–69, 171–72
Confucian ethics, 22, 45, 52–54, 67, 87, 92–93
consort, 6, 91, 119, 126, 190, 217–18
cosmetics and cosmetology, 7, 107, 112–13, 132, 249–50; eyebrow ink, 126, 140, 167–68, 185–87; powder, 24–26, 59, 65, 78, 90, 107, 114, 116–18, 126–27, 129, 135, 140, 159, 177–78, 209, 236; rouge, 24, 26–28, 59, 78, 90, 111–16, 118, 120–22, 127, 129, 135, 140, 159, 178, 196; safflower, 111, 113–16, 120–22, 168, 146, 152, 168
courtesan, 23, 26, 47, 57–58, 73, 82, 88, 90–92, 109, 135, 169, 190–92, 194, 197, 207, 209, 225
court women/lady, 6, 10, 22, 28, 95–100, 102–4, 119–20, 160, 174, 188
"crimson face, hapless fate," 55–56, 58, 60, 66, 92
criteria of beauty, 1, 2, 5, 7–12, 16, 18, 37, 54, 107, 110–12, 132, 154, 160, 247
cruelty and destruction associated with women 61–65
Cui Bao, *Commentaries on Things Now and Old*, 114–15
Customs, Manners, and Fashions of the Capital, 18, 200–201, 215–16

da Cruz, Gaspar, 3
Daoism, 64–65
Diao Chan, 190

Diary of Izumi Shikibu, The, 161
Diary of Murasaki Shikibu, The, 145, 149, 160–61, 164, 167
didacticism in literature, 44, 51, 65, 187, 220
disguise as attractive women, 41, 46–50, 62–63, 175, 190
Dream of Red Mansions, A, 29, 38, 48–49, 51, 59–60, 121, 148

elegance, 101, 145, 153, 167–69, 174, 190, 195, 204, 206, 209, 210, 221
emaciation, fragility, ill health, 29, 43, 50, 58–60, 138, 145, 147, 165–167
Empress Consort Wu, 51, 120
Empress Xiao Xianchun, 7
enchantress, 48, 50, 61, 66–67, 85
Erya, 114–15
Essential Skills for Commoners, 117–18, 121–22
evil or wicked woman, 11, 41–42, 45–46, 49–52, 56–57, 61–62, 64, 66–67, 92
eyebrows: crescent moons, 206, 210, 220; distant hills or mountains, 194, 211, 204–5, 223–24, 229; moth-feeler eyebrows, 15, 22, 45, 99, 101–2, 119, 135, 139, 153; shaven or plucked eyebrows, 90–91, 118, 141, 143, 152, 211, 216; short or thick eyebrows, 98, 119–20, 175–76; thin eyebrows, 180–81, 199, 201, 210
eyes and eyelids: black eyes, 235; bright or clear eyes, 7, 15, 16, 18, 20–21, 139, 148, 217, 220; cool-looking eyes, 16, 185–86, 216, 222, 224–25; double eyelids, 6, 15, 73, 102, 103, 199–200, 216, 218, 249–50; downcast eyes, 215; large or wide open eyes, 15, 18, 215, 226, 244, 247; "red hair, jasper eyes," 4; single eyelids, 73, 200, 216, 219; slim, narrow eyes, 16, 19, 73, 99, 101, 215; small eyes, 19; willow eyebrows, 77, 152, 201, 203

face: deep-sculpted, 244, 247; oval face, 6, 20, 73, 100, 102, 216, 218, 244; round or plump face, 30, 97, 150, 197, 210; white face, 199, 223–24, 232

Index

Fan Jing's Wife, Surname Shen, "Water Reflections," 139
female demon type as a category of Noh drama, 66
femme fatale, 43, 61, 64, 67; Bao Si, 44, 50; Daji, 44, 50, 66; Empress Dowager Lü, 50; Lady Xia, 50; Li Ji, 44, 50, 56; Pan Jinlian (Golden Lotus), 49, 51, 56, 64, 199, 203; Wang Xifeng (Sister Phoenix), 48–52; Xi Shi, 9, 56, 59, 176, 195, 208; Zhao Feiyan, 56, 58–60, 224
Fernweh, 239
Five Miscellanies, 56, 66
flowers as metaphors for feminine beauty, 201–3, 206–8, 221, 232
fragrance, 170, 190, 194, 196–97, 201, 204, 206, 208, 222–23
Futabatei Shimei, 237; *Drifting Clouds*, 225–26, 232; "Tryst" (from Turgenev's *Sketches from a Hunter's Album*), 227–28, 230; "How I Came to Use Genbun Itchi," 228

gazoku setchūtai (eclectic style combining the literary and the vernacular), 205, 223, 225–26, 233, 237
Ge Hong, *Baopuzi*, 65
Geographical Compilation, 115
gesaku (playful writing), 226
Gleanings of the Daye Era, 126
Glories and Graces (*Bunka shūreishū*), 134, 143, 188
goddess, 10–11, 16, 20–22, 25, 29, 39, 41, 94–95, 98, 102, 104, 112, 132, 190, 198, 204–206, 223
Gold and Jewels Fill the House, 78, *81*
gracefulness, 9, 54, 103, 138–39, 144, 150–51, 153–55, 161–63, 166–67, 169, 173, 187–88, 190–91, 195–97, 199–201, 203, 221–22, 227, 229, 232
"Grand Beauty, The" (in *The Book of Songs*), 20
Great Learning for Women, 67
Great Mirror, The, 164–65
Gu Hongzhong, *Han Xizai's Night Revels*, 35, *35*, 100–103

Gu Kaizhi, "Goddess of the Luo Illustrated," 94–95, 98, 104, 112, 132

hair: Afro hair, 5; black hair, 21, 145, 161, 163, 165, 168, 173, 189, 196, 199–200, 208–210, 231, 244; "brown hair" (*chapatsu*), 148; coiffed hair, 90, 95, 129, 163–64, 171, 198, 201, 210, 209, 211, 223; glossy hair, 137, 163–65, 167, 200; golden or blond hair, 4, 148–49, 220, 223, 230, 232; green hair, 185–87, 204; hair ornaments, 77, 196, 209, 203; in disarray, 177, 181, 220, 224; naturally let-down long hair, 154, 163–65, 169; side locks like the wings of autumn cicadas, 135, 204–5
Han Palace at Spring Dawn, The, 122, *124*
Heian narrative literature, 155–56, 160, 187, 234
hierarchy and power relations, 5, 10–11, 37, 47, 112, 251
Higuchi Ichiyō, *Child's Play*, 234

Ihara Saikaku, *The Life of an Amorous Man*, 191–92, 201
Imperial Readings of the Taiping Era, 115
Isoda Kōryūsai, *Beautiful Woman in the Snow*, 87–88

"Jealous-Woman River, The" (in *Miscellaneous Morsels from Youyang*), 49
Jeweled Chamber Secrets, 19

Kaempfer, Engelbert, 4
Kaibara Ekiken, *Life-Nourishing Principles*, 65
kanazōshi, 62, 185, 190
Kang Tao, *After Bathing in the Huaqing Pool*, 85, *86*
Kikukawa Eizan, *Cooling Off in the Evening*, 78, *80*
Kitagawa Morisada, *Morisada's Rambling Writings*, 90–91

Kitagawa Utamaro: *Array of Supreme Beauties of the Present Day: Takikawa*, 84; *Five-Color Ink of the Northern Region*, 217; *Ten Types of Women's Physiognomies*, 82, 211, *212*; *Twelve Hours of the Green Houses: The Hour of the Bull*, 84, 85; *Young Women's Sundial: The Hour of the Horse*, *81*, 82
Kunikida Doppo, "Musashino," 228
"Kurokawa Genda-nushi Enters the Mountains and Gains a Path to Longevity" (in *Garland of Heroes*), 64

Ladies-in-Waiting at the Go Board, 26–28, 122, *123*
Ladies' Pocket Notebook, 240
Lady Li, 55, 176–77, 179–80
Lady Shezhi, 177
lasciviousness, 45, 50, 61, 66, 85, 92
"Legend of Dame Ren" (mentioned in *Tales of Overgrown Fields*), 64
Legends of the West River, 115
Leng Mei, *Out in the Garden on a Moonlit Night*, 76
Lessons with Illustrations for Admonishing Women, 42
Lévi-Strauss, Claude, 2
Li Bo (Li Bai), 194
Li Gonglin, *Beautiful Women's Outing*, 34, 36
limbs: bound feet, 2, 23, 29, 87, 199, 201, 216, 223; delicate hands or fingers, 135–36, 144, 199–201, 209–10, 216, 221; long, slender legs, 199–201, 209–210, 217, 239–242, 247–48; lotus steps, 203, 222–24
lips and mouth: cherry, 111, 194, 196, 198, 203; large mouth, 160; peach blossom, 220; red lips, 20, 111, 139–41, 187, 199, 201–2, 210, 222; small lips and mouth, 73, 77, 95, 99, 160, 222
Li Shi, *Sequel to a Treatise on Curiosities*, 113–14
Li Shizhen, *Compendium of Materia Medica*, 126

Literary Gems of Japan, 143
literati paintings, 73, 75–76, 85, 92, 173, 255
Liu Bang, 178
Liu Xi, *Etymological Dictionary of Names*, 24, 118
Liu Xiang, *Biographies of Exemplary Women*, 44–45, 52–53
Liu Yiqing, *Records of Light and Dark*, 117–18
Li Yu, *Occasional Contemplations*, 11, 16, 20, 55, 215

Ma Gao, *Commentaries on Things Now and Old in the Central States*, 113
makeup, 78, 116, 132; blackened teeth, 2, 20, 90, 142–43, 175–76, 211, 216; eyebrow makeup, 20, 24, 98, 99, 118–20, 126, 135; eye makeup, 200; "immortal moth makeup," 119; "intensely dark" (*ganguro*), 251–52; lip makeup, 120–21; makeup as a method of artificially constructing beauty, 107–8; meanings attached to makeup, 108–10; no makeup, 223; plum blossom makeup, 205, *206*; powder applied by men, 26, 116; powdering exposed areas of the neck, breast, hands, 25–26, 90; red cheeks, 26–27, 129, 136, 177, 223, 244; "sob makeup," 126–29
Mandarin-Duck Coverlet, 55
Mao Qiang, 17
marriage beyond one's means, the horror of, 51
Mary Pickford, *238*
mass production, media, and consumer culture, 9, 47, 110, 159, 247, 250–51
Memorabilia of the Kaiyuan and Tianbao Eras, 27, 126–27, 129
modern technology, 8, 217–19, 249, 253
Mori Ōgai, *Dancing Girl*, 233
mother as a beautiful woman, 43, 85, 87–92, 202, 224
Murasaki Shikibu, 145–46, 149, 152, 161, 165. See also *The Diary of Murasaki Shikibu* and *The Tale of Genji*
Music and Fun at Court, 31

Index

Nagai Kafū, *Flowers of Hell*, 228
Natsume Sōseki, 239; *Literary Theory*, 236; *Red Poppy*, 67; *Sanshirō*, 235–36; *Ten Nights of Dream*, 67
New Account of Tales of the World, A, 26, 148
New Lamp-Wick Trimming Stories, 186, 200; "The Account of Peony Lantern," 186
New Songs from a Jade Terrace, 188
New Year's woodblock prints (Ch. *nianhua*), 71, 73, 76, 82, 87, 92
ninjōbon (books of human feeling), 189, 201, 209–210, 220–21, 223, 228, 232, 234
Niwa Jun'ichirō, *Love Story of Flower and Willow*, 220–22
nose, 160; long nose, 161; straight or tall nose, 6, 8, 21, 95, 100, 102, 161, 192, 215–17, 223–24; well-shaped, 231

Ōe no Asatsuna, "Nuptial Song for Man and Woman," 140
"Oil-Peddler Wins the Queen of Flowers" (in *Stories to Waken the World*), 57
Okajima Kanzan, *A Popular Account of Loyal Outlaws of the Marsh*, 195–96, 19, 200–202, 220
Ono no Komachi, 175–78, 180, 192, 208
Origin of Things, The, 24
Osada Shūtō, *The Lady of the Camellias* (translation), 228–31
"Outcast Orphan Woman" (in *Biographies of Exemplary Women*), 53
Outlaws of the Marsh, 49, 51, 64, 196–99, 202–4, 207, 211
Outlaws of the Marsh, a Sequel, 211
Ovid, 22
Ozaki Kōyō, *The Golden Demon*, 230–32

"Permanent Lump Woman" (in *Biographies of Exemplary Women*), 53
"Pledge of Mandarin Ducks unto Death, The," 45
Plum in the Golden Vase, The, 21, 49, 51, 56, 85
"Powder Girl" (in *Records of Light and Dark*), 117–18

"Priest Kyata Goes to the Land of Rākasana" (in *Stories Gleaned at Uji*), 62
Princess Yontai, 119–20

Qu Yuan, "The Lament," 45–46

"reading books" (*yomihon*), 187, 189, 195, 198, 200–202, 208–210, 220–24, 228, 231–32, 234
Record of Ancient Matters, 133
Records of the Grand Historian, 44, 50, 108, 111
Records of the Three Kingdoms, 25
Remarkable Stories Old and New, 193
rhyme-prose (*fu*), 55, 94, 132, 140, 155, 165, 174–75, 177, 200
Ricci, Matteo, 3
Rise and Fall of the Minamoto and the Taira, The, 178
Romance of the Western Bower, 55, 59–60

"Saiki," 187
Santō Kyōden, 195, 203, 220; *An Account of the Loyal Vassal Utō Yasukata*, 205; *The Full Account of Sakurahime*, 66, 204; *Tale of Udumbara Flowers*, 187, 204–6
Scott, Walter, *Ivanhoe*, 222
"Seven Explications," 58
Shi Jianwu, "Viewing a Beauty," 26
Shikitei Sanba, 226; *The Barbershop of the Floating World*, 211
Sikong Shu, "Viewing a Courtesan," 26
sixteen (twice eight) as an ideal age, 64, 175, 187–89, 204, 206, 208, 220, 222–23, 233
Songs of the South, 46, 118
Song Yu: "On Deng Tuzi as a Sensualist," 20; "The Divine Woman," 16, 21–22
Standing Female Figures with Bird Feather Ornaments, 165, *166*
Stealing Immortals; Herb, 122, *125*
Stories Gleaned at Uji, 171
Stories Old and New (Gujin shiaoshuo), 193

Stories to Awaken the World, 193; "Over Fifteen Strings of Cash, a Jest Leads to Dire Disasters," 208; "The Golden Eel Brings Calamity to Officer Ji," 50;
Stories to Caution the World, 191, 193–94, 196; "Qiao Yanjie's Concubine Ruins the Family," 63; "Secretary Qian Leaves Poems on the Swallow Tower," 209; "With a White Falcon Master Cui Brings an Evil Spirit Upon Himself," 63, 209
"Story of Huo Xiaoyu, The," 50
"Story of Yingying, The," 50
Story of Yoshitsune, The, 180, 199
Strange Tales from the Make-Do Studio, 47
Strategies of the Warring States, 22, 24
Suehiro Tetchō, *Plum Blossoms in the Snow*, 223
Sugawara no Michizane, 134–143, 147, 149, 151–52
Sugawara no Takasue's daughter, *The Sarashina Diary*, 169
Su Little Sister Thrice Fools Her Bridegroom, 78–79
Supplementary Lamp-Wick Trimming Stories, 186, 200
Su Shi, "Poem on a Hapless Fate," 55
Suzuki Harunobu, 88, 91

Taiheiki, The, or *Chronicle of Great Peace*, 169, 174–75, 177–78, 188, 203, 207
Takebe Ayatari, 201; *Japanese Outlaws of the Marsh*, 198–200; *Tale of Nishiyama*, 195, 199
Takehisa Yumeji, *Nostalgia for Hirado*, 239, *239*
Takizawa Bakin, 189, 195, 201, 203, 209–10, 220, 224; *The Crescent Moon*, 206–8, 210; *Eight Dogs Chronicle*, 66–67, 208, 211
Tale of Genji, The, 142, 144–46, 149–55, 159–63, 166–68, 171–72, 175–76, 187, 202, 207; picture scrolls, 122, 131
Tale of Matsura Palace, The, 170
Tale of Ochikubo, The, 146, 153
Tale of Sagoromo, The, 153–54, 161, 169
Tale of the Heiji War, The, 178

Tale of the Heike, The, 169, 172–74, 176–77, 187–88, 207
Tale of the Hōgen War, The, 178
Tale of the Hollow Tree, The, 153
Tales for Comfort, 62, 189
Tales of the Riverside Middle Counselor, The, 21, 162; "Eyebrow Ink," 167; "Lady Who Loved Caterpillars," 143, 172
Tales of Yamato, The, 153
Tamenaga Shunsui: *The Love-Tinted Garden of Fukagawa*, 210–11; *The Love-Tinted Plum Calendar*, 189, 209–10
Tanba no Yasuyori (compiler), *The Essence of Medical Prescriptions*, 19
Tang Xianzu, *Peony Pavilion*, 55, 60
Tang Yin, *Four Beautiful Women*, 78, *79*, 85, 92, 104
Tanizaki Junichirō, *Naomi*, 236–37, 242
Tao Gu, *Record Clarifying Different Names*, 121
teeth: blacking, 2, 20, 142–43, 159, 211, 216; decayed, 144, 156n; white or lustrous, 15, 139–43, 152, 222–23, 238; white teeth not mentioned or avoided, 210–11
Three Words and Two Slaps, 63–64, 189, 194–95, 199–200, 209
Thunberg, Carl Peter, 3–4
Tōkai Sanshi, *Strange Encounters with Beautiful Women*, 223–24
Tokutomi Roka, *Namiko*, 232
tomb murals and burial accompaniments, 93
Torii Kiyonaga, 88, 90
Tosa Diary, The, 161
Treasury of Great Learning for Women, 42
Tsubouchi Shōyō, 231; *The Essence of the Novel*, 224–25; *Mirrors for Wife and Husband*, 224; style, 226; *Temperaments of Contemporary Students*, 224, 226, 232
Tsuga Teishō, 63; *A Garland of Heroes*, 192–93, 195–96; *Tales of Overgrown Fields*, 194–96

Ueda Akinari, "A Serpent's Lust" (in *Tales of Moon and Rain*), 66, 195
ugly woman, 49, 52–53
ukiyo-e, 6, 75, 78, 88, 92, 122, 225; eyebrows intentionally drawn, 91
"unity of written and spoken languages" (*genbun itchi*), 222
Ushiyama Ryōsuke, *Lingering Fragrance of Plum Buds*, 221
Utagawa Kunimasa: *Three Fashionable Beauties Cooing Off in the Evening*, 78, *80*; *Young Woman and a Cat at a Kotatsu*, 78, *80*
Utagawa Toyokuni, *A Beautiful Woman Wiping Rouge*, *77*, 78

Venus, 132
virtue versus beauty, 53–54
von Siebold, Philipp Franz Balthazar, 3–4

Wang Can, "Seven Explications," 165
Wang Zhaojun, 56, 134–35, 176, 190, 195
Western cultures, aesthetic premises of, 215
Western influence 12, 73, 122, 218, 244–45
westernization, 224, 242, 251
Western literature, 210
Western regions, 3, 113–14, 126
white skin, 24–25, 28, 137, 140, 144–49, 152, 160, 168–69, 171–74, 176, 181, 209–210, 216, 218, 224; polished with rubbing bran, 209; snow, 111, 146–47, 168–69, 191, 200, 203, 208, 209–10; wheat-colored skin, 147, 249; white skin viewed negatively, 146–47
wicked women, Western examples of, 61

Xiang Yu, 178
Xiao Xianchun, Empress, 7
Xie Lingyun, "On Composing a Poem under the Tomb of King Luling," 139
Xiongnu people, the (the Huns), 115
Xi Shi, 9, 56, 176, 190, 195, 208

Yang Guifei, 27, 30–31, 39n17, 56, 85, 92, 104n1, 132, 139, 146, 152, 155, 175–80, *179*, 190, 195
Yearnings for the Ancient Chinese Style, 143
Yinzhen Fei's Outing, 103, 112

Zhang Hua, *A Treatise on Curiosities*, 113–15
Zhang Lihua, 193
Zhang Mi, *Accounts of the Dressing Chamber*, 116
Zhang Qian, 113–14
Zhang Shoujie, *Annotations on the Records of the Great Historian*, 115
Zhang Wencheng, *Grotto of Immortals*, 18–19, 38, 134, 137–38, 155, 165
Zhang Xuan, *Spring Outing of the Lady of the State of Guo*, 31, 33–34, 97
Zhao Binzhen, *Overnight on a Lotus Boat*, 17
Zhao Feiyan, 56, 58–60, 194, 224
Zhongli Chun (ugly woman and accomplished speaker in *Biographies of Exemplary Women*), 52
Zhou Fang, 96, 97; *Court Ladies with Floral Hair Ornaments* (ascribed to Zhou Fang), 98–99, 102, 119–20; *Court Lady Holding a Fan*, 96–99
Zhuo Wenjun, 194